SECRET
SOCIETIES

SECRET
SOCIETIES

INSIDE THE WORLD'S MOST
NOTORIOUS ORGANIZATIONS

John Lawrence Reynolds

ARCADE PUBLISHING ❖ NEW YORK

FIRST U.S. EDITION

First published in Canada under the title *Shadow People* by Key Porter Books Limited

Library of Congress Cataloging-in-Publication Data

Reynolds, John (John Lawrence)
Secret societies : inside the world's most notorious organizations / John Lawrence Reynolds. —1st U.S. ed.
         p. cm.
Includes bibliographical references and index.
ISBN-13: 978-1-55970-826-5 (alk. paper)
ISBN-10: 1-55970-826-3 (alk. paper)
1. Secret societies. I. Title.

HS125.R49 2006
366—dc22   2006018635

Published in the United States by Arcade Publishing, Inc., New York
Distributed by Hachette Book Group USA

Visit our Web site at www.arcadepub.com

10 9 8 7 6 5 4 3 2 1

Designed by Martin Gould

EB

PRINTED IN THE UNITED STATES OF AMERICA

For Anna P.,
of course.

Cruelty has a human heart,
And jealousy a human face;
Terror the human form divine
And secrecy the human dress.

WILLIAM BLAKE

The more things you know, or pretend to know,
the more powerful you are.
It doesn't matter if the things are true.
What counts, remember, is to possess a secret.

UMBERTO ECO

CONTENTS

INTRODUCTION
FOOLS, FEARS AND FANATICS

THEY WERE AMONG THE MOST FRIGHTENING OF EARLY SECRET societies, a furtive group both feared and hated by citizens of the Roman Empire. Many suggested killing every man, woman and child who were members. Others proposed caution, having heard tales of bloody vengeance taken against enemies of the group. Some grew worried that their own neighbors might be society members, infecting their children with dangerous ideas and engaging them in revolting practices. A few were fascinated by the outrageous antics attributed to this secret organization; their curiosity piqued, their imaginations running rampant, they asked themselves: could these people really be so depraved?

Tales exchanged among the Romans were almost beyond belief. The members of this secret group, it was said, were cannibalistic, eating human flesh and drinking human blood during secret rituals, and their gory feasts often included newborn babies. They promoted sexual orgies among brothers and sisters, and engaged in bizarre ceremonies, met in clandestine locations, avoided contact with respectable society, and identified themselves by flashing the image of an instrument of torture when they met.

"An infant covered with their meal that it may deceive the unwary," one Roman wrote, "is placed before him who is to be stained with their rites. This infant is slain by the young pupil, who has been urged on as if to harmless blows on the surface of the meal, with dark and secret wounds. Thirstily—O horror!— they lick up its blood; eagerly they divide its limbs. By this victim they are pledged together; with this consciousness they are covenanted to mutual silence. Such sacred rites as these are more foul than any sacrileges..."

Throughout the Mediterranean region during the first century of the first millennium, especially among Romans, who valued nobility above all qualities, these stories were equally repulsive and fascinating. Roman politicians began demanding elimination of the sect, without question or exception. Most citizens agreed, and crowds began to gather in the marketplace where they exchanged tales, confirmed evidence, and embellished the more unpleasant aspects of the secret society's behavior. Over time, a consensus was reached: something must be done to break the cult's bonds and rein in these scoundrels, these perverts, these insurgents, these...Christians.

From our perspective two thousand years later, the tales of disgusting Christian practices sound like propaganda created by members of the Roman senate as a strategy to eliminate the sect. Perhaps by spreading vile stories among the populace, we assume, citizens would be dissuaded from joining the ranks of Christians, and Rome's harsh treatment of the new religion's followers would be supported.

In reality, the Roman senate had little to do with the outrageous tales. While the general populace may have been scandalized by reports of cannibalism and incest, public opinion mattered little to politicians, who were concerned with more practical matters, including the refusal of Christians to worship the emperor. Tolerant of religious disparity generally, Rome's major objection addressed this single unacceptable behavior, considered an act of disloyalty to the Empire. When Christians began converting others to their point of view, their actions represented an insurgency that could not be ignored. At that point, Roman leaders encouraged stories of their scandalous activities, employing them as a weapon to suppress the movement.

But Rome's senate and other leaders did not originate the stories of bizarre behavior by Christians. These yarns, spun in the imaginations of ordinary citizens, were based on information provided by Christians themselves—information subject to exaggeration and malignment that grew directly out of the twin mills of ignorance and suspicion. Consider the clues that inspired the tales:

SECRECY. Christians kept to themselves, did not admit strangers to their ceremonies without the approval of a known member, and demanded that new members undergo a test of faith before being admitted. But there were valid reasons for all these actions. Following Christ's crucifixion, declaring that you were a Christian was akin to signing your death warrant. When Christians began concealing their activities in response, paranoia over their goals and practices grew deeper and more widespread, stimulating a more desperate need for members to mask their identity. And so spun the cycle of oppression, leading to deeper secrecy and generating greater paranoia, inviting new oppression.

CANNIBALISM. Didn't Christians conduct ceremonies in which they consumed the flesh of a man, and drank his blood? Of course they did. To Christians, the Communion sacrament represented an allegory of oneness with the spirit. To unbelievers, it sounded suspiciously like repulsive reality.

EATING BABIES. Lacking effective methods of contraception and abortion, poor Roman citizens set unwanted infants outside to die of starvation and exposure. As abhorrent as this may be to modern sensibilities, it was acceptable practice in a culture where unwanted mouths to feed presented a major burden on the family. When Christians began rescuing these infants from certain death, baptizing them into their faith, Romans grew confused. Why would someone choose to raise another's child? The idea defied logic. Or perhaps they were not being raised at all. Perhaps, given their practice of consuming flesh and blood, Christians gathered abandoned babies as a source of raw material for their disgusting ceremonies. The fact that these children were being cared for and raised as

Christians was not considered plausible. Nor, of course, was it nearly as intriguing.

ORGIES AND SEXUAL INCEST. When reports of Christians engaging in Love Feasts began spreading among the Romans, it was an easy leap to assume that the "love" aspect was not entirely spiritual in nature. Certain Gnostics, another secretive society, participated in ritual sex and regarded semen as a sacred fluid, consecrating each member's status with it. Christians and Gnostics varied widely in their beliefs and practices, but it's easy to imagine an average citizen of Rome shrugging and commenting the Latin equivalent of, "Christians, Gnostics, what's the difference? They're all the same."

The incest factor? It grew from the practice of Christians referring to each other as "Brother" and "Sister" in expressions of fondness and support. In other cultures, sisters and brothers were born of the same parents, an undisputed fact, and no allegorical reference applied.

AN INSTRUMENT OF TORTURE AS SYMBOL AND IDENTITY. In Roman times, the cross was a widely employed instrument of torture and death. To Romans, there was nothing reassuring about displaying a cross or drawing its shape in the air with your hand, a gesture that could be interpreted as a threat. Visualize a modern-day clandestine group of people employing a hangman's noose, a guillotine, or an electric chair as a symbol of unity and values, and imagine your reaction.

This view of Christians as a menacing secret society remains as fitting a lesson about collective fear and repulsion today as it was then. In spite of advances in technology and communication, our fascination with secret societies remains powerful and abiding. When prodded and inspired by popular culture's twisted depiction of esoteric organizations in films and novels, our belief in their existence and dangers may match or exceed the flawed visions Romans harbored about Christianity.

As the Christian example proved, the most common responses to secret societies by outsiders are suspicion and fear, born in the belief that *anything that is good should not be kept secret, and anything kept secret cannot be good.*

We crave secrets, along with societies to maintain and perpetuate them, as much as we desire honesty in our dealings with others. We expect important business and military decisions to be made in secrecy. We accept back-room politicians arriving at decisions about candidates and policy while striving to remain anonymous. And we harbor secrets from our friends, our children and our lovers. Yet we also strive to fathom all the mysteries affecting our lives, demanding access to information that has been denied us, whatever the motive. If secrets are being kept from us, we insist, they must be shared. And if they are being shared by a definable group exclusively, the group's motives must be suspect.

Secret societies have changed, gradually but significantly, over time. In the ancient world they were primarily philosophic and religious in nature. By the medieval period, politics began to replace the philosophical quotient, although religion remained the dominant element. By the mid-eighteenth century, the societies had evolved in one of two directions: either towards *political and fraternal associations*, retaining remnants of philosophical and religious trappings from the ancient world; or in the direction of *outright criminality*, using secrecy to achieve clandestine ends and acquire enormous wealth.

The differing objectives influenced the manner in which the societies were constructed and operated, because their secrecy became necessary either as a means of creating exclusivity for members or as a defense against discovery and harassment. Among members of fraternal organizations, exclusivity added distinction; for organizations subject to harassment by law enforcement or society as a whole, secrecy became a tool for self-preservation. Either way, the effect was to generate mistrust among nonmembers. Mistrust led to assumptions, the assumptions were invariably negative, the negative perceptions aroused hostility, hostility strengthened the organization's secrecy, and the circle revolved ad infinitum. Little has changed.

This circle of suspicion and response launches a fever of assumptions that resists any attempt to insert a dose of reality, a process as powerful and predictable today as it was when Nero took music lessons. Secret societies, you will be lectured by adherents of conspiracy theories, control the world's destiny. The declaration of wars, the onslaught of global epidemics, the election of national leaders, and the presence of alien life on earth are controlled by societies whose power and purpose are as rampant and evil as any James Bond villain concocted by Hollywood. Fanatics trot out and display proof with all the authority of a prosecuting attorney making a case to a credible jury, while serious objections are twisted into evidence that the Devil's power is so all-embracing he can convince you that he does not exist.

It's fine entertainment for those who suspect that their lives are manipulated by unseen powers. They seek evidence like seedlings craving light, even when the source of light is somewhat less illuminating than the sun. According to conspiracy buffs, every decision regarding your economic well-being, your position in society, the condition of your health, and the institution that governs your life rests in the hands of enigmatic men—they are almost always men—whose identity is either concealed from view or hidden behind a mask of benign public service. Nothing you think or do is yours alone to decide, you will be lectured. The world's destiny is determined by Freemasons or Gnostics, Wicca or Druids, the Bilderberg Group or the Illuminati, the Mafia or members of Skull & Bones. Economic disasters? Vanishing resources? Wars and famine? Only fools believe these occur naturally. To conspiracy theorists, they are the result of conscious actions taken by robed grandmasters, Sicilian warlords, plotting Rosicrucians, followers of Kabbalah, or other menacing factions.

The most rabid believers assume that all groups are equally involved, exchanging responsibilities like merchants in a marketplace of schemers. Most people are more sanguine. Many secret societies, they point out, are benign or even beneficial. Others may be deceptive, although this doesn't mean they are dangerous, just fraternal. Some, admittedly, are utterly treacherous in intent, but the risk they represent may be minimal. Should we worry about the Ku Klux Klan, for example, a once feared gang of lynchers that has morphed into a ragtag assembly of racist fools? Not very likely.

Yet it would be foolish in the extreme to treat every clandestine group as though it were nothing more than a collection of adults playing childish games. If the price of liberty is indeed vigilance, then the prudent ones among us should be aware of societies that may be acting entirely in their interests and totally against our own. The challenge lies in knowing who is who. Or what.

Taking the long view, this book will examine the most prominent secret societies that have endured down through the ages. In every case their influence, and at least vestiges of any notorious actions, exists today. As we'll see, most are fraternal and benign, several remain tantalizingly suspicious, and some deserve to have their dark cloak of secrecy yanked away with a brilliant light shone upon them as they wriggle and squirm in an unfamiliar beam of exposure.

ONE

THE ASSASSINS
NOTHING IS TRUE, EVERYTHING IS PERMITTED

IN AD 1191 CONRAD OF MONTFERRAT ASCENDED THE THRONE as King of Jerusalem, appointed to this position by the celebrated hero of the Crusades, Richard the Lion-Hearted. After instructing Conrad to rebuild Christian forces in preparation for his return, Richard departed for home, destined to achieve immortality as a fair-haired idol in tales of Robin Hood and fables of great heroics.

Conrad, who had campaigned against Henry, Count of Champagne, for the throne, planned to glorify his reign as King of Jerusalem by driving Muslims from the Holy Land forever, earning a hallowed place in history as a Christian hero, and a seat in heaven near the right hand of God.

He had precious little time to do it. Soon after Richard departed the Holy Land, three Christian monks entered Conrad's campsite, bowing and making the sign of the cross to all they encountered. Their pious actions persuaded Conrad and his warriors to let down their guard, a fatal mistake. As soon as the monks were within reach of Conrad, they withdrew daggers from beneath their cloaks and cut him to pieces, slashing and stabbing in a violent display of butchery before the guards could intervene. With Conrad dispatched, the young men, who were not Christian monks but devout Muslims, made no attempt to escape. Surrendering to Conrad's guards, they suffered silently through a ghastly ordeal that included first flaying them alive, then slow-roasting them to death. Such were the penalties in that unforgiving world.

Later, while mourning the loss of their leader, Conrad's followers whispered among themselves about the odd behavior of his killers, especially their passivity after the deed was accomplished. It was strange how they dropped their weapons and simply stood awaiting capture while the king's death rattle faded. Even when informed of the agony that awaited them, the young men actually appeared to welcome the grisly experience of a torturous death. No one had seen such behavior before. No one could explain it. No one knew what it meant.

Henry, Count of Champagne, spent little time pondering the manner of the young killers. Conrad's premature death may have proved a tragedy to some, but it was an opportunity for Henry who, had he been born eight centuries later, might have become an outstanding corporate CEO. Soon after the last shovelful of Holy Land earth had been tossed onto Conrad's coffin, Henry took strategic action by marrying Conrad's widow, hoping to inherit the title that had eluded him and cost her husband his life. Whether through lack of support within Conrad's court or simple bad luck, Henry failed to win the crown as king of Jerusalem, settling instead for an administrative position that required him to make several trips east from Jerusalem into Persia. During one of these journeys, he encountered the source of Conrad's demise, and tapped one of history's most chilling secret societies.

It occurred when Henry and his entourage were following a rarely traveled road through the rugged Alborz Mountains, north of Tehran in modern-day Iran. During the Crusades, this land was occupied by Shiite Muslims who permitted Christians to pass with relative safety. Nearing a large fortress poised on the brink of an elevated bluff, Henry and his guards were met by representatives of the castle's resident, the Dai-el-Kebir. At first apprehensive, the Christians were reassured when the servants displayed every mark of honor to them before extending an invitation from their master to view the fortress and sample the Dai-el-Kebir's hospitality. Such an invitation could not be ignored without insulting the host. Besides, the impressive fortress captured Henry's interest. The prospect of both a tour of the intriguing structure and a good meal was irresistible.

Henry and his men followed the servants to the heights of the castle entrance, where their host greeted them with warmth and fanfare. The Dai-el-Kebir, a man of obvious wealth and power, took some pleasure in displaying the fortress to his guests, escorting them through extensive gardens and drawing their attention to the many stone towers that soared high above the rocky valley. At one point, he gestured at the tallest of the towers, asking if Henry was impressed by its height and magnificence.

Henry agreed it was an imposing sight, rising almost a hundred cubits over the edge of a steep rocky cliff. At the tower's summit, two sentinels dressed in immaculate white robes stood watching the Dai-el-Kebir's every move. Henry had noticed similar young men positioned atop other towers of the fortress, each smiling and nodding at their master and his guests, all apparently happy and contented. "These men," the Dai-el-Kebir said, "obey me far better than the subjects of Christians will obey their masters."

His guest appeared confused by his host's words. They had not discussed anything to do with armies or obedience.

At the sight of Henry's puzzled expression, the Dai-el-Kebir smiled, said, "Watch," and waved his arms in an obviously pre-arranged signal. Immediately, the men on the peak of the highest tower threw themselves from the ledge and into the air, dashing their bodies to pieces on the rocks below.

Henry was appalled. The two young men had been content and physically fit, yet they had died at the whim of their master without hesitation.

"If you wish," the Dai-el-Kebir said, "I shall order the rest to do the same. All the men atop my towers will do likewise at a signal from me."

Henry declined with thanks, shaken at the sight of the senseless waste of life.

"Could any Christian prince expect such obedience from his subjects?" the Dai-el-Kebir asked.

The count replied that no Christian leader he knew could exert such power over his men. His own warriors, like the warriors of other leaders, would march into battle drawing bravery from their dedication to honor, devotion and loyalty, willing to sacrifice themselves for a greater good. They would die, if necessary, defending themselves and their honor, with the opportunity for victory and glory. But none would act with such apparent delight in the manner that the two young men had, responding to a simple wave of their master's hand.

"By means of these trusty servants," the Dai-el-Kebir said with an attitude of unmistakable superiority, "I rid our society of its enemies."

Henry, Count of Champagne, had encountered the organization that had murdered his predecessor and would terrorize lands from Persia to Palestine for more than a hundred years. He had met the Assassins.

The Assassins were neither among the earliest of secret societies nor the most widespread and enduring. Their actual power lasted little more than a hundred years, waning with the advance of the Mongol hordes, and by the fourteenth century they were no longer a viable force in Middle East politics. Yet so terrifying was their reputation for ruthlessness that many European nations believed the killers were responsible for political murders well into the 1600s, and some evidence suggests that descendants of the Assassins remained active in India as late as 1850. Their legacy extends down to this day in two significant measures.

One is their name. In English, *assassin* identifies the killer of a prominent individual, usually in a violent manner. The other provides a timely motive for probing their origins, because the methods and motivations of the Assassins, initiated almost a millennium ago, serve as the model for the most deadly and prevalent terrorist group at large today. Spiritual descendants of the Dai-el-Kebir and the smiling white-robed men who joyfully threw themselves to death have formed a small secret society that terrorizes the globe. Its members scurry among the hills and waddis of Afghanistan, meet in clandestine cells from Karachi to Cologne, and threaten the world's only remaining superpower. It is called *Al Qaeda*.

The Assassins grew out of a seventh-century schism among Muslims that produced two warring factions, Shiites and Sunnis. No event in any other religion, even the Christian Reformation, produced the enmity created by this division following the death of Mohammed.

Born in AD 570, Mohammed is believed by Muslims to be the last messenger of God, following Adam, Abraham, Moses and Christ. His visions and teachings, acquired in a cave near Mecca around 610, form the basis of the Koran and represent the foundations of Islam. Driven from Mecca for his beliefs, he fled to Yathrib, now called Medina (City of the Prophet) in 622, returning to conquer Mecca on behalf of Islam in 630. Muslims date their calendars from the Prophet's arrival in Medina. At the time of Mohammed's death in 632, Islam had spread across Arabia and into Syria and Persia.

With Mohammed gone, his followers had to deal with the question of naming his successor. Sunnis, who take their name from the Arabic phrase *ahl as-sunnah wa-l-ijma* (People of the Sunnah and the consensus), are considered today as the orthodox branch of Islam. They believed authority should be handed down to the Prophet's closest and most trusted advisers, or caliphs. Shiites ("Followers of Ali") insisted that the bloodline must be rigorously sustained and proposed Mohammed's cousin Ali, who was also his son-in-law, as the Prophet's successor.

It is impossible to overstate the impact of this rift among Muslims, for it extends beyond the question of legitimate succession. Each group disagrees about numerous social and cultural mores, including the date and meaning of sacred ceremonies, the legitimacy of temporary marriages, and the use of religious compromise to escape persecution and death (Shiites accept it, Sunnis consider it apostasy).

Christianity's Reformation wars were mere skirmishes compared with battles between Shiites and Sunnis—battles that usually ended in defeat for the Shiites, who have always been outnumbered about ten to one. Not long after the death of Ali, his grandson Husayn and every member of his family were brutally murdered by the Umayyads, an opposing faction. All Muslims were horrified by this event, which further solidified the split between Sunnis and Shiites; it also provided the Shiites with a sense of tragedy and persecution that colors their beliefs and inspired their melancholy mood down to this day. In Western vernacular, Shiites see themselves as underdogs, an oppressed minority willing to sacrifice themselves if necessary for their convictions. And, as current events demonstrate, they often do.

In the period leading up to the Crusades, individual Shiites living among Sunnis risked death upon discovery. Forced to live in a clandestine manner to survive, they became adept at maintaining secrecy and demanding that members be totally obedient to instructions from their leaders. With time, Shiites arranged themselves into factions, scattered throughout the Middle East, to promote their beliefs and protect their adherents, and while the differences between the factions may appear inconsequential, they fueled enmity and suspicion that helped spawn the Assassins.

Two of the most significant splinter groups were the Twelvers and the Ismailis. The Twelvers believed only twelve true imams (the word means "leader" in Arabic) existed in the Muslim faith and the twelfth imam has remained alive and in hiding for the past thousand years. The Ismailis are further split into various segments including the Seveners, who believe in only seven imams, and the Nizaris, who insist that the imams will never vanish from the earth and identify the Agha Khan as their imam. While the Twelvers are substantially larger in numbers than the Ismailis, comprising 90 percent of the current population of Iran and perhaps 60 percent of Iraqis, the Ismailis have tended to be more violent in response to their minority status within a larger minority.

These divisions, unfamiliar and confusing to non-Muslims, grew insistent upon even the smallest distinction between actions and philosophy, often to the point of violent dissent. In preparation for prayer, for example, purification rituals must be performed. Shiites accept wiping the feet with wet hands to be sufficient, but Sunnis insist that a total cleansing is necessary. In the standing position of prayer, Shiites believe that hands must be held straight down; Sunnis (with the exception of the Malikis group) insist that the hands be folded. Minor concerns? Not to sincere Muslims. These and dozens of other issues remain contentious today; in the Islamic world of a millennium ago, they led to enmity that was often resolved in pitched battles to the death, a fact that must be understood in order to appreciate how the Assassins developed and maintained their ruthless character.

Around AD 1000, a group of Ismailis in Cairo founded the Abode of Learning and began attracting acolytes with promises of secret techniques that would enable believers to carry out divine missions on behalf of Allah. The movement became known as Ismailism, and teachers in the Abode of Learning acted under direct orders of Egypt's ruler, the Caliph of the Fatimites, a direct descendant of Mohammed.

Much of the faculty at the Abode of Learning was drawn from the caliph's own court, and included the commander-in-chief of the army and various ministers. To ensure the Abode's success, the caliph bestowed on it a collection of advanced scientific instruments and an annual endowment of a hundred thousand gold pieces. In its early stages, the group welcomed both men and women into its movement, although the genders remained segregated.

Along with opportunities to acquire an education, students of the Abode were promised that elevations to the highest degrees of learning would earn them a similar level of respect as their teachers. In a culture where government officials and teachers were drawn from the same class, this opportunity held enormous attraction for young people eager to rise above their lowly state, and the prospect of improving their lot while learning to strike back at their Sunni tormentors must have been especially exciting for hot-headed young men.

Whatever goals the caliph may have had for the Abode of Learning, it failed to achieve them directly. Nothing within the Muslim world was altered by the Abode's existence. Its impact, however, continues to resonate to our present day, and the structure it pioneered and implemented became a model employed, with minor variations, by secret societies through the centuries.

Government organizations and large corporations traditionally organize themselves in a pyramid configuration, with one individual at the apex. Immediately below is a small, generally cohesive group of advisers—think of the cabinet in a democracy, and a board of directors in a corporation. From the summit down, in steadily decreasing levels of influence and authority, layers of bureaucracy extend towards the wide base, which consists of the lowest-paid and least-recognized workers. This common means of corralling and controlling power remains familiar and understandable to us today. It is not the only method of structuring an organization, however, and in the case of secret societies it is far from the most appropriate.

Instead of pyramids, many secret societies and religious cults tend to be organized at the epicenter of a series of concentric circles, with the ultimate power residing somewhere in the hub. Circular organizations are not nearly as easily understood or penetrated as pyramid structures are because their internal mechanism remains concealed. In addition, the number of circles can vary, meaning that outsiders are never aware of how close they may be to the actual center of power. From the foot of a pyramid, you can see the summit, but from anywhere within a circular organization you can never accurately measure your proximity to authority. In this manner, circular organizations conceal and protect their centers more effectively than pyramid structures.

The circular configuration of the Abode of Learning, copied by religious-based secret societies over the years, began with study groups called Assemblies of Wisdom, designed to discard candidates lacking sufficient dedication.

Successful graduates of the Assemblies of Wisdom entered a nine-stage initiation procedure built upon the characteristic circle structure. This initiation process represents a classic method of securing allegiance to a group's cause and building a foundation of unquestioned obedience.

In the first initiation stage, doubts were planted in the minds of students about the values and concepts they had been taught to respect throughout their lives. Applying false analogies, teachers began to dismantle their students' entire system of beliefs and any who were unable to deny their beliefs and values were dismissed. Those who accepted the teachings—essentially emptying their minds—were warmly congratulated by their instructors. Today, we refer to this technique as *brainwashing*. With no value system in place, students were forced to rely upon their teachers as a source of knowledge and the means to apply it. The most dedicated students swore a vow of blind allegiance to their masters, elevating them to the second degree.

Students who reached the second degree were informed that seven great imams represented the source of wisdom and knowledge delivered by the prophet Mohammed, and these imams had personally communicated that knowledge to the teachers. Teachers in the Abode of Learning were all highly placed officers in the caliph's administration, meaning that students could trace divine inspiration directly from the Prophet to the very people who were passing His wisdom to them. With this awareness, the students moved through the second degree with enthusiasm.

In the third degree of initiation, the names of these seven imams were revealed, along with secret words to summon them for assistance and protection.

Revelations continued through the fourth degree, when the teachers added the names of the Seven Mystical Law-givers to the seven imams, along with magical properties attributed to each. The names of the Mystical Law-givers were Adam, Noah,

Abraham, Moses, Jesus, Mohammed and Ismail, and they had seven mystical helpers: Seth, Shem, Ishmael, Aaron, Simon, Ali and Mohammed, son of Ismail. Through further lessons other names were revealed, including those of the twelve apostles under the seven prophets, along with their individual functions and magical powers. Finally, students learned the existence of a mysterious deputy known as the Lord of the Time, who spoke only through the caliph.

Qualifying students moved to the initiation's fifth degree, where they acquired the ability to influence others through the power of personal concentration. Documents suggest this was actually a form of deep meditation, with students required to repeat, for endless periods of time, a single word: AK-ZABT-I. Meditation can be an effective means of relaxation because it effectively blocks the thinking process. Extend the technique long enough and intensely enough, however, and it severely damages the ability of individuals to think for themselves, which was the goal of the fifth degree.

The sixth degree consisted of instruction in analytical and destructive arguments, precisely the technique used by teachers to disarm students in the first degree. Successfully passing an examination qualified students for the seventh degree, where they were informed that all humanity and all creation were one, including both positive and negative powers. Students could use their power for either creativity or destruction, but the power was available only from the mysterious Lord of the Time.

Now they were prepared to accept the teachings of the eighth and ninth degrees even though, to our eye, *the teachings appear in total contradiction to the spiritual values that motivated the movement in the first place.*

Reaching the eighth degree required students to recognize that all religion and philosophy were fraudulent; the primary force on earth was the will and dedication of the individual; and individuals could attain true fulfillment only through servitude to the imams. This prepared students for the ninth degree, which taught there was no such thing as belief; all that mattered in life was action, taken in direct response to instructions from the leader, who alone possessed the reasons for carrying out these orders.

Throughout the levels of instruction, the lesson of the nine degrees could be summed up in a single declaration: *Nothing Is True, Everything Is Permitted.*

The Abode of Learning created an organization populated with members willing to perform any task assigned by their leaders. Its most significant achievement was the taking of Baghdad in 1058 by a graduate of the Abode, who crowned himself sultan and coined money in the name of the Egyptian caliph. No other achievement by a student from the Abode of Learning compared with this feat, but the glory proved short-lived, as was the graduate himself. He was soon slain by the Turks, who swore that anyone associated with the Abode of Learning would pay with his life. Along with other events, including a weakening of moral and financial support from the caliph's descendants, the society's operations began to dwindle until, in 1123, they closed forever.

The Abode's demise may have ended the formal training procedure of the movement, but it did not end the secret society, whose members remained underground for many years, each describing its operations and achievements to the next generation. One of those who listened with wonder was a remarkable man named Hasan, son of Sabbah, whose family originated in Khorasan, the vast open regions of eastern Iran bordering Afghanistan. Sabbah, a prominent politician and learned man, was descended from Abode members who had achieved the ninth degree of Ismailism, and he passed at least some of this knowledge to his son.

As a young man, Hasan was placed under the tutorship of Imam Muwafiq, who chose to instruct only the most promising students and taught them the secrets of achieving power. There must have been something to the Imam's teaching techniques because among Hasan's colleagues at the school were the future poet and astronomer Omar Khayyam and a brilliant youth

Hasan Sabbah. His creation of the Assassins launched
a terrorist technique that functions to this day.

named Nizam-al-Mulk, who rose to
become prime minister of Persia. While
studying with the Imam, these three young
men agreed that whoever rose to power
first would assist the other two.

Nizam kept his promise. After achieving
a position of authority and influence among the Persians, he
secured a pension for Khayyam, enabling the poet to live a life
of ease in his beloved Nishapur region, where the *Rubaiyat* was
composed. For his friend Hasan, Nizam obtained a ministerial
post in the shah's palace.

Hasan proved to be an excellent administrator, winning first
the favor and later the trust of the shah, who assigned him the
duty of managing the regime's wealth. Whether Hasan was larcenous from the beginning or his ethics became blinded by the
sparkle of gold and jewels, the shah's trust was misplaced for
Hasan embezzled enormous amounts of the kingdom's riches.
Fleeing just ahead of the shah's guards, Hasan escaped to Cairo,
remembering his father's tales of the Abode of Learning, where
he believed he would be safe from certain execution. There he
encountered a group of Ismailis who comprised the remaining
nucleus of the old society. They had been waiting generations
for both an opportunity and a leader to restore its power. Hasan
was that man.

Charismatic, cunning, ruthless and intelligent, Hasan gathered a number of adherents, convincing them that he possessed
magical powers awarded by the Prophet himself. Their devotion
to him grew stronger when, on a sea voyage to Africa, Hasan and
his followers encountered a sudden violent storm. Soon waves
were towering over the small ship, lightning flashed, thunder
rumbled, and winds threatened to smash the craft against the
rocks if the water didn't first engulf the vessel and its occupants.

Everyone on board panicked, and began to wail and pray.

Everyone except Hasan, who remained calm and undisturbed. When they asked how he could remain tranquil when facing almost certain death, Hasan smiled and replied, "Our Lord has promised that no evil shall befall me."

And no evil did. The storm soon passed, the sea grew calm, and Hasan's devotees regarded him with even greater awe and respect. Back in Cairo, the tale of Hasan's stoic nature was repeated over and over again. Hasan was a blessed man protected from evil, a man to heed, and a man to follow. Hasan himself tended the tale with all the care and patience of a shrewd farmer anticipating a rich harvest.

Meanwhile, he continued to absorb the training techniques employed by the Abode of Learning, recognizing that the power available to anyone who could refine the Abode's methods could be applied in a different context, with different goals. After a few months Hasan, accompanied by his most trusted supporters, returned to the region of his father's birth. He had found his destiny. Investing the riches he had stolen from the shah, and applying the brainwashing procedures of the Abode, he would construct a murderous society around a spectacular deception.

Hasan's plan was based upon building trust and loyalty among a cluster of young followers by adapting methods pioneered at the Abode of Learning. After arriving in the Alborz Mountains, he traveled to a massive fortress shadowed by high mountain peaks north and west of the present Iranian city of Qazvin. The land here is exceptionally rugged, with nearby volcanic Mount Damavand soaring almost 6000 meters in height, creating a natural barrier between the Caspian Sea and the gently flowing plains of central Iran. For many years, Shiites fleeing persecution from Sunnis fled to the Alborz for safety. Tehran, the capital, may be barely a hundred kilometers distant, but the region remains remote to this day.

Crowning a rugged mountain crest almost half a kilometer long and in some places only a few meters wide, the fortress appeared as a natural wall of rock from a distance, blindingly white in the afternoon sun, blue-gray in the dusk light, and blood-red at dawn. Approaching the structure, travelers encountered a steep gravel slope that foiled any attempt to reach its vertical walls. In fact, the fortress was inaccessible except by a steep spiral stairway designed so that it could be defended by a single archer guarding its summit.

Hasan was familiar with both the terrain and the castle, and he knew many of its guards were sympathetic to Shiite extremists. With the cooperation of these backers, Hasan won entry to the fortress and confronted the owner, demanding that he turn the fortress over to him. Surprisingly, considering later developments, Hasan paid the man a reasonable sum for his property and sent him on his way, winning total control of the bastion without drawing his sword. He renamed the fortress Alamut, meaning Eagle's Nest, and began converting it into a training facility and operations center dedicated to the murder of Hasan's chosen enemies.

The remains of the Assassins' original stronghold, Alamut, in northern Iran. At one time, over twenty such fortresses dotted the landscape.

Hasan's next step was to transform a secluded corner of the valley into a walled garden out of the castle's view. Diverting streams through the garden, he constructed numerous fountains and settled beautiful young *houris* there. According to the *Siret-al-Hakem* (*Memoirs of Hakem*), an Arabian historical romance from that era, Hasan

> caused to be made a vast garden in which he had water conducted. In the middle of this garden he built a kiosk raised to the height of four stories. On each of the four sides were richly ornamented windows joined by four arches in which were painted stars of gold and silver. He had with him twenty slaves, ten males and ten females, who had come with him from the region of the Nile, and who had scarcely attained the age of puberty. He clothed them in silks and the finest linens, and gave them bracelets of gold and silver....
>
> He divided the garden into four parts. In the first of these were pear trees, apple trees, vines, cherries, mulberries, plums and other fruit trees. In the second were oranges, lemons, olives,

The view from Alamut.

pomegranates and other fruits. In the third were cucumbers, melons, leguminous plants and so on. In the fourth were roses, jasmine, tamarinds, narcissi, violets, lilies and anemones....

Marco Polo passed through the region some years later, and described the scene in detail:

> In a beautiful valley was a luxurious garden stored with every delicious fruit and every fragrant shrub that could be procured. Palaces of various sizes and forms were erected in different parts of the grounds, ornamented with works of gold and paintings and furniture of rich silks. Streams of wine and pure honey flowed in every direction. Entry to the garden was restricted to a secret passage out of the castle fortress.
>
> The inhabitants of these places were elegant and beautiful damsels accomplished in the arts of singing, playing musical instruments, dancing, and especially games of dalliance and amorous allurement. Clothed in rich dresses, they sported and amused themselves in the gardens and pavilions.
>
> The object of the chief was this: Mohammed had promised that those who obeyed his will would enjoy the pleasures of Paradise forever. In Paradise, every species of sensual gratification would be found, including the company of beautiful and willing nymphs. The chief, claiming to be a descendant of Mohammed and thus also a prophet, had the power of admitting to Paradise after their deaths those whom he favored, which included those who had sacrificed their life on this earth in the fulfilling of his orders.

With his earthly paradise in place, Hasan attracted young men between ages twelve and twenty to Alamut, choosing those whom he believed could become killers. He also pur-

Marco Polo accurately described the chilling control Hasan held over his young Muslim disciples.

chased unwanted children from their parents, raising them with all the fixed purpose of a contemporary horse trainer shaping a future winner for the Derby. Along with techniques drawn from the Abode of Learning that elevated students towards a promised position within a circular command structure, Hasan added further motivation among the young men with repeated descriptions of the pleasures of Paradise. Once their curiosity was sufficiently heightened, Hasan revealed that he was able to transport the youths to Paradise for a short time so they could sample its pleasures without having to undergo the inconvenience of dying first.

Those who appeared to believe his tale were drugged with hashish and other narcotics until they sank into a deep, almost comatose sleep. In that condition, they were carried through a secret passage to the kiosk in the hidden garden. Once Hasan and his trusted assistants had returned to the fortress the *houris*, obeying Hasan's instructions, splashed the young men with vinegar to wake them. The confused youths were told they had entered Paradise, a concept that, in their drugged condition, appeared plausible. With fruit and wine in abundance, they lay back on plush satin cushions while the *houris* filled—and probably exceeded—all of their adolescent fantasies. Reportedly, the maidens would whisper into each aspirant's ear,

> We are only waiting for thy death, for this place is destined for thee. This is but one of the pavilions of Paradise, and we are the *houris* and the children of Paradise. If thou were dead, thou would be forever with us. But thou art only dreaming, and will soon awake.

After a day of this illusion, the youths would be drugged to unconsciousness again and returned to the fortress, where they were permitted to slowly awake.

When asked by Hasan, and later by the chiefs who replaced him, where they had been, they would reply, "In Paradise, through the favor of Your Highness." Then, encouraged by their leader, they would describe their experience in great detail to others. The envy of those who absorbed these testosterone-fueled tales of beautiful and willing young women, and endless supplies of fruit and wine, must have been spectacular.

"We have the assurance of the Prophet," Hasan and his later deputies would promise the youths, "that he who defends his lord shall inherit Paradise forever, and if you show yourself to be obedient to my orders, that happy lot is yours." The most gullible could hardly wait.

How convincing was this subterfuge? Convincing enough that some followers committed suicide in the belief that they would be instantly transported to Paradise and all its rumored delights, a practice Hasan suppressed by explaining that only those who died in obedience to his orders would receive the key to Paradise. These were the young men who, posing as Christian monks, slaughtered Conrad of Montferrat and endured horrific tortures in silence following their capture. They were the men who launched themselves from high towers at their leader's command as a demonstration of their unflinching obedience. And they were the first to be known as the *hashshashin* or assassins, instruments of revenge and political expediency throughout the Middle East.

A few historians have questioned the likelihood that twelfth-century men could be so gullible and trusting, suggesting the tale is an allegory or at best apocryphal. In response, others note that these were impressionable youths and point to the accounts of Henry, Count of Champagne, and Marco Polo as evidence that Hasan's deception actually worked. From today's perspective, recent events imply not only that Hasan's techniques were successful, but also that they continue to be effective on a regular, almost daily, basis. On the streets of Baghdad, Beirut and Tel Aviv young men and, increasingly, young women carry out terrorist activities by sacrificing themselves as human bombs, many in the belief that they will be transported instantly to Paradise. Knowing this, we can hardly doubt the authenticity of those tales of Hasan and his fanatical followers. Muslim youths of a millennium ago rarely encountered any nubile females outside their own family. An afternoon with a barely clad girl willing to engage him in carnal delights would have the usual impact on a pubescent boy, heightened even more by his narcotic-induced state of mind.

Hasan's manipulation of his young followers spawned more than an efficient killing machine. It also spawned other fables that may or may not be rooted in reality.

As described in the ancient work *Art of Imposture* by Abdel-Rahman of Damascus, Hasan strengthened his power over the trusting disciples by digging a deep, narrow pit in the floor of his chambers. Within the pit he positioned a young man, known to others in the fortress, so that only the youth's head appeared above the level of the floor. Then, after filling in the space surrounding the young man's body, Hasan had a two-piece circular dish with a hole in the middle set on the floor around the man's neck as though the head were resting on a plate. To add to the subterfuge, fresh blood was poured on the plate, completing the realistic impression of a severed head.

Recruits, perhaps drugged with hashish, were brought into the room and, in their presence, the "head" explained that he had followed the Master's instructions, earning himself a place in Paradise. While his awed compatriots listened, the much-alive young man described all the pleasures he was enjoying there—endless fruit and wine, luxurious surroundings, and beautiful and willing young virgins.

"You have seen the head of a man who died while carrying out my commands," Hasan told the undoubtedly wide-eyed onlookers. "He is a man you all know. I willed him to speak with his own tongue of the pleasures that his soul is enjoying even now. Go and fulfill my orders." It was pretty persuasive stuff, made even more plausible when, after the recruits departed, Hasan chopped off the talking head—no doubt to its owner's surprise—and displayed it on the parapet of the fortress for everyone to see. Their former colleague, Hasan's followers believed, was indeed enjoying the pleasures of Paradise, even as they remained on earth. How soon could they join him?

None of the reported techniques used by Hasan and those who replaced him is surprising to contemporary experts. Psychiatrist Robert Jay Lifton, in his book *Thought Reform and the Psychology of Totalism*, outlines three primary characteristics of secret societies that are as effective today as they were in Hasan's time. They are the following:

1. A charismatic leader who becomes an object of worship when the general principles that originally sustained the group lose their power.
2. A process such as coercive persuasion or thought reform.
3. Economic, sexual and other forms of exploitation of group members by the leader and ruling coterie.

The Assassins were not overly selective in choosing their victims. During the Crusades, they supported whichever side suited their purposes while maintaining a vendetta against Sunnis. On at least one occasion they combined forces with the Knights Templar, hated enemies of Saladin and his Islamic defenders of Jerusalem. And by charging fees from others in a murder-for-hire operation, the Assassins built a substantial income over the years.

When their reign of terror against selected targets rose to a crest, a mere rumor that an individual had somehow offended Hasan or had been selected for death was sufficient for the man to flee for his life. Few managed to escape.

Added to the certainty of death was the uncertainty of its time and place. The sultan's own prime minister, Nizam-al-Mulk, was cut to pieces by an Assassin posing as a dervish while Nizam was being carried in a litter to his harem, his mind likely diverted with expectations of carnal delights even as the dagger was plunged into his chest. The Atabeg[1] of Hims warned that

[1] *Atabeg* was a title of nobility commonly used in Mesopotamia from the twelfth century. The term indicated a governor of a nation, below an emperor or king in rank but above a khan, as well as a military advisor to a young and inexperienced prince.

he had been selected for murder by the Assassins, kept a contingent of armed guards always at his side. As the atabeg entered a mosque for prayers, the guards relaxed their vigil, for who would dare offend Allah by committing murder at such a time? In an eye blink, the atabeg was surrounded by Assassins who cut him to ribbons. And when a Christian, the Marquis Corrado di Montefeltro, was named for death, he was attacked by two Assassins posing as monks even as the marquis was being entertained by the Bishop of Tyre at a banquet. They managed only to wound the marquis before one of the Assassins was killed. The other managed to escape and hide in the chapel, where he knew the marquis would arrive to give thanks for his deliverance from certain death. He did, and as the marquis knelt in prayer, the surviving Assassin emerged from behind the altar and finished the job before dying in bliss at the hands of guards.

When it served their advantage, the Assassins chose intimidation over outright murder. After the Assassins dispatched the son of Nizam-al-Mulk with their daggers, the father declared he would lead an army unlike any in history, march on Alamut, and destroy it and all of its inhabitants. One evening, arriving within sight of the fortress and making camp in the foothills of the Alborz, Nizam-al-Mulk went to sleep confident that he would rise the next day to lead his warriors against the Assassins, wiping them from the face of the earth. When he awoke in the morning, he found a dagger buried to its hilt in the sand next to his head, the blade piercing a note warning that nothing but massacre awaited him and his army.

None of Nizam-al-Mulk's entourage could explain how the dagger and note had been placed there. No one had been seen approaching his tent. Had it been ghosts or spirits? Whatever it was, Nizam-al-Mulk decided to call off his attack, instructing his forces to avoid the region in the future, and providing Hasan and his followers with a free hand throughout the Muslim world.

As Hasan increased both his power and wealth he expanded his authority, acquiring and strengthening fortifications among the crags of the Alborz, each impregnable to all but the largest, most dedicated armies. And as the years passed, Hasan acquired a description that sounds almost paternal to today's ears. He and each of his descendants who led a group of Assassins, including the Dai-el-Kebir, became known as the Old Man of the Mountain.

The Assassins did not restrict themselves to political or spiritual figures, nor did they lack an appreciation for the power of psychology to achieve their goals, as they proved with their intimidation of the sultan. The Imam Razi, one of the great Muslim intellectuals of his era, was foolish enough to insult the Assassins by declaring they were not qualified theologians, until visited by an envoy of the group who offered the Imam a choice: death by dagger or an annual pension of a thousand gold pieces. The imam's condemnation promptly ceased, causing a colleague to ask why the wise man was no longer criticizing the Assassins. The old man glanced quickly around. "Because," he whispered, "their arguments are so sharp. And pointed."

Fear of the Assassins grew not only out of their ruthlessness but also from the unpredictability of their actions, and the near impossibility of preventing an attack once a command was issued. Hasan and his successors originated and perfected the strategy of "sleeper cells," dedicated killers dispatched to communities hundreds of miles away and instructed to meld into local society until ordered to act. These devotees might wait for years until contacted by an envoy. By this time, they could approach the victim without raising suspicion about their identity or intention. Adding to the difficulty would be the assassin's demeanor—calm, almost pleasurable, not fearing reprisal but actually welcoming it as his entry into Paradise.

The Assassins, under the direction of Hasan and his lieutenants, terrorized the Middle East into the thirteenth century. Hasan's son and loyal followers assumed leadership after the founder's death, and at least three generations of his descendants carried on his work. But not even the Assassins could resist the brutality of the Mongols.

Hasan's grandson provided the first break with the murderous tradition. Upon his elevation to the position of Imam in 1210, Hasan III did the unthinkable by converting to the Sunni faith, restoring Islamic law and even inviting Sunni teachers to visit Alamut. The apparent conversion had less to do with theology than with practicality and survival: hordes of Mongols, whose legendary ferocity made even the Assassins quake in their boots, were beginning to flow across the steppes into Persia. Faced with a common enemy, both Shiites and Sunnis set aside their differences to launch a mutual defense.

Hasan III's sense of discretion was not, unfortunately for his followers, passed on to his son Muhammad III, also called Aladdin (Height of the Faith). Muhammad returned the group to Shiite beliefs and exceeded all previous Assassin leaders for cruelty, to the point where most historians consider him mad. He was so intolerable that his followers quickly transferred their allegiance to his son Khurshah, who attempted to negotiate an understanding with the Mongols now heavily infiltrating the mountainous area.

It was too late. In the mid-thirteenth century, the Mongol leader Hulagu Khan began methodically attacking each mountain stronghold of the Assassins. Using trickery, brutality and the force of overwhelming arms, the Mongols seized each fortress one by one, slaughtering the inhabitants and laying waste to the carefully contrived Paradise on Earth.

The Assassins were too devoted, too fanatic, and too numerous to be totally eliminated, even by the Mongols who swept through the region like a tsunami of slaughter. A few managed to escape to India, where they became known as the *Khojas* (honorable converts) and resumed their practices on a limited scale. Remnants of the sect reportedly still exist in Iraq, Iran and Syria, but they are little more than splinter groups of militant Shiites.

The Assassins were more than an early prototype of Murder Inc. Their influence extends, in both benign and malignant versions, through the present day. The concentric circular construction of the Abode of Learning, adapted by Hasan, became a prototype for restricted organizations and secret societies. Most notable are the Freemasons, who drew inspiration for their organizational structure from the Knights Templar, reputed allies of the Assassins during the Crusades.

The most extreme and trustworthy followers of Hasan and his successors became known as *fidayeen*. The name continues to be attached to Islamic fanatics battling enemies of the Prophet, whether infidel Westerners or Muslims following a wrong path. For most of them, including the fanatical young men who flew hijacked American aircraft into the World Trade Center on September 11, 2001, the motivation continues to be the promise of eternity in Paradise, an incentive that seems to work even without the persuasion of Hasan's contrived "previews."

The tactic of embedding followers into a targeted society as "sleepers," suicidal fanatics prepared to slaughter as many people as necessary in the name of their cause, is another element inherited from a millennium ago. Both the promise of Paradise and adherents immersing themselves for years in the very culture they have vowed to destroy are familiar to everyone aware of Al Qaeda.

Al Qaeda does not entirely duplicate the design first established by the Assassins. Their assumed leader Osama bin Laden is a Sunni, not a Shiite, although extreme elements from both factions stand united against much of the Western world. And while the Assassins recruited young men as suicidal killers on the promise of immediate dispatch to Paradise and the arms of waiting *houris*, violent Muslim factions recently have succeeded in recruiting young women to carry out similar missions based, apparently, solely on dedication to the group's success. Clearly, however, the link between Hasan's Assassins and bin Laden's Al Qaeda remains unbroken. Were Hasan, the Old Man of the Mountain, to meet with Osama bin Laden, the leader of Al Qaeda, they would see each other as compatriots, brothers under the skin.

TWO
TEMPLARS, ILLUMINATI AND FREEMASONS
THE SECRET SEAT OF POWER

WHO ARE THE MOST DANGEROUS MEMBERS OF THE VARIOUS secret societies skulking the earth, people with power to change our lives and direct the course of history? According to sources claiming inner knowledge of the group's true purpose, they are Freemasons. Masonic conspirators choose international leaders, launch wars, control currencies and infiltrate society, among other applications of their hidden powers, or so the tales propose. When anyone questions this premise, conspiracy theorists trot out an impressive array of proof, beginning with a recital of influential men through history who were undeniably associated with Masonry, including many signers of the U.S. Declaration of Independence. Who holds higher positions in the American pantheon of heroes and great thinkers than Benjamin Franklin, George Washington and Andrew Jackson? All were Freemasons. In fact, at least twenty-five U.S. presidents and vice-presidents have been active and enthusiastic supporters of Masonry. Two of them—Harry Truman and

Masons dominated Western politics and cultures for years. Among their members were U.S. presidents George Washington and Harry S. Truman, British prime minister Winston Churchill, and the elegant Duke Ellington.

Gerald Ford—could boast 33rd Degree status, the highest level of recognition within the organization.

It is a remarkable achievement, this elevation of a private club with secret rituals into an incubator of leaders, visionaries and intellectuals. On the face of it, the Masons appear to inspire men of exceptional talent far beyond that of any other organization ranging from the Boy Scouts to Rhodes scholars. What is it about their values and systems that breeds such overachievers?

To a few fanatic historians—almost all of them Masons—at the root of their achievements is a historic and inspirational link with the Knights Templar, who began as Defenders of the Christian Faith, became the bankers of medieval Europe, and succumbed to the machinations of a greedy king and a complicitous pope.

Once acclaimed and admired for chivalrous deeds and good works on behalf of Christianity, the Knights Templar safeguarded pilgrims on their way to the Holy Land and battled Islamic armies for control of Jerusalem. Genuine knights in an era when that title brought respect and admiration, they obeyed rules of chivalry and asceticism, dedicating their lives to the glory of God and the protection of Christian pilgrims.

That was the admirable side of the society. The darker side hid rumors of associations between Templars and the Assassins,

the replacement of Templar moral values with outright greed, a decline in commendable character traits and the pursuit of various obscene and blasphemous practices. These attributes are not a model for any high-profile organization seeking respect, let alone

In their early years, Knights Templar were identified with chastity, piety and bravery. Later, their reputation grew less admirable.

one that prides itself on providing world leaders and community benefits. But dark complexity and suspicion provided the necessary intrigue and color for a later group whose original objective was to protect the secrets of tradesmen. Along the way, the Templars' spiritual leader managed to be compared to, and perhaps even mistaken for, Christ himself.

The Templars were a product of the Crusades. And the Crusades, contrary to popular belief, were the result not of chivalrous intent or even a dedication to the Christian faith, but of feudalist obligation.

Historians, as is their manner, vacillate as much about the definition of feudalism as they do about its structure, and a few now reject the notion of a "feudalistic age." Whatever title is hung upon it, Europeans living during the period between AD 800 and 1300 experienced a way of life that bridged inchoate barbarianism and the roots of democracy. During this time, kings may have claimed wide authority over lands we now know as France, Germany, Britain, but the countryside was effectively ruled not by monarchs but by individual lords and barons. Dominating the lands encompassed by their estates, the lords dispensed justice, levied taxes and tolls, minted their own currency, and demanded military service from citizens occupying their lands. Most lords, in fact, could field larger armies than could the king, who was often a figurehead ruler.

The social structure was many layered and clearly defined. Serfs represented the lowest level, performing basic labor and having no claim to any wealth they created. Vassals worked the land on behalf of the lord; knights, whose primary qualities included sufficient funds to own both a horse and armor, performed services on behalf of the lords; and the clergy administered spiritual assistance as required. Lords, in turn, were considered vassals to more powerful rulers, and all were formally considered vassals to the king.

Feudal loyalty flowed in two directions. The citizens made an oath of loyalty to the lord, paid taxes imposed by him, and attended the court when summoned. The lord's obligation included protecting the vassals from intruders, an act that was admittedly as much in the lord's interests as in the vassals'.

Out of this linear arrangement, subjected to the influence of Christianity, came the concept of chivalry. Vassals and knights, heeding the rights and property of their feudal lord, elevated the notion through terms such as "proud submission" and "dignified obedience" inspired, perhaps, by Biblical tales of Christ's actions. Phrased in this manner, behavior that appears to mirror a master–slave relationship was spun into something more reputable and uplifting. As contradictory as it may sound, individuals could elevate their status by lowering their position on behalf of some splendid goal. Popular literature suggests that the incentive for chivalrous behavior was romantic interest in an elegant lady who had stolen the knight's heart, and to whom he pledged eternal reverence. In reality, a knight's "proud submission" was made either to God or to the lord who controlled the knight's destiny. The romantic aspect of chivalrous behavior, glorifying womanhood in a manner that combined worship of the Virgin with suppressed sexual desire, remains an inspirational source for much fiction but was basically a by-product of a deeper motivation.

Chivalric demands were rigid. Obligations were expected to be fulfilled, and vassals and knights accepted a sacred duty to defend by arms the honor and property of the class above themselves. Since the pyramid structure of medieval society set Christ at the apex, lords, knights and vassals alike were equally obligated to defend His rights and honor.

With feudalism solidly established throughout Europe, lords and knights, accompanied by a retinue of servants, began the practice of making pilgrimages to Jerusalem as a means of expressing their Christian faith. Reviving a concept dating back to early Greeks, who trekked to Delphi in search of wisdom, European Christians began setting off on pilgrimages to the Holy Land, first in honor of Christ, later as a means of cleansing their sins, and later still in response to direct instructions from the pope.

Prominent early pilgrims in search of spotless souls included Frotmond of Brittany, who murdered his uncle and younger brother; and Fulk de Nerra, Count of Anjou, who burned his wife alive, which was evidence of serious marital discord and abuse even in those tumultuous pre-feminist times. Both men sought forgiveness with a pilgrimage to the Holy Land, and both achieved success, albeit in contrasting measure.

After years spent wandering the shores of the Red Sea and searching the mountains of Armenia for relics of Noah's Ark, Frotmond returned home swaddled in the warmth of forgiveness for murdering his relatives, and passed the remainder of his days in the convent of Redon. For his sins, Fulk de Nerra wandered the streets of Jerusalem accompanied by a retinue of servants who beat him with rods while he repeated the words, "Lord, have mercy on a faithless and perjured Christian, on a sinner wandering far from his home." His apparent sincerity impressed the Muslims so much that they granted him entry into the room of the Sacred Tomb, normally forbidden to Christians, where he threw himself prostrate upon the bejeweled floor. While wailing for his wretched soul, de Nerra managed to detach and pocket a few precious stones from the site.

The examples set by Frotmond, de Nerra and others had their impact on devout Christians. Around AD 1050, making a pilgrimage to the Holy Land was considered a duty for every able Christian as a means of assuaging guilt and appeasing the wrath of God, and the Church began assigning a pilgrimage as a common means of penance. By 1075, pilgrimage trails had become as well defined and well traveled as trade routes.

The pilgrims' trek, usually tracing the Adriatic coast before turning overland to Constantinople and across Asia Minor to Antioch, was neither more nor less dangerous than any other journey of similar length. Their established route, however, proved a factor in 1095 when Byzantine emperor Alexius Comnenus pleaded for Pope Urban II to help in defeating a group of Muslim tribes known as the Seljuk Turks. After seizing Anatolia, the Byzantine Empire's richest province, the

Seljuks occupied Antioch, Tripoli and finally Jerusalem. Now, it seemed, they had their eye on Constantinople itself. If the pope could organize an army of dedicated Christians to assist Byzantine troops, Alexius suggested, together they could retake Antioch and restore Jerusalem itself to Christian rule.

The promise of Christian rule over the Holy Land, bolstered by expectations of wealth tapped from the Byzantine emperor's own treasury, was enough to inspire Urban II to launch the first papacy-sanctioned holy war. Thus, almost two hundred years of horrific slaughter on both sides began with a goal as much mercenary as it was spiritual, and in 1096 the first of nine crusades set off, inspired by Urban's cry *Deus vult!* (God wills it!)

Deciding to take part in a crusade was a serious decision, even for the most devout of Christians. It meant at least two years of travel across rugged and often hostile country, although later crusades reduced the time by sailing eastward along the Mediterranean from Provence. Seeking food and shelter during the long journey from Europe to Palestine and back, pilgrims and crusaders had to deal with open hostility from both the Muslims and Greek Orthodox administrators. In response Gerard de Martignes established a hospital in Jerusalem to serve as a refuge. Consisting of twelve attached mansions, the facility included gardens and an impressive library. Soon local merchants created an adjoining marketplace to trade with the pilgrims, paying the hospital administrator two pieces of gold for the right to set up stalls.

This was too good for feudal entrepreneurs to ignore. When the flow of pilgrims swelled to an endless flood, a group of Italian traders from the Amalfi region established a second hospital near the Church of the Holy Sepulcher, this one operated by Benedictine monks, with its own profitable marketplace. Soon the second facility began overflowing, promoting the monks to create yet another hospital, dedicating it to St. John the Compassionate.

The men of St. John the Compassionate elevated the concept to a new spiritual status. They devoted their lives to

The two Templars on horseback, as shown on their seal, indicated brotherhood, but later generations spied a sexual reference.

providing safety and comfort for pilgrims by treating their patients as their masters, creating a prototype for every charitable organization that followed them, although none matched their dedication and humility. This practice, of course, reflected the true origins and goals of chivalry, attracting many knights who set aside their military objectives in favor of emulating the most charitable of Christ's teachings. Their military bearing and discipline were never wholly discarded, however. Among those they served, the knights were liberal and compassionate; among themselves, they were rigid and austere. They pledged vows of poverty, chastity and obedience, and their dress became a black mantle bearing a simple white cross on the breast. They were called the Sovereign Military Order of the Hospital of Saint John of Jerusalem, of Rhodes and of Malta, known simply as the Hospitaliers.

Vows of poverty, chastity and obedience may have suited their obligations to chivalrous behavior (and, they no doubt anticipated, facilitated their entry into heaven), but they did little to protect the Hospitaliers from the dangers of attack by various factions in the Holy Land. With time, the Hospitaliers grew focused almost as much on their military actions in defense of their order as on their acts of benevolence. Most were armed knights, after all, noble of birth and adhering to the high standards of true chivalry.

They were also as human as anyone else, of that era or ours, and when powerful European duchies expressed admiration for the Hospitaliers by awarding them extensive lands in Europe, the members accepted the donations gladly. In addition to this source of income, they assumed the right to claim booty seized from defeated Muslim fighters, and by the time Gerard died in 1118 the Hospitaliers had acquired substantial assets from their patrons, and exceptional independence from Church authority. What began as selfless dedication to the poor, injured and diseased had evolved into an organization more akin to a modern-day service club, whose well-heeled members were at least as interested in fraternal association and public status as they were in helping their neighbors.

The Hospitaliers may have been capable military men, but their raison d'être continued to be public service. Battling Muslims while fulfilling their obligations was proving a distraction from their primary goal, and others were needed to direct as much energy into fighting the enemy as the Hospitaliers were investing in caring for Christians.

It may be cynical to imply that the wealth accrued by the Hospitaliers as a result of their charitable services inspired their more celebrated brethren, but history suggests it played a role. In any case, a new society was formed within ten years of Gerard's death. Comprised originally of nine knights led by Hugh de Payens, the followers claimed the same ascetic and pious characteristics that distinguished the original Hospitaliers. This new group, however, focused on the hazards faced by pilgrims and Crusaders—by now the distinction was growing blurred and almost meaningless—during their trek to the Holy Land and their stay in Jerusalem.

The hazards arose from multiple threats. Egyptians and Turks resented passage and intrusion through their countries, Islamic residents of Jerusalem objected to the pilgrims' presence, nomadic Arab tribes attacked and robbed the travelers, and Syrian Christians expressed hostility towards the foreigners.

Much of the group's early reputation for humility and valor was rooted in de Payens' personality, described as "sweet-tempered, totally dedicated, and ruthless on behalf of the faith." To a modern sensibility, the concept of being sweet-tempered and ruthless may appear contradictory, but to medieval observers they were perfectly compatible. A battle-hardened veteran of the First Crusade, de Payens took delight in recounting the number of Muslims he had slain without, apparently, souring his day-to-day charitable mood. And why should he? The even more pious Bernard of Clairvaux had declared that the killing of Muslims was not homicide but malicide, the killing of evil. Thousands of dead Muslims in the Holy Land may have begged to differ, but their opinions were rarely sought.

So de Payens, single-minded to the exclusion of everything except the worship of God and the slaughter of Muslims, gathered men around him who committed themselves to protecting pilgrims from danger in the same manner that Gerard's Hospitaliers were healing and feeding them. The new group, de Payens announced, would combine the qualities of ascetic monks and valiant warriors, living a life of chastity and piety, and employing their swords in the service of Christianity. To aid them in achieving this somewhat contradictory role, they chose as their patroness La Dolce Mère de Dieu (The Sweet Mother of God), and vowed to live according to the canons of St. Augustine.

Baldwin II, then ruling as King of Jerusalem, was sufficiently impressed with the group's character and goals to award them a corner of his palace for their living quarters, and an annual stipend to support their work. Access to their quarters was through a passageway adjoining the church and convent of the Temple, and so they anointed themselves as Soldiery of the Temple, or Templars.

With time, the Templars impressed various noblemen who proffered the same kinds of financing arrangements as the Hospitaliers enjoyed. When one French count announced that he would contribute thirty pounds of silver annually to support the Templars' activities, others followed suit, and soon the nascent movement was awash in the kinds of riches it originally planned to reject.

To their credit, for the first several years of their existence the Templars resisted temptations to use their growing wealth for anything except the support and defense of pilgrims. Seven years after the group's formation, Bernard of Clairvaux wrote of the Templars,

They go and come at a sign from their Master. They live cheerfully and temperately together, without wives and children and, that nothing may be wanting for evangelical perfection, without property, in one house, endeavoring to preserve the unity of the spirit in the bond of peace, so that one heart and one soul would appear to dwell in them all. They never sit idle or go gaping after news. When they are resting from warfare against the infidels, not to eat the bread of idleness they employ themselves in repairing their clothes and arms, or do something which the command of the Master or the common good enjoins.

No unseemly word or light mocking, no murmur or immoderate laughter, is let to pass unreproved.... They avoid games of chess and tables; they are adverse to the chase and equally so to hawking, in which others so much delight.

They hate all jugglers and mountebanks, all wanton songs and plays, as vanities and follies of this world. They cut their hair in obedience to words of the apostle.... They are seldom ever washed; they are mostly to be seen with disordered hair and covered with dust, brown from their corselets and the heat of the sun....

Thus they are in union strange, at the same time gentler than lambs and grimmer than lions, so that one may doubt whether to call them monks or knights. But both names suit them, for theirs is the mildness of the monk and the valor of the knight.

This was not exactly a life of beer and skittles. Even the Cistercian monks, who represented a model for the Templars, sought pleasure from life while managing to avoid the risk of death on the battlefield. Under these circumstances, only men of the highest character and most sincere virtue could endure a career as a Templar, but among ambitious and pious young men the call of chivalry was difficult to ignore. Impressive numbers of them sought membership in the Templars, swelling the ranks and raising the group's profile among European nobility, who expressed their support by pledging money and land, and sometimes their own sons.

As membership in the Templars grew, a formal structure was imposed on the organization. Three classes were established: knights, who were men of noble families, neither married nor betrothed, and who bore no personal debt; chaplains, who were required to take vows of poverty, chastity and obedience; and serving brethren, men of wealth and talent who lacked the noble birth requirement of the knights. Eventually the brethren were divided into brethren-in-arms, who fought alongside the knights; and handicraft brethren, who performed menial chores of baking, smithing and caring for the animals, but were held in the lowest esteem within the order.

Both knights and chaplains were required to undergo a rigid initiation process and this practice, extending in modified form down to the present day, forms the root of the perception of Templars and their descendants as a secret society.

On the evening of a nominee's reception into the order, he was inducted in the presence of other knights within a chapel. No one else could be in attendance, nor could the candidate divulge when, where or even if the ceremony was taking place.

The procedure focused on warning the aspirant of the difficulties he was about to encounter, and demanding that he swear allegiance to the Templars' purpose before God. Reading an account of the ceremony today suggests the initiation was a form of Middle Ages boot camp. When he wished to sleep, the candidate was told, he would be ordered to watch. When he wished to watch, he would be ordered to bed. When he wished to eat, he would be ordered to work. Could he agree to these conditions? Each demand was to be answered, clearly and loudly, with the response, "Yea, sir, with the help of God!" The initiate was to promise never to strike or wound a Christian; never to receive any service or attendance from a woman without the approval of his superiors; never to kiss a woman, even if she were his mother or sister; never to hold a child at the baptismal font or be a godfather; and never to abuse any innocent man or call him foul names, but always be courteous and polite.

Who could resist an order dedicated to such chivalrous behavior and high Christian principles? Not the Church. In 1146 Pope Eugenius III declared that Templar knights could wear a red cross on their white tunic (chosen in direct contrast with the Hospitaliers) in recognition of the martyrdom they faced, and that they were henceforth free of direct papal supervision, including the risk of excommunication. This generated an even greater flow of lands, castles and other assets into their treasury from impressed patrons.

There is no infinite resistance to perpetual temptation, and the seeds of the organization's downfall were soon sown. Rumors spread that the Templars were engaged in extortion from the Assassins. The claim arose from the murder of Raymond, Comte de Tripoli, assumed to have been carried out by the Assassins. In response, the Templars entered territory controlled by the Assassins, but instead of challenging the Assassins in battle they demanded a tribute of 12,000 gold pieces. While there is no record that the Assassins made any such payment, some time later they dispatched an envoy to Amaury, then King of Jerusalem, offering to convert to Christianity if the Templars would forego the tribute. Clearly, some sort of accommodation had been reached.

Later, Templars intercepted Sultan Abbas of Egypt as he fled into the desert with his son, his harem and a goodly portion of stolen Egyptian treasures. After killing the Sultan and seizing the treasure, the Templars negotiated a deal with the Sultan's enemies to return the son to Cairo in exchange for 60,000 gold pieces. This may have been business as usual for the times, except that the son had already agreed to convert to Christianity, which should have been enough justification to spare his life. Instead, when the Templars' deal with the Egyptians closed, the son was placed in an iron cage and sent back to Egypt where, as he and the Templars knew, he faced death by protracted torture.

Incidents such as these marked the decline of the Templars from an ascetic order dedicated to the protection of the poor and helpless into an organization as focused on material gain as is any modern-day corporation. In fact, they set up an extensive banking system expressly to transfer money and treasures between Palestine and Europe, an action totally unrelated to their purported oaths of charity and poverty.

Their corruption did not end with money, and their change from strict asceticism to expansive materialism parallels any contemporary rags-to-riches tale. In place of modesty and humility, they grew haughty and rapacious, and they employed any deception at hand to build their impressive treasures to greater heights. In 1204, word spread throughout Palestine that an image of the Virgin near Damascus was issuing a juice or liquor from its breasts, and consuming the liquid was proving miraculous at removing sins from the souls of pious victims. The location, unfortunately, was a fair distance from Jerusalem, along a road often raided by bandits. The Templars proposed a solution. They would risk making the journey to the image, milk it of the miraculous liquor, and bring it to the pilgrims— for a price, of course. Both the demand and the price, as might be expected, shot skyward, and the magic elixir generated substantial income for an organization launched on the basis of maintaining total poverty.

Not all of the Templar treasures could be spent on the poor or on battling Muslims. A good deal of it appears to have been invested in wine and other delights of the flesh. Soon "drink like a Templar" became a common phrase to describe someone with an excessive taste for the grape, and the Germanic language acquired a new description for a house of ill-fame: *Tempelhaus.*

With a life of ease and fulfillment, who wanted to wear hair shirts among Muslims in Palestine? Not the Templars, who appeared more interested in acquiring wealth than in defending the Christian faith. Their original brothers-in-arms, the Hospitaliers, had also shifted their values towards mercenary rather than spiritual incentives. They had also abandoned their emphasis on sacrifice and charity, becoming as effective on the battlefield as the Templars themselves. For several years both groups of knights sniped at each other until, in 1259, they engaged in a battle launched by the Templars reportedly in pursuit of their rival's treasure. More zealous (and perhaps more numerous), the Hospitaliers won, cutting to pieces every Templar who fell into their hands. Soon after, the Templars retreated to Europe where, after all, the money was.

By 1306, the Templars were nicely settled on Cyprus, close enough to Palestine to maintain the premise that they were still involved in their original mission, and far enough away from raiding Muslims to enjoy safely the benefits of their wealth. In that year Pope Clement V, who had assumed the papal throne only months before, decided to address rumors about the Templars engaging in "unspeakable apostasy against God, detestable idolatry, execrable vice, and many heresies." He summoned the Grand Master of the Templars, a charismatic man named Jacques de Molay, to Rome for an explanation.

De Molay, one of history's most colorful figures, stood over six feet tall with an appearance and bearing that might have qualified him as a medieval show-biz celebrity. Born about 1240 in Burgundy of a minor noble family, de Molay joined the Templars at age twenty-five and served valiantly in Jerusalem before being elected Grand Master at age fifty-five.

Arriving in Rome with sixty Knights Templar, de Molay also brought 150,000 gold florins, and substantial quantities of silver, all acquired by the Templars during their various forays in the Middle East. He left several days later with the papal equivalent of an apology, Clement explaining, "Because it did not seem likely or credible that men of such religion who... showed so much great and many signs of devotion both in divine offices as well as in fasts... should be so forgetful of their salvation as to do these things, we are unwilling to give ear to this kind of insinuation." De Molay may have departed Rome with Clement's approval ringing in his ears, but he left behind the gold florins and silver.

Sensing a bribe, Philippe le Bel, the French king, grew outraged. Once a supporter of the Templars, he now turned against them, partially in reaction to their flagrant lifestyle, and partially because of their growing power and wealth; he feared the former and lusted after the latter. The Templars, Philippe determined, were to be dissolved and their treasury, the bulk of it stored within Philippe's domain, would be placed in the hands of the Crown. To achieve this, Philippe employed a device familiar to fans of contemporary crime stories: a jail-house snitch.

A former Templar named Squin de Flexian, imprisoned on charges of insurrection and facing a certain death sentence, learned of Philippe's dislike of the organization. Calling his jailer, de Flexian announced that he had dire, dark secrets of the Templars to pass on to the king. This was enough to earn de Flexian a junket to Paris, where he rambled through a litany of charges against the Templars, including secret alliances with the Muslims, initiation rites that included spitting on the cross, impregnating women and murdering their newborn babies, and ceremonies involving various acts of debauchery and blasphemy. As expected, de Flexian's tales entranced the monarch and his court, who could not hear enough of the fascinating details. Debauchery? Blasphemy? Alliances with the enemy? Secret ceremonies? What monarch could refuse to take action against these fiends, especially with several thousand gold florins, untold treasures of silver, and extensive lands and castles waiting to be seized?

On October 13, 1307,[2] in an action worthy of a gifted military field commander, Templars were arrested in coordinated raids all across Europe, with the most brutal apprehensions occurring in France. Under torture many Templars, including de Molay, confessed to activities similar to those described by de Flexian (who was hanged for his troubles). For several years the imprisoned Templars tried to defend themselves against vile charges brought against them by the French king until, in 1313,

---

[2] This fell on a Friday, giving rise to the superstition of unfortunate events occurring on Friday the thirteenth.

the pope announced that the Templars were to be abolished. Depending on their rank, their admissions of guilt and their sincerity in rebuking their sins, members were either banished or set free, with the exception of de Molay and three of his closest confederates.

Brought before a papal tribunal on a stage in front of Notre Dame cathedral, the four Templars were about to be sentenced to spend the rest of their lives in prison when de Molay rose to speak. In direct and inspirational language, the Templar Grand Master protested his innocence and decried the confessions made under torture, many incriminating other Templars. His adamant refusal to admit wrongdoing and his demand for an opportunity to plead his innocence to the pope was supported by the brother of the Dauphin of Auvergne, one of the three other high-ranking Templars charged with similar crimes.

The tribunal was dumbfounded. They expected the Templars to receive their fate in silence and be grateful that their lives had been spared. The French king, upon hearing the news, was not dumbfounded at all. He was outraged, and demanded that the two Templars not only be burned at the stake, but that it be done slowly so that the men suffered as much agony as possible.

The following day, de Molay and Guy of Auvergne were trundled to the downstream point of the Île de la Cité, a site now known as the Square du Vert-Galant, one of the most attractive locations in all of Paris. Still declaring their innocence they were stripped naked and bound to posts. Then, in the words of one Templar scholar,

> The flames were first applied to their feet, then to their more vital parts. The fetid smell of their burning flesh infected the surrounding air, and added to their torments; yet still they persevered in their declarations [of innocence]. At length, death terminated their misery. Spectators shed tears at the view of their constancy, and during the night their ashes were gathered up to be preserved as relics.

Jacques de Molay died a martyr's death and helped elevate the organization's tarnished reputation.

The Templars' treasury was seized by Philippe, who claimed the majority of the prize to cover expenses incurred in trying and executing its members. The leftover amount he distributed to the Hospitaliers and King Edward II of England, who had somewhat reluctantly agreed to banish Templars from his own realm.

Legend has it that de Molay, while being tied to the stake for his execution, predicted that Pope Clement would follow him within forty days and the king would join them all within a year. If so, he was correct. Clement died of colic the following month and, while his body was lying in state, a fire swept through the church and consumed most of his corpse. A few months later, Philippe was thrown from his horse and broke his neck.

In another, more contemporary incident, de Molay has been identified as the figure imprinted on the mysterious Shroud of Turin. First displayed in 1357, the shroud was claimed to have been recovered from Constantinople by crusaders who sacked the city in 1307. The apparent imprint of a bearded figure on the material was attributed to Christ, suggesting the shroud had been used to wrap his body after it had been removed from the cross. Carbon dating, however, revealed that the shroud material dated only as far back as the late thirteenth century, initiating new speculation that de Molay had been wrapped in the material following one of his torture sessions during his years of imprisonment. The size and appearance of the image on the shroud could as easily be de Molay's as anyone's, adding to the mystique of de Molay's martyrdom.

The actions of Philippe, Edward and other rulers who were persuaded to follow the French lead failed to annihilate the Templars, and remnants of the society retained the organization's structure in a deeply clandestine manner lest they share the same fate as de Molay and Guy of Auvergne. Secret activities that had been conducted under de Molay's leadership were enhanced and sanctified. A few sources claim that documents prepared by de Molay shortly before his death appointed Bertrand du Guesclin to succeed him as Templars Grand Master, and the leadership position was filled over time by a succession of prominent French citizens, including several princes of the house of Bourbon.

More enduring, especially among French citizens, has been a suspicion that Philippe failed to seize all the Templars' treasures. Stories have abounded for centuries that immense troves of gold and jewels lay waiting for someone to locate them. One tale concerns pretty Rosslyn Chapel near Edinburgh, whose intricate stone carvings are claimed by some to be a secret code understood only by Templars and Freemasons. When deciphered, the code supposedly identifies the location of the Holy Grail and the Templars' fortune, both hidden nearby. The chapel's link to the Templars is questionable, because it was built 170 years after the death of de Molay, yet the story persists in spite of the fact that extensive investigation and excavation have revealed nothing remotely of value or interest around or beneath the chapel. Another legend suggests that much of the Templars' wealth was buried on Oak Island, in the Atlantic Ocean off the coast of Nova Scotia.

Tales of Templar treasure may be rampant, but real-life Templars today are not—except, perhaps, via a lineage extending down to modern-day Freemasons. Masons have been of two minds about the linkage with Templars. On one hand, the idea of Masons as direct descendants of the martyred Templars adds an aura of mystique and grandeur to the organization; whatever their faults, the Templars' image has benefited from the burnishing of time, and they are now widely viewed as noble knights sacrificed to a larcenous king and a perfidious pope. On the other hand, no direct historical association can be found between the Templars and Masons—which, of course, has not prevented widespread speculation and garish fable from connecting the two. Should an organization like the Masons, striving to be recognized and admired for maintaining a high level of scrupulous behavior, foster a relationship that has no basis in fact? The latter point is no longer a serious concern, because given their declining membership and recent debacles, the Masons could benefit from bathing in reflected glory from the Templars.

The Masonic movement has fallen far and hard, especially in the United States where its greatest glory and most enduring strength once lay. Any review of U.S. history encounters Freemasons lurking behind every treaty, battle and statute, and their members holding the offices of Secretary of State, General of the Army and Supreme Court Justice. From George C. Marshall, through Generals John J. Pershing and Douglas MacArthur, to Supreme Court Justices Earl Warren and Thurgood Marshall, Freemasons dominate seats of American power in greater numbers than does any other organization. No fewer than sixteen U.S. presidents have proudly declared their Masonic status.

Nor is this an exclusively American phenomenon. Sir Winston Churchill, Canadian prime minister John Diefenbaker, and at least four presidents of Mexico all held high positions within Freemasonry. Can any other closed society claim such extensive influence on seats of power over so many years?

Proof that Masons exert enormous power over world events, should you choose to believe conspiracy buffs, can be found in pockets, purses and billfolds around the world. Every U.S. dollar bill bears the Great Seal of the U.S. on its reverse, a symbol many believe confirms Freemasonry's dominance and control of the country. The seal's

The Great Seal on the U.S. dollar—is it proof of a Masonic plot?

design includes an eye within a triangle floating above an apparently unfinished pyramid. On the base of the pyramid are engraved the Roman numerals for 1776 (MDCCLXXVI), and the design is framed by two Latin phrases: *Annuit Coeptis* (Providence Has Favored Our Undertakings) and *Novus Ordo Seclorium* (A New Order of the Ages). According to those who fear the Masons, the eye and pyramid are Masonic symbols, and the manner in which the emblem is flaunted proves their power remains unchallenged.

Or does it? Masons have long used a triangle as a symbol of their membership but only because it represented a set-square, a tool used by the stonemasons who created the organization. In any case, the Great Seal of the U.S. depicts not a triangle but a pyramid, chosen because it represents strength and stability, important qualities for a nascent country. The eye represents the all-seeing vision of God, nothing more, and while it is indeed framed within a triangle, triangular shapes have been popular among Christian societies for centuries, representing the Trinity of the Father, Son and Holy Spirit.

Historical evidence supports this view. Writing on behalf of the Freemasons in 1821, Thomas Smith Webb noted that the Masons did not adopt either the eye or the triangle as a symbol until 1797, fourteen years *after* the U.S. Congress approved the Great Seal. Webb explains the components of the seal in fine early-Victorian prose:

> Although our thoughts, words and actions may be hidden from the eyes of man, yet that All-Seeing Eye, whom the Sun, Moon and Stars obey, and under whose watchful care even comets perform their stupendous revolutions, pervade the inmost recesses of the human heart, and will reward us according to our merits.

Some skeptics believed him. Most did not.

Freemasons have been trying to shake off this connection with the Great Seal of the U.S. for two centuries without success. They have also attempted to disprove the theory that

Freemasons are determined to carry out acts of revenge on the Templars' behalf for abuses committed against the group almost 800 years ago. In the process, they also deny an association with the Illuminati, an organization of free-thinking intellectuals whose goal, two centuries before CNN, was nothing less than global control of social and political thought; or that they installed popular personalities in positions of power to carry out secret Masonic strategies.

Crusading knights, revenge-driven descendants, subversive currency, global tyrants, celebrity insurgents—what is really behind the Masonic movement? As with all secret societies, the reality suggests both more and less than the eye reveals.

While a few fringe commentators declare that Adam was the first Mason (the same crowd who claim that remnants of de Molay's group escaped to America 200 years ahead of Columbus), the origin of the Freemasons is as simple and direct as their name. In seventeenth-century England, craft organ-izations began forming as a means of concealing specialized knowledge of their trade from outsiders who might profit from it. The craft guilds declared that they were setting quality stan-dards among the craftsmen; they were less open about their goal of ensuring higher incomes for members by restricting the num-ber of people qualified to join and elevating wages accordingly.

Among the most powerful craftsmen of their time were stonemasons, who possessed the tools and skills to build strong, straight walls. The proof of their talents is evident throughout Britain, where many stone structures remain as solid as the day they were constructed 400 years ago. Mason skills were rated according to three levels: Entered Apprentice, Fellowcraft and Master Mason. Each level of skill elevated the mason to a higher rank of recognition, or degree, entitling him to earn appropriately higher wages. Secrecy became para-mount among the masons, who chose their companions carefully and swore new initiates to silence about the tech-niques they had perfected over centuries. To provide control

over their members and ensure that the secrets remained
hidden, masons were organized in small community-based
lodges with each lodge electing a leader or master.

What began as an organization of craftsmen evolved into
something quite different in June 1717, when the leaders of four
London lodges gathered at the Apple Tree Tavern to form the
Grand Lodge of Freemasons. The goals of the Grand Lodge
extended beyond those of the original craft guild to encompass
the status of a pseudo-religion, reflecting established Protestant
values. Members vowed to work within Christian principles,
rationalize the teachings of Christ, and empty Christianity of its
mystery through the application of logic and scientific analysis.
This marked the beginning of Freemasonry as a global power.

The Freemason concept spread to France and the rest of
Europe, and in the process it also spread its recruitment net to
snare a wider range of members. No longer restricted to tradesmen, Freemasonry began to welcome all men of qualified social
stature, providing them with a fraternal organization where
they could exchange ideas, pursue common interests, and make
important business and professional contacts. Retaining the
oath of secrecy among its members, the movement added a
mystical initiation ceremony. Soon after, the historical intrigue
tying Masons to the Templars began to spread.

A historical link with romantic martyrs garnered as much
status for organizations and individuals 300 years ago as it does
today. Adding color to the fraternal basis of their organization,
Freemasons began to claim descendancy from the Knights
Templar. The hypothetical combination transformed an organization originally based on the practical concerns of tradesmen
into a fraternal assembly of upper-class businessmen and
professionals.

Once their association with the Templars took hold, many
enthusiastic Masons began to build an aura of mystique around
their group. Like all mystiques, this one acquired a patina of
authenticity with time. Scottish Freemasons claimed that several of de Molay's most dedicated followers had escaped France

and fled to Scotland following their leader's execution. A few went further, maintaining that de Molay himself had escaped execution and arrived in Scotland, where he fought with Robert Bruce at the Battle of Dupplin in 1332 and the Battle of Durham in 1346.[3]

Masonic records trace the Templar–Mason connection back to an oration delivered in 1737 in the Grand Lodge of France by a Mason named Chevalier Ramsay. Ramsay claimed Freemasonry dated from "the close association of the order with the Knights of St. John in Jerusalem" during the Crusades, and that the "old lodges of Scotland" preserved the genuine Masonry abandoned by the English. From this rather dubious historical connection spun the Scottish Rite or, as the Masonic constitution identifies it, the Antiquus Scoticus Ritus Acceptus, the Ancient and Accepted Scottish Rite. A more likely explanation stems from the mid-eighteenth–century emigration by Scottish and Irish Masons to the Bordeaux region of France, where they were identified as the *Ecossais*.

The *Ecossais* extended the original three degrees of Masonry first to seven degrees and later to twenty-five degrees, eventually evolving into thirty-three degrees today. Masons who choose to advance beyond the basic three degrees join the Scottish Rite.

American colonists established a Masonic lodge in Boston, Massachusetts, in 1733. Memberships in this first American lodge grew spectacularly, and by the American Revolution over 100 lodges were listed. In fact, members of the St. Andrew Masonic Lodge effectively kick-started the revolution with the Boston Tea Party, when they dressed as Mohawk Indians and dumped British tea into the harbor to protest unfair taxation. As in England, American Freemasons represented the most ambitious, gifted and powerful men in society, so it is no surprise that

---

[3] In recognition of de Molay's leadership and martyrdom, the International Order of de Molay was founded as a fraternal organization for young men aged 13 to 21. Operating under the direction of Masonic advisers, it is essentially a recruiting service for the parent organization.

fifty-one of the signers to the Declaration of Independence supposedly identified themselves as Masons. With so many prominent rebels actively involved, it's reasonable to claim that Freemasons, more than any other single group, instigated the revolution. The list included luminaries such as George Washington, Benjamin Franklin, John Adams, Patrick Henry, John Hancock, Paul Revere, John Paul Jones, Ethan Allen, Alexander Hamilton and, to the later chagrin of his fellow American Freemasons, Benedict Arnold. With independence achieved, American Freemasons cut all ties with Britain and launched an exclusively American Grand Lodge in 1777.

Freemasons in the U.S. strengthened their organization, refined their procedures, and extended their influence beyond the lodge halls more than members in any other country. Along with an emphasis on rituals and secrecy, their growth and authority produced speculation about their true motives, encouraged at the outset by Masonic practices and policies; the more mystery attached to the order, the more they would be regarded as powerful men engaged in shadowy activities. Decisions were made not to dilute this vision, but to enhance it in every way possible. The location for the Supreme Council of Scottish Rite Freemasonry, for example, was chosen as Charleston, South Carolina, because that city is located on the 33rd parallel, reflecting the thirty-three degrees of Masonic membership.

To outsiders, this kind of conscious effort to create inscrutability proved either amusing or menacing, and over the years a number of outlandish claims were made about the true goals of Freemasons. Some rather astonishing practices and achievements were credited to them, including the following:

FREEMASONS ARE IN LEAGUE WITH THE ILLUMINATI. Like Russian dolls, secret societies are reputed to exist within each other, large groups concealing smaller, more concentrated divisions through ancient alliances. Among the most persistent claims by conspiracy buffs and anti-Masons generally is the allegation that Freemason lodges secretly harbor members of the Illuminati.

In the view of these alarmists, the Illuminati are the people who pull the strings on puppeteers who believe they themselves are pulling strings attached to other puppets. Shadows within shadows, Illuminati members supposedly hover in the background among Masons and other groups, including the Priory of Sion, followers of Kabbalah, Rosicrucians and, in a test of theological extremes, the Elders of Zion.

Launched in 1776 by Adam Weishaupt, a Bavarian Jesuit scholar described as "an unpractical bookworm without necessary experience in the world," the Illuminati ("Enlightenment") was created as a secret society the true objectives of which would be revealed to its members only after they achieved a "priestly" degree of awareness and understanding. Those who managed to survive Weishaupt's process of selection and preparation eventually learned they were cogs in a political/philosophical machine regulated by reason, an extreme extension of the founder's "reason over passion" Jesuit education. Thanks to the Illuminati, people would be liberated from their prejudices and become both mature and moral, outgrowing the religious and political restrictions of church and state.

Achieving this utopia would be a gain not without pain, however. Illuminati members were to observe everyone with whom they came into social contact, gathering information on each individual and submitting sealed reports to their superiors. By this means, the Illuminati would control public opinion, restrict the power of princes, presidents and prime ministers, silence or eliminate subversives and reactionaries, and strike fear in the hearts of its enemies. "In the bosom of the deepest darkness," wrote one of the movement's early critics, "a society has been formed, a society of new beings, who know one another though they have never seen one another, who understand one another without explanations, who serve one another without friendship. From the Jesuit rule, this society adopts blind obedience; from the Masons it takes the trials and the ceremonies; and from the Templars it obtains subterranean mysteries and great audacity." Without a doubt, this was a force to be reckoned with.

One of Weishaupt's early strategies was to ally himself with the Freemasons, a move that initially proved successful. Within a few years "Illuminated Freemasons" were active in several European countries. But as details of their true aims escaped, public attitude turned against them until, in August 1787, Bavaria declared that recruiting Illuminati members was a capital crime. This managed to drive the society more deeply underground, but it also persuaded Weishaupt that his vision was seriously flawed. After renouncing his own order and writing several apologies to mankind, Weishaupt reconciled with his Catholic religion and spent his last few years helping to build a new cathedral in Gotha.

During the Illuminati's limited tenure, tales circulated that it was responsible for the outbreak and progress of the French Revolution, a claim that is almost laughable in view of the group's emphasis on reason instead of passion. Few events in history were propelled by raw passion more than the overthrow of the French throne.

The short-lived dance between the Illuminati and Freemasons launched a fable that persists among some conspiracy addicts to this day. Various anti-Mason commentators continue to insist that Masters of the Illuminati remain in control of the Freemasons and other secret societies, dedicated to bringing Weishaupt's original plan for world domination to reality. Yet, while the Illuminati appears as a shadowy presence within or among other secret societies, no one seems able to identify specific acts attributable to them. And, unlike every other secret society to be examined here, no one within the Illuminati has ever broken the oath of silence to reveal its inner workings. If you resort exclusively to logic, you suspect that the Illuminati is a phantom organization with neither goals nor members. If you fear secret societies, you believe they are powerful enough to deny their own existence.

FREEMASONS MURDERED U.S. PRESIDENT GEORGE WASH-
INGTON. According to this theory, Washington resigned from the
Freemasons and intended to expose the group's more reprehensi-
ble actions to the world. Supposedly, he was outraged at plans by
the Masons to erect a monument in his name, in a form that the
plotters called an obelisk but the president considered something
quite different, referring to it as the Phallus of Baal. To silence the
Father of His Nation, so the story goes, he was bled four times by
Masonic doctors on the day he died. The Freemasons had already
agreed that this would occur on December 31, 1799, the last day
of the eighteenth century. In spite of Washington's objections, the
phallic Washington Monument was erected, reaching a height of
555 feet—coincidentally equaling the code number signifying
assassination in the Luciferian religion.

This fanciful idea is transparent enough to be almost
amusing. Bleeding was an accepted medical procedure in the
eighteenth century, Washington died December 14, 1799, not
December 31, discussions regarding the Washington Monument
did not begin until at least a week after his death, and no credible
reference exists regarding either a Luciferian religion or its use of
5 as a symbol of death and 555 as a code for assassination.

THE STREETS OF WASHINGTON DC DEPICT MASONIC AND
SATANIC SYMBOLS. Like most of his colleagues, architect Pierre
Charles L'Enfant was a Freemason when asked to design the seat
of federal government in Washington D.C. in 1791. Various
sources claim L'Enfant was pressured by both Washington and
Jefferson to create a series of satanic occultic symbols representing Freemasonry and labeling its dominance over American
politics forever. Among the symbols impressed on Washington's
street layout are the evil pentagram, the classic Mason pyramid
and a representation of the devil himself, all of them declaring
the evil intentions of Freemasons and their absolute power over
the United States.

The absurdity of such claims should be self-evident. The
pentagram is not a uniquely evil symbol, nor does it play any

role in Freemasonry documentation. Moreover, how could its presence make any impact on U.S. affairs, let alone global concerns? Triangles—pyramids are three-dimensional forms that cannot be replicated on street plans—can be traced in the street plan of any community anywhere in the world, and the claimed replication of Satan might be at home in a kindergarten art class, but not among mature adults.

FREEMASONS MURDER THOSE WHO THREATEN TO REVEAL SECRET POLICIES AND AGENDA. Not much is known about William Morgan, but it can be assumed that he was a man of many faults. Born in 1774 in Culpepper County, Virginia, he and his young wife moved to Canada, where they launched a distillery. A mysterious fire destroyed the operation, driving Morgan back to the U.S., where he settled in upstate New York and, after several failed attempts, managed to join the Freemasons. When he was turned down for membership in a

In an effort to prove Freemasonry's dominance of U.S. life, theorists find satanic images in the street plan of Washington D.C.

new Freemason chapter in Batavia, N.Y.—he was accused, with some justification, of being a swindler—he took revenge by writing and publishing a book attacking Freemasonry. This launched a long chain of events starting with a mysterious fire in the print shop that produced the book, the imprisonment of three Freemasons charged with arson, a series of arrests involving threats against Masons made by Morgan, and an ongoing battle between him and the organization.

Morgan vanished in 1826, an event that apparently pleased most local residents who hoped life would return to normal. A month later, when a badly decomposed body was found floating in Lake Ontario, many citizens claimed it was Morgan's remains. His wife first denied it was her husband, then admitted it was, and finally denied it again before fleeing New York to become one of several wives claimed by Joseph Smith, founder of the Mormon Church. Later, witnesses reported that Morgan was seen in Boston, Quebec City and other locations, having assumed a new identity and a new wife.

Whoever the floating corpse belonged to, the incident was enough to fuel claims that Morgan had been prepared to reveal deep, dark secrets of Freemasonry activities not mentioned in his book. Nothing captures the public's imagination like a good mystery, especially one that defies solution, and the mystery of William Morgan has been durable enough to support a belief in murderous Masons for almost 200 years.

FREEMASON RITUALS ARE SATANIC AND SUBVERSIVE. To many people who do not share the fraternal goals of Freemasons, a more accurate description of their rituals might be silly and juvenile.

Masons chart their status by degrees ranging from 1 to 33, the 33rd Degree representing the pinnacle of personal achievements as a Mason. The 1st Degree, conferring membership, is granted after the initiate dresses in a particular fashion, submits to a blindfold, and is led to a locked door. His knock on the door and its entry to him symbolize his departure from the outside world and access to the Inner Sanctum of Freemasonry. After answering questions about his ability to follow Masonic principles, and promising never to reveal the organization's secrets, the initiate experiences the point of a compass being pressed against his chest, and he is asked, "What do you desire?" With the ritualistic reply "More light," the blindfold is removed and the applicant can see his fellow members for the first time, again very symbolic.

Silliness is carried to extreme by Shriners, a group within Freemasonry whose origins date back to the late nineteenth century. Shriners just wanta-have-fun, and they justify their antics by performing charitable work on behalf of children's hospitals. Recently, their image has been tarnished by revelations suggesting that barely 25 percent of their $8 billion charity endowment is spent on actual charitable activities.

FREEMASONS ARE ADEPT AT DECEIVING THE PUBLIC. "Deceiving" in this case means "hoodwinking," and for once the charge is true, even if the reality is not what it appears.

The initiation ceremony that includes covering the candidate's eyes during interrogation originally involved placing a hood over his head. "Wink," an archaic term for "eye," was associated with this procedure; thus, initiates were said to be "hoodwinked." Over the years, the meaning of the term has evolved to indicate a deception, spawning the claim that Freemasons consistently present themselves as something they are not.

The early success of Freemasons produced critics, who feared the aggregate power of so many Masons holding high political office, and imitators such as the Oddfellows, who adapted secret procedures of the Masons while ignoring their pseudo-historical and mystical origins.

Among the most vociferous of Masonry critics has been the Catholic Church, launching levels of enmity and suspicion between Masons and Catholics almost from the beginning. As early as 1738, Pope Clement xii condemned Freemasonry, saying, "We command to the faithful to abstain from intercourse with those societies...in order to avoid excommunication, which will be the penalty imposed upon all those contravening this order." Obviously the Church wasn't merely annoyed; it was outraged and, perhaps, threatened.

A few years later Clement's successor, Benedict xiv, identified six dangers Freemasonry posed to Catholics: (a) the Interconfessionalism (or Interfaith) of Freemasons; (b) their secrecy; (c) their oath; (d) their opposition to church and state; (e) the interdiction pronounced against them in several states by the heads of such countries; and, (f) their immorality.

This is no mere academic or theological difference; for almost 300 years the Catholic Church has practically equated Masons with a stampede of Satans. Leo xiii, in the late nineteenth century, described Masonic lodges as "Bottomless Abysses of Misery which was [sic] dug by those conspiring Societies in which the Heresies and Sects have, it may be said, vomited as in a privy, everything they held in their insides of Sacrilege and Blasphemy." Obviously, Leo's concept of Christian charity had its limits.

This eighteenth-century acrimony is not diluted by twenty-first-century enlightenment, nor is it limited to traditional Catholic animosity. In November 2002 the Archbishop of Canterbury, Dr. Rowan Williams, condemned Masonry as incompatible with Christianity due to its secrecy and "possibly Satanically-inspired" beliefs. An earlier statement by the U.S. Southern Baptist Convention accused Masons of conducting pagan rituals based on the occult, leading the 16-million-strong assembly to brand Masonry as "sacrilegious."

Religious leaders are not the only people quick to condemn Masons. From a secular point of view, Masonry is also susceptible to charges of racial segregation and gender bias. Corners of the movement continue to maintain separate white and black lodges, with many white groups resisting not only integration but full recognition of their black brethren. They conveniently ignore the fact that black Masons have included, in addition to Duke Ellington, such celebrated individuals as singer Nat "King" Cole, U.S. Supreme Court Justice Thurgood Marshall, author Alex Haley, and political gadfly Reverend Jesse Jackson among their members.

Both black and white members dismiss any suggestion that Masons admit women to their membership rosters, as the Rotary Club has since been ordered to do by the U.S. Supreme Court in 1987. "Freemasonry is a fraternity," sputtered Douglas Collins, a Texas Mason with Worshipful Master status. " 'Frater' meaning male brothers. Period. Any mainstream grand lodge in the United States that pulls that stunt [allowing women], they're going to be dropped from fraternal relations by the rest of them. They're going to be an outcast grand lodge."

Or maybe it will all die away on a rapidly shrinking vine. Membership in all service clubs for men peaked during the 1920s and 1930s in North America, entering a long decline in the years after World War II. During the 1960s, the number of U.S. Masons was estimated at 4 million; by the year 2000 it had declined to about 1.8 million as society turned away from lodges in pursuit of other means of group identification such as professional sports teams and musical groups. In numbers, and especially in power, Freemasons are a shadow of the organization that wielded influence through the nineteenth and much of the twentieth centuries.

Despite their shrinking numbers and lower profile, Freemasons are still considered by some to be a threat to the world generally and the U.S. in particular, and they remain for many people the first organization that comes to mind when asked to define a "secret society." Yet, how secret can an organization be when its various meeting places are clearly identified along with its more prominent members? And how deadly can the intentions of a secret society be when it boasts among the highest-ranking members in its history the great Duke Ellington, one of the least likely candidates for performing anything more subversive than a piano solo?

The distant association of Freemasons with Templars and Illuminati, along with the large number of members who have held high political office, fuels wild assumptions among those inclined to assume that anything concealed must, by definition, be evil. Yet this is nothing but extreme speculation. Almost no one claims evil deeds or intentions for the Shriners, elevated Masons whose antics may be tiresome to some, and whose charitable activities may be less all-embracing than its members suggest.

The mainstream media rarely address negative aspects of Masonry or claims of the global powers attributed to it. In fact, media coverage of Freemasonry occurs only in response to shocking events such as an incident that took place in the basement of a Long Island Masonic lodge in March 2004. On that evening William James, 47, gathered at the lodge with about a dozen confirmed Masons to initiate him into the order. Knowing the process would be designed both to frighten him and build confidence in his lodge brothers, James arrived that evening filled with excitement and anticipation.

After enduring the blindfolded knock at the lodge door and the request for "More light!" James was asked to place his nose alongside a mock guillotine. When the guillotine left his nose intact, he was ordered to step carefully among several scattered rat traps, followed by walking a plank.

Nothing surprising occurred until the most dramatic part of the ceremony, which consisted of James being set in front of a shelf holding two empty tin cans. At a signal, a Masonic brother was to fire a pistol in James's direction, and the two tins cans would tumble noisily from the shelf, convincing James that the gun had actually been loaded.

The shots were to be fired by 77-year-old Albert Eid, who arrived for the ceremony carrying a .22 caliber revolver in one pocket and a .32 caliber revolver in the other. The smaller pistol was loaded with blank cartridges, the .32 with real bullets. At a signal from one of the brothers Eid reached into his pocket, withdrew a pistol and, instead of aiming it at the empty tin cans, he pointed it directly at William James and fired. He had chosen the wrong pistol. The bullet entered James's head and he died instantly.

Freemason leaders quickly distanced themselves from the tragedy, noting that the procedure had nothing to do with true Masonic traditions or ceremonies. Anti-Freemasons had little to say at first. After such a tragedy, how could anyone seriously consider the Masons a dangerous society? Then came the revisionists. Within a year, stories circulated on the Internet and elsewhere that James's death had been no accident at all. Eid had been ordered to eliminate James because the about-to-be-initiated Mason had planned to infiltrate the organization and reveal its true clandestine activities. Ignoring the fact that Eid was one of James's oldest and closest friends, and thus the least likely person to be assigned the murder, theorists pointed to the gentle manner with which Eid was treated by the courts, who called the death a senseless tragedy and handed down a five-year suspended sentence. This, they said, was proof that Masons controlled both the media and the justice system.

A new legend was born. If Freemasons endure for a few more centuries, William James may well be associated with William Morgan as another tragic victim of the Freemasons and the machinations of their secret society.

THREE

PRIORY OF SION
KEEPERS OF THE HOLY GRAIL

IF ALL FAMILIES HAVE SECRETS, THEN SOME SECRETS ARE more common than others. Surely among the most familiar of family secrets is a clandestine marriage (or no marriage at all) that produces a child whose existence is never acknowledged. That's the basis for the Priory of Sion, whose members are legion, whose adherents are fanatic and whose history, according to serious researchers, is either mundane or absurd.

Mind you, the tale has its understandable appeal. Who could resist a story involving a fake death, a reformed prostitute and a bloodline traced through individuals as eminent and gifted as Leonardo da Vinci, Sir Isaac Newton, Claude Debussy, Jules Verne and Victor Hugo? Toss in the Templars, the Nazis, a vast hidden treasure and the promise of retrieving an artifact of Christ's crucifixion (the grail), and the epic grows more enticing than anything a Hollywood scriptwriter could create. For this reason alone, the Priory of Sion boasts thousands of adherents who allege proof of its existence and contend that it has influenced world events for 2000 years.

In spite of many celebrated names associated with the Priory, reality suggests that the tale revolves around three primary characters: a poor parish priest who needed an explanation for his accumulation of personal wealth; an anti-Semitic Frenchman searching for a way to fulfill his wartime dreams; and a charming medieval princess. Not to mention Jesus Christ and his wife and child.

The basis of the tale, which has more variations than the works of Mozart, is this:

Despite certainty among Christians, Mary Magdalene was no Jerusalem strumpet but the middle-class Jewish wife of Jesus, their union either never divulged or conducted in a manner described today as common-law. Depending on the source, Christ's crucifixion was faked and he and his wife fled Jerusalem to escape death, or Mary Magdalene escaped alone from Palestine following Christ's death. Either way, she arrived on the Mediterranean coast of France, suggesting she traveled by boat, and she was pregnant. Moreover, her pregnancy resulted in the birth of a healthy baby whose offspring, traced through two millennia of history, have influenced world development to an enormous degree even while their existence has been hidden from the general populace.[4]

It is difficult to imagine a story more capable of tilting virtually every tenet of Christianity into a cocked hat than the suggestion that Mary Magdalene gave birth to a descendant of God through Christ. That premise alone has spawned dozens of explanations for historical events, including those for which no "explanation" would otherwise be deemed necessary. The creation and initial success of the Templars, for example, is traced by some to the French-based line of Christ's descendants. Proponents of this theory point to France as the acknowledged root of the Templars' strength and to the fact that their destruction was organized by a French monarch, who perhaps had learned the truth of their blood heritage. In partnership with a newly elected pope aware of the dangers to the Church if the truth were revealed, the French king grew determined to eliminate the Templars. He was motivated not by fear of the Templars' power and his avarice for their wealth, but by the need to purify Christianity.

Indeed, a lengthy list of descendants of Jesus may be found on "secret dossiers" written on ancient parchment and placed in

[4] According to proponents of the priory's existence, the term "holy grail" refers not to a chalice or other utensil used at The Last Supper, but to the bloodline traced from Christ through descendants.

the care of the Bibliothèque Nationale in Paris. Many names in the dossiers are obscure. Some are recognized by scholars for being associated with the occult, especially during medieval times. A few qualify as first-rank historical celebrities: Robert Boyle, Isaac Newton, Victor Hugo, Claude Debussy, Jean Cocteau and, of course, Leonardo da Vinci.

Why maintain records of such a distinctive lineage and keep it secret for twenty centuries, only to make it public at the end of the second millennium? Perhaps to restore the dynasty established by Mary Magdalene, a bloodline that extends not only to the throne of France but to thrones of other European nations, creating an international cabal tied by common lineage and devoted to controlling world events. This family line, known as the Merovingian dynasty, took control of France about AD 475, filling the power gap created when the Roman empire collapsed and extending its influence across history ever since.

"Merovingian" is derived from Meroveus, father of Childeric I, who became the first non-Roman ruler of Gaul, the region now known as France. Meroveus, so the legend goes, could trace his ancestry back through Joseph of Arimathea to Christ. Or maybe not. While some monastic records identify Meroveus in this manner, the historian Priscus claims he was sired by a mysterious sea creature, explaining the source of his esoteric knowledge and skills in the occult. This relationship with a sea-beast is seen as evidence that (a) Mary Magdalene stepped out of a sailing vessel onto the shores of France, where she gave birth to the son of Jesus; (b) an effort has been made to obscure this same historical fact by immersing it in fable; (c) an attempt has been made in the opposite direction, identifying Meroveus's ancestor with Christ, because the fish is a symbol of Christianity.[5]

The tale remains murky until 671, when the Merovingian prince Dagobert II marries Giselle de Razes, daughter of the Count of Razes and niece of the Visigoth High King, thus

5 Or, if you prefer, (d) the Merovingians were descendants of extraterrestrial beings who bred with chosen Israelites, creating a true superrace.

uniting two powerful forces that had long struggled against each other for control of France.

Dagobert appears to be an erudite man for his time. Educated in an Irish monastery, he married Mathilde of York, a Celtic princess, and settled in England, where he became friends with Saint Wilfrid, the Bishop of York. Upon the death of Mathilde, the bishop guided him into the marriage with Giselle. Based on a description of Giselle as a ravishing beauty skilled in the arts and educated beyond the level of women of her day, it sounds like a marriage made in heaven, or at least in Languedoc, the area of France bordering the Mediterranean between Marseilles and the Spanish border. Here, in an old Visigoth chapel dedicated to Mary Magdalene, near the city of Rhaede, they were wed.

Thanks to several geographic advantages, Rhaede boasted a population at the time of more than 30,000 inhabitants. Situated at the intersection of roads extending across adjoining valleys, with several fresh-water springs nearby, the town dated back to pre-Roman times. It was a natural location for celebrating the union of two powerful families.

Things went reasonably well at first, especially for a Dark Ages warrior. Dagobert managed to wrest what is now modern-day France away from the clutches of three brothers who had claimed the land after the death of their father, and Giselle rewarded him with a son and heir, an important achievement in those times. Meanwhile, Dagobert began to consolidate his power, which angered both the Church and his old friend Wilfrid. Like most rulers of his time, Dagobert created enemies, so many that few of his subjects were surprised when he was murdered while on a hunting expedition, and it was only through luck, perception or divine intervention that Giselle and their son Sigisbert, accompanied by a small group of faithful knights, escaped a similar fate. From that point on, Sigisbert and his descendants kept their lineage a secret from others, even while recording it among themselves so that members could recognize the holiness of their ancestry and employ it to achieve greatness of one kind or another.

Soon after, Rhaede began a long decline from its status as a major center. After being devastated during battles with Spain, its inhabitants suffered terribly during the plague years. Repeated sacking and burning by Catalan bandits persuaded the remaining residents to abandon the city entirely. Most fled inland, while a hardy few remained, rebuilding their community as a village named Rennes-le-Chateau.

Meanwhile, a monastic order was founded in Jerusalem. Known as Our Lady of Mount Zion, the order later transferred its headquarters to St. Leonard d'Acre in Palestine, and later still relocated in Sicily. It operated there for some time before being absorbed by the Jesuits in 1617, its history easily confirmed through authentic Church records. Everything we know about it appears to verify that this Priory of Sion functioned like dozens of similar facilities of its time. As a center for meditation and salvation, it interacted with the community around it, playing the usual feudal/medieval role of social hub, inspirational retreat and cultural resource. Nothing suggests that it seethed with conspirators, harbored Templars plotting revenge against the Church, or served as a genealogical resource for latter-day Merovingians. Its only role in history has been to provide a name for a society that claims 2000 years of threatened yet influential existence.

The next chapter of the tale begins in 1885 when a Catholic priest named Francois Berenger Saunière is dispatched to the parish surrounding the village of Rennes-le-Chateau. Over 1000 years had passed since the wedding of Dagobert and Giselle that bound the Visigoth kingdom and the Merovingian blood line. The old strategic city of Rhaede that had been the site of that marriage was now a backwater village housing barely 200 residents.

Saunière[6] is an interesting historical figure, made more interesting by his involvement in perhaps the most compelling

[6] Alert readers of *The Da Vinci Code* will recognize that the book's author employed this name to identify the mysterious individual whose death, at the beginning of the book, sets the novel's plot in motion.

Francois Berenger Saunière. Keeper of the Holy
Grail or ecclesiastical swindler?

secret society legend of our time.
Well educated and ambitious, the
handsome Saunière could only have
been disappointed, if not crushed,
upon arriving at his new posting.
Located about forty kilometers from
Carcassonne in the shadows of the
Pyrenees, Rennes-le-Chateau might
as well have been on the moon as far as a priest with high aspi-
rations was concerned. At thirty-three years of age, Saunière
probably saw the assignment as the end of the road, if not the
end of his dreams.

To make things worse, Saunière inherited not a parish church
but a pitiful ruin. Much of the chapel roof was missing, permitting rain to pour directly onto the altar. The windows were
covered not with stained glass but with rough boards, the presbytery was virtually uninhabitable, no housekeeper had been
assigned to him, and his monthly salary of 75 francs was barely
enough to buy bread for his table. The only thing more surprising than the state of Saunière's church was his decision to remain.

At least part of this decision may have been inspired by carnal rather than ecclesiastical notions. While priests were
permitted to recruit women as housekeepers, the Church suggested that thirty years or more separate their ages, indicating
that Saunière's live-in housekeeper should be in her sixties. But
Saunière swung the age compass in the other direction, and
soon sixteen-year-old Marie Denarnaud began sharing the run-
down presbytery with him. Over time, it became accepted that
the couple shared both the building and its bed, a situation that
the community and Saunière's superior, the lenient and amiable
Bishop of Carcassonne, appear to have tolerated.

Marie Denarnaud may have been attracted to the priest for
reasons other than his handsome appearance. Perhaps it was

Marie Denarnaud. As housekeeper/mistress to the
mysterious Father Saunière, how many secrets
did she keep?

Saunière's passionate nature, which he
demonstrated within a few months of
arriving at his new posting. During
state elections held in October 1885,
Father Saunière became a rabid oppo-
nent of the ruling Republican party,
haranguing and practically ordering his parishioners to vote
against it. His scolding sermons made little difference to the
outcome; the Republicans won, and when stories of Saunière's
rabid sermons against them became known, they pressed for
revenge and got it. As punishment for his political indiscretion,
Saunière's small salary was suspended. He appealed to the
bishop who, having forgiven the priest's unapproved living
arrangements with his nubile housekeeper, extended his charity
by appointing Saunière to a professor's post at the nearby Petit
Seminaire de Narbonne, where the fiery priest stalked the halls
and classrooms for six months until his suspension was lifted.

If Church leaders believed they had slapped Saunière down,
they were mistaken. In fact, Saunière returned to the village and
his dilapidated structures, this time with the backing of a
wealthy supporter and plans to improve the fortunes of his
parish and himself.

Perhaps in admiration for his political stand, which may
have coincided with her own, the influential Countess of
Chambord bestowed 3000 francs on Saunière upon his return
to his parish. The figure is significant, because Saunière had
reportedly obtained an estimate of 2800 francs to make repairs
to the church. To his credit, he appears to have dedicated all of
the countess's largesse towards rebuilding and restoring it.

Somewhere along the way, Saunière grew fascinated by the
legend surrounding his church's supposed historical significance. A few sources claim the tale of the church was already

well known among the local citizens; others say no one was aware of its historical importance until the restoration work was well advanced. As things turned out, neither explanation is significant.

Saunière's church, dedicated to Mary Magdalene, had been constructed on the site of the marriage between Dagobert II and Giselle de Razes, the story went, and Saunière made an amazing discovery while assisting in its reconstruction. A heavy stone that had served as an altar in the original edifice was mounted on four pillars. Saunière himself moved the slab to discover that one of the pillars was hollow. From within that space he gently removed four ancient parchments, keeping them hidden from the eyes of others working around him. Two of the parchments traced a genealogical line, while the other two were written in a mysterious code that took experts in Paris some time to decipher. When they did, the words were electrifying. *A Dagobert II Roi et à Sion est ce tresor et il est là mort*, the message came back. To King Dagobert II and to Sion belongs this treasure, and he is dead there.

Treasure? What treasure? The answer appeared when a second stone slab was unearthed. Something was concealed behind it, something only Father Saunière saw. One glance told him his dreams of being assigned to Bordeaux or Paris or even Rome were nothing compared with the wealth that lay before him. Soon Saunière and two trusted helpers were busy as gophers, unearthing sites all around the church and on the outskirts of the village.

Father Saunière may have had to beg for funds to repair his old church in the beginning, but from that point forward the building activity at Saunière's church was intense and extravagant enough to generate envy in every prelate from the Bishop of Paris down. The little church was rebuilt to magnificence, decorated with paintings and sculptures purchased by Saunière on expeditions to Paris. Some were traditional, like *The Shepherds of Arcadia*, illustrating a group of people gathered around a sarcophagus in a landscape eerily similar to Rennes-le-

Chateau. Others were obscure in style and meaning, including a statue near the church entrance that bore the Latin inscription *Terribilis est locus iste*—This place is terrible.

The priest accumulated enough riches to purchase more than artifacts for his church. He bought several acres of land adjacent to the property, and began construction of the Tower of Magdala in honor of Mary Magdalene, and a multi-roomed mansion named Villa Bethania for himself and Marie. The expenditure was enormous—40,000 francs for the tower, 90,000 francs for the mansion and 20,000 francs for an adjoining garden. In total, Saunière spent an estimated 200,000 francs, paid out by a man who a few years earlier had received a pitiful monthly salary of 75 francs. In contemporary terms, 200,000 francs in 1900 would equal almost 7 million francs or about 1.25 million U.S. dollars.[7]

Saunière may have been dispatched to a backwater location in an uninspiring corner of France, but he was living like a combination of Vatican cardinal and eastern potentate, a man whose every desire—material, spiritual, cultural and carnal—appeared satisfied thanks to an apparently endless source of funds. He fed special biscuits to his flock of ducks to produce a milder flavor when they were roasted, boasted a well-stocked wine cellar, and had seventy liters of rum brought in each month from Jamaica. In June 1891 Saunière staged a procession through the village to display a newly acquired statue of the Virgin of Lourdes, which he installed on a pillar in the elegant new church gardens. The following year, he added a new confessional and pulpit, and mysteriously designed Stations of the Cross set in an unusual circular pattern that was believed to represent a coded message. The water stoup soon boasted an elaborate guardian devil, a commissioned statue of Mary Magdalene and numerous other items that elevated his tiny church far above the expected level of taste and culture for such an otherwise insipid community.

The ambitious priest began decorating more than his beloved church. The villagers delighted in his plans to construct

[7] Other estimates of the value of Saunière's expenses range up to 250 million francs (over $50 million), a figure that strains credulity to the extreme.

In addition to an elaborate restoration of its dilapidated church, Rennes-le-Chateau soon boasted an impressive tower dedicated to Mary Magdalene.

a grotto near a life-sized image of Christ on the cross in the town square. Marie Denarnaud took equal delight in wearing the latest Paris fashions in her strolls through the marketplace, sometimes carrying a purse containing deeds to property that Saunière had purchased in her name.

Local citizens were curious about the source of Saunière's riches, but not especially so. After all, he was providing employment for local artisans, and adding a measure of distinction that the community had been sorely lacking. Besides, their interest was sufficiently satisfied with a tale that explained things reasonably while appealing to their somewhat rebellious nature. Here is what the local folk believed:

Saunière had unearthed something more valuable than gold and jewels during his excavations. The treasure of Dagobert, and the identity of the buried man ("...and he is dead there") was not the long-deceased Merovingian king himself but the body of Christ, its location pinpointed by a coded parchment hidden in the pillar beneath the altar.

Consider the import of that discovery. The existence of Christ's body in an insignificant French village would destroy every tenet of Christianity, scatter every foundation of its faith, and demolish every institution from the Vatican down. Either Christ had not died on the cross, or he had not arisen from the dead and been elevated to heaven three days later. Each theological principle of Christianity would have to be rethought and rewritten or discarded entirely, along with 2000 years of piety and sacrifice.

What was Saunière to do? A deeply religious man might have kept the secret forever, clinging to the faith he had lived by and refusing to shatter the spirituality of millions. A rationalist would have made his discovery public, challenging old ideologies and assisting to replace them, and the faith they represented, with a new order.

Saunière was neither of these. He was a materialist who, quietly disclosing his discovery to a small group of selected Church leaders, promised to conceal the facts in exchange for a generous stipend, paid by the Church while they plotted their next move. In effect, Christianity was being blackmailed by an obscure French priest living openly with his young house-keeper/mistress.

If this were the case, the Church's ultimate response after several years of meeting his demands might be first to discredit Saunière, and later slap him down and be done with it. Which is what happened, but not before various mysterious events occurred, the kind that set small-town tongues wagging and conspiracy fans salivating.

The process began dramatically with the strange deaths of two local church officials. On the eve of All Saint's Day 1897 Abbé Gelis, a reclusive priest in the nearby village of Coustaussa, was found brutally murdered in the kitchen of his presbytery. Beaten with a pair of fire tongs and an ax, the priest had been reverently positioned on the floor with his hands neatly placed on his chest. While the residence had been ransacked, robbery appeared not to be the motive because 800 francs were found in an easily accessible drawer. The murder was never solved.

Five years later, the placid Bishop Billard of Carcassonne was also murdered. Billard, who not only failed to question Saunière regarding his wealth and extravagant lifestyle but appears to have encouraged it, suffered a fate as brutal as Abbé Gelis. His murder also remains unsolved.

Bishop Billard's successor, Abbé de Beauséjour, was not as forgiving to Saunière as Billard had been, especially after delving into the priest's background. Accusing Saunière of unspecified outrageous acts, the new bishop demanded explanations for Saunière's actions and an audit of the parish's income and expenses, demands Saunière ignored before attempting to placate his superior with faked and incomplete records.

By 1909, the bishop had had enough. He ordered Saunière to leave his post at Rennes-le-Chateau. When Saunière refused, he was promptly defrocked. For eight years, the disgraced priest remained in the village, cared for by the faithful Marie Denarnaud to whom he willed all of his earthly possessions when he died in 1917. Saunière's estate consisted of a few books and a handful of worthless trinkets, but Marie was assured of a reasonably comfortable existence because Saunière had transferred Villa Bethania to her. She survived for the next thirty years by renting rooms within the mansion, finally passing ownership of the property her lover priest had acquired in her name to a local businessman in exchange for a lifetime annuity. This income source supported her for the rest of her uneventful life until her passing in January 1953. The man who purchased the land and provided the annuity was Noel Corbu, a local entrepreneur. Mark that name.

Through the period between the two world wars, while Marie Denarnaud lived quietly with her memories and secrets, France was jostled by two competing political factions. Royalists, who supported a return to a monarchist government and enjoyed open support from the Catholic Church, were opposed by republicans, who favored democratically elected governments. Many leaders of the republican movement were Masons, who had dominated French politics since the 1880s.

The conflict remained relatively benign until France encountered the upheaval of the late 1920s that brought Hitler to power in neighbor-

By 1900, Rennes-le-Chateau and the Bethania Mansion shown on this postcard had begun to grow in fame and notoriety.

ing Germany. Assuming many of the postures that characterized the Nazis, groups composing the French far right grew more racist. Along with the wave of anti-Semitism sweeping Europe, French right-wing extremists added Masons to their list of likely traitors and subversives. Given the turmoil of Europe and the global economic crisis produced by the Great Depression, scapegoats were found everywhere, and coalitions congealed whenever a common enemy was identified. Extreme monarchists joined forces, presenting themselves as knightly orders assigned to redeem a lost society now dominated by Jews and Masons. The election of Leon Blum, a Jew, as the country's first socialist prime minister, drove monarchists and the far right into a coalition that paved the way for the Vichy regime and France's collaboration with occupying Nazis during World War ii.

Among the monarchist/fascist groups shaped during this swirl of political commotion was Alpha Galates (The First Gauls). The organization generated little interest and made even less impact until its members elected, as its titular head, a teenager named Pierre Plantard. Either very precocious or well connected, Plantard achieved fame and notoriety exceeding both his working-class origins and his mediocre intellect.

Plantard sometimes assumed the clichéd manner and appearance of French underworld characters: gaunt and dark, with a perpetual sneer and a Gauloise hanging from his lips. At other times, he posed as an intellectual, an existentialist comfortable in the company of a Malraux or Sartre. The best depiction of Plantard, who identified himself variously as Pierre de France and Plantard de St. Clair, is chameleon-like; he altered whatever aspect of his life and values necessary to achieve whatever goal happened to fall within his vision at the time. Other descriptions of the man are

Pierre Plantard (with his son Thomas in 1979) was a convicted con man whose most successful hoax spawned a best-selling novel.

less neutral, including charlatan, fraud artist and convicted criminal. The latter is easily confirmed via French police archives revealing he had been found guilty of extortion and embezzlement, and sentenced to six months in prison.

During the Vichy regime that ruled Nazi-occupied France from 1940 to 1944, Plantard and his Alpha Galates group published *Vaincre* (To Conquer), a magazine dedicated to French nationalism and restoration of the monarchy. Many of the publication's articles were openly anti-Semitic and anti-Masonic, an accusation that Plantard later justified by claiming it avoided censure by the Gestapo. If that were indeed the strategy, it failed miserably; *Vaincre* was shut down and Plantard imprisoned in 1943 because, according to Nazi records, he was too openly supportive of French fascist views over those of Germany. Plantard, in later years, had a more flattering explanation: The Nazis discovered that his articles in *Vaincre* contained secret codes for French Resistance fighters.

Whichever side Plantard was on, he was clearly a firebrand when it came to French nationalism, a role he pursued with even greater vigor after hostilities ended in 1945. Two years later, Plantard created The Latin Academy, whose avowed purpose was to conduct historical research but whose more apparent goal was to continue the right-wing activities of Alpha Galates. As a mark of the group's questionable success, documents incorporating the "academy" listed Plantard's mother as its titular head.

Plantard became a familiar figure among certain Catholic leaders in Paris, particularly the seminary of St. Sulpice, and it was there in the mid-1950s that he began claiming to be the Merovingian pretender to the French throne. Later, in 1956, he extended that identity by proclaiming himself leader of a divinely guided organization founded by Godfrey de Bouillon during the time of the Crusades, and whose members had been influencing world events since the days of Christ. It was called The Priory of Sion.

The organization's title may have changed, borrowed from the medieval monastery that began as Our Lady of Mount Zion, but in most ways it remained Alpha Galates attached to a new face and a new magazine, this one titled *Circuit*. Plantard's publication soon began carrying stories of Father Saunière, hinting at secrets the priest uncovered in the remote Pyrenees village. The articles eventually formed the basis of a book by Plantard detailing Saunière's discoveries, implications that Christ's body had been buried near the little church dedicated to Mary Magdalene, the uniting of Christ's descendants and French gothic blood with the marriage of Dagobert and Giselle, and the astounding secret that had been maintained through the lives of great men of history.

It was an intriguing story, but Plantard's writing style was less than gripping because no one appeared interested in publishing his book. In an effort to generate support for his literary work, Plantard announced that he had obtained two of the parchments discovered by Saunière in the hollow pillar supporting the altar, and with some fanfare he bestowed them on the Bibliothèque Nationale, the French National Library. The existence of these parchments represented a vital link between Saunière's strange behavior and the existence of the Priory of Sion. Suddenly there were a few believers where only skeptics had stood smiling and shaking their heads.

Both parchments provided by Plantard contained hidden messages, one honoring Dagobert's marriage to Giselle and the other, more cryptic, referring to the Priory of Sion. Once their contents, if not their

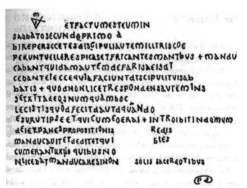

The clue to the truth behind the Priory of Sion lies within this complex code on parchment, but not in the manner you might expect.

authenticity, were confirmed, Plantard stunned scholars and historians by announcing that the documents proved he was a direct descendant of Dagobert and Giselle, thus explaining his role as Grand Master of the Priory of Sion.

The parchments were followed by a revised version of the book, now made publishable thanks to the parchments and some serious rewriting by co-author Gerard de Sède. Titled *L'Or de Rennes* and published in 1967, the book detailed the story of the Priory's beginnings with Mary Magdalene and Christ's children, accompanied either by Christ or his corpse, escaping across the Mediterranean to Gaul. From there it traced the bloodline through Giselle de Razes, tracked her descendants across 1300 years of world history, and ended with the discovery of the parchments and other paraphernalia by Saunière.

The book's revelations generated two distinct and equally fervent points of view. One found the story indisputable, relying on various sources for its authenticity including the mysterious wealth accumulated by Saunière, the existence of the parchments, historical references to Dagobert and the Merovingian line, and Plantard's own convincing accounts. The imaginations of these believers galloped towards conviction that a secret society had carried one of mankind's greatest mysteries through generations of descendants whose intellectual superiority and creativity could be explained through a direct connection with the Creator. These adherents scurried to locate historical references that supported Plantard's claims. Inevitably they found some, and with each apparent confirmation, momentum grew among the believers.

The other side remained skeptical, and over time they discovered a few realities of their own.

The first speed bump on the Priory road occurred when two of Plantard's associates, Gerard de Sède and Philippe de Chérisy, sued Plantard to recover royalties promised them from the book's sale. De Sède's role as co-author was acknowledged, but who was de Chérisy? He was revealed as a well-educated academic with a reputation as something of a prankster. By the time *L'Or de Rennes* was published, he had acquired a drinking habit that would later kill him. More important, de Chérisy claimed that the parchments submitted to the Bibliothèque Nationale were forgeries. He knew they were, because he had produced them as a means of generating publicity and authenticity for Plantard's book.

Plantard, by now riding a wave of publicity and sales from *L'Or de Rennes*, quickly agreed with de Chérisy. The parchments were not authentic, he admitted, but they were not forgeries either. They were meticulous copies of the original parchments which, due to their value, Plantard was storing in a safe place whose location he refused to reveal. He also announced that his family had suppressed the fact that their origins were not entirely French. Plantard's ancestors, he declared, included a distinct lineage with the St. Clairs, anglicized as Sinclair, who had founded Scottish Rite Freemasonry. This alleged link explained the means of maintaining the secrecy of the Priory of Sion's existence down through the centuries. The revelation satisfied believers, but prompted skeptics to dig deeper into the tale, with remarkable results.

The first discovery involved a close examination of the pillars that had supported the altar in Saunière's church, easily located in Rennes-le-Chateau, where they were displayed as part of the town's heritage. None of the pillars was hollow. In fact, all three were quite solid, with the exception of a crack in one that may have concealed a postcard or two but nothing more. An even more disturbing revelation was to follow.

Remember Noel Corbu? He purchased Villa Bethania, the mansion Saunière had built with money earned from his supposed discovery of either bones or treasure. Following Saunière's death, Marie Denarnaud converted the mansion into a rooming house before exchanging it for the lifetime annuity from Corbu. After Marie died in 1953, Corbu transformed Villa Bethania into a small hotel and restaurant. With nothing to attract tourists to Rennes-le-Chateau beyond tales of Saunière's eccentricities and his mysterious wealth, Corbu's investment in his operation would never amount to much. He solved the problem with nothing less than a marketing tool, a device that owed everything to entrepreneurial strategy and almost nothing to the truth.

Corbu concocted a dramatic tale of the legend behind Saunière's mysterious accumulation of riches, populated with characters who would be quite at home in a Harry Potter novel and delivered with the flair of a campfire ghost story. Recording the narrative in his own voice, he played it in his restaurant as a diversion for diners, later publishing it in pamphlet form as a souvenir of their visit.

The story of Saunière and Rennes-le-Chateau was hardly Joseph Conrad quality, but it amused visitors dining on their *pol au pot* and *cassoulet*. They absorbed facts about the town's Roman and gothic roots, its destruction during various battles with Spain, the arrival of Berenger Saunière in 1885, his poverty-stricken early years and his sudden, unexplained accumulation of wealth.

To this point Corbu, who never denied being the author, remained reasonably close to confirmable facts. When he began to explain the source of Saunière's fortune, however, fiction trampled fact into obscurity.

According to Corbu, files in Carcassonne confirmed that Saunière had stumbled upon a fortune buried beneath his church in 1249 by Blanche de Castille, mother of Louis ix, the last great Crusader and the only French king declared a saint. A mini-revolt led by power-seeking barons and oppressed vassals began soon after the king departed for Palestine. His mother, sensing that Paris was not the safest place for the royal treasury, secretly shipped the monarch's gold and jewels to Rennes-le-Chateau. When Louis returned from the east he subdued the revolts and left Paris again several years later, this time to lead the Eighth Crusade. He never returned, dying in Tunis and leaving his son Philippe le Hardi as his successor. Philippe, deciding that the country's treasury was safer in this remote village than in the capital, improved the town's defenses. Perhaps he forgot to tell *his* son, Philippe le Bel, destroyer of the

Templars, about the country's mobile riches, because from that point forward, according to Corbu, the treasure was forgotten.

Forgotten? How does even a French king from the Middle Ages forget 180 tons of gold plus jewels and art objects worth, according to Corbu's 1956 estimate, "4000 billion francs"? Even more basic, how did the king's servants transport 180-plus tons of gold and other goodies more than 650 kilometers (400 miles) in the first place? And why, of all places, to Rennes-le-Chateau, one of the furthest locations from Paris, on the border with one of France's enemies?

No one appears to have questioned this feat, distracted perhaps by Corbu's next revelation:

> The treasure was found twice. In 1645 a shepherd named Ignace Paris fell in a hole and brought back golden coins. He then claimed he saw a room filled with gold. He finally went mad, trying to protect his gold. The owner of the castle searched for it but could not find [the gold]. Later came Saunière, who found the gold....
>
> It is in this small village with a superb landscape and a prestigious history that one of the most fabulous treasures in the world is hidden!

This kind of fable was probably more effective than a rave review in *Paris Match* at drawing patrons to Corbu's hotel and restaurant. Corbu knew it, and he took advantage of contacts in the media to spread his tale among newspapers and magazines. Rennes-le-Chateau did not become a new Monaco overnight, but it seems to have drawn its share of intrigued visitors, and among them was Pierre Plantard, perhaps in search of a scam. The meeting between Corbu and Plantard is not speculation; photographs confirm that the two men met around 1960, shortly before Plantard wrote his first draft of the book eventually published as *L'Or de Rennes*.

The most notable absence in Corbu's fable is any mention of the lovely Giselle, whose marriage to Dagobert joined the power of the Visigoths with the bloodline of Christ. How could Corbu overlook such a vital episode in the historical legend? The answer is startlingly simple and revealing: *Giselle de Razes never existed*. She is as fictional as Snow White. She did not exist in either flesh or spirit in the seventh century, and exists in the twenty-first century only in the minds of deluded followers, conspiracy buffs and gullible readers of a recent best-selling novel. Despite claimed records tracing a family lineage before and after Giselle, in the opinion of Aviad Kleinberg, noted medieval scholar and professor of history at Tel Aviv University, the beautiful, intelligent and charming Giselle remains "an invention of the 20th century."

Without the existence of Giselle, Plantard's entire fabrication collapsed beneath him like a paper porch, so he simply created her as the Visigoth connection with the Merovingian bloodline. Plantard admitted as much from time to time—consistency was not one of the Frenchman's notable virtues—and launched a new version of the Priory tale in 1989. At that time, he claimed a man named Roger-Patrice Pelat, an acquaintance of then Prime Minister Mitterrand, was the current Priory Grand Master of the Priory of Sion and not Plantard himself, as he had been claiming for thirty years. Pelat's status was never confirmed, but he had at least one thing in common with Plantard: both had been convicted of fraud and embezzlement, Plantard's trial taking place soon after his apparent elevation to Grand Master status.

In September 1993, during an official investigation into Pelat's activities Plantard, who never encountered a media moment he didn't like, came forward in his friend's defense. It was a move he regretted after the presiding judge ordered a search of Plantard's dwelling. The search uncovered reams of documents, many proclaiming Plantard as king of France, which was enough for the judge to order Plantard to answer questions under oath. Whatever Inquisition techniques might have been used, Plantard quickly admitted that the entire undertaking was a hoax, that he had made up all the details regarding the bloodline, including the marriage of Giselle and Dagobert, the discovery by Saunière of either a treasure or a corpse beneath or near his church, and his own identity as a Priory of Sion Grand Master. The judge, lenient perhaps due to Plantard's age and broken spirit, called Plantard a harmless crank and released him with a warning not to play games with the French judicial system. Plantard left the courtroom and wandered into relative obscurity until his death in February 2000.

These events—the investigation of Pelat, the claims of Plantard about Pelat's Grand Master position in the Priory of Sion, the phony documents and Plantard's admission of fraud— were widely reported in the French media at the time. No one has disputed them; they are as authentic and confirmable as the fable of Giselle is imaginary.

Of course, there is just enough truth to the story of Saunière and the supposed holy bloodline to suggest that Plantard lied not when he told his often-altered tale but when he claimed the Priory was a fabrication. Perhaps his original tale was true after all. Perhaps his claim under oath that it had all been a fabrication was a brave man's effort at concealing a sacred truth. How, for example, could this somewhat simple-minded man create such a complex structure as the Merovingian bloodline, supported by documents from the past?

The answer lies in the maelstrom of political upheaval that swept Europe during the 1920s and 1930s, when Plantard was first building his reputation as an imaginative sycophant of fascist principles. During those years, an Italian fanatic named Julius Evola attracted the interest of far-right proponents, including Heinrich Himmler and Oswald Mosley, when he published an Italian version of the *Protocols of the Elders of Zion*,[8] claiming that Jewish leaders had met in the nineteenth century to frame their strategy for ruling the world. Evola supported a philosophy similar to the Divine Right of Kings, promoting the old system of power based on the acceptance of a true monarch

[8] For more on the *Protocols*, see Chapter 11 herein.

as a sacred being from whom divine virtues and powers flow to his subjects. He especially admired Godfrey de Bouillon, the first European ruler of Palestine and, supposedly, the founder of the Priory of Sion.

Around the same time, a German scholar named Walter Johannes Stein published *The Ninth Century: World History in the Light of the Holy Grail*, a doctoral dissertation that included a genealogical chart Stein labeled "The Grail Bloodline." Although the bloodline was a symbolic representation of historical figures who had demonstrated a high spiritual nature and paranormal capacities, someone skimming the surface of Stein's premise could easily mistake the symbols for real people—especially when Stein's lineage chart included Godfrey de Bouillon and the French royal family.

These and other esoteric documents accessible in libraries across France could easily have stimulated Plantard's imagination. Spiced with his confirmed penchant for fraud and his hunger for public recognition, Plantard shaped a core of history, with a cover of esoterica wrapped around a substantial amount of fiction, into a ball of a fairy tale that he rolled down a mountain, the ball growing in weight and stature until it swept up three British writers, who molded it into a best-seller titled *The Holy Blood and the Holy Grail.*[9]

One mystery remained. Where did Father Saunière find the money for his extravagant construction and lifestyle? Unlike other aspects of the tale, this was no myth; Saunière's Magdalena Tower, extravagant church interior and Villa Bethania mansion exist to this day. How could he amass so much money without finding Louis ix's treasure or blackmailing the Church with Christ's bones? The confirmed answer is common and familiar: simple fraud.

Until the practice was outlawed by Vatican ii, Catholic priests could claim a stipend for celebrating a Mass to heal an illness suffered by a living person, or to hasten the passage

9 For more on this book and its shaky premise, see Chapter 11 herein.

through purgatory to heaven for a departed soul. Income from these Masses was an acceptable and even encouraged form of financial support for the priest and his parish.

In time, however, unscrupulous priests saw these commissioned Masses as a source of substantial income from Catholics beyond their community, and even beyond their country. Soon Masses were being marketed like any mail order item, advertised in newspapers and Catholic journals. The faithful could have a Mass said on behalf of whomever they desired by forwarding money and details to the priest whose name appeared in the advertisement.

No one, except God and the priest himself, could confirm that the Mass actually occurred. A priest might receive literally thousands of mailed requests, each accompanied by a few francs in cash, to celebrate Masses in the same week or even on the same day. The practice was called "trafficking in Masses," and it appears that Saunière mastered the process. Advertisements appearing in various publications throughout Europe were traced back to the priest in the Pyrenees, and an examination of his books, recording the responses to his marketing campaign, revealed that Saunière could not possibly celebrate all the Masses that he had been paid to conduct, even if he were employed at the task twenty-four hours a day, seven days a week.

The volume of Mass requests and the money enclosed over the years between 1895 and 1904 easily exceeded the 200,000 francs needed to achieve all the construction Saunière directed, as well as goodies such as the rum shipments from the Caribbean.

Correspondence seized from Saunière's church when he was defrocked revealed the enormous extent of his industry. One family sent 250 francs to pay for 125 Masses celebrated for each of their two departed sisters. A widow forwarded 45 francs to pay for 30 Masses for her dead soldier husband, and members of a convent paid 16 francs for Masses for their recently deceased abbess, who herself had paid Saunière for several Masses.

Saunière may have had a silent mentor for his Mass marketing scheme. Investigations revealed that Monsignor Billard,

Bishop of Carcassonne, had been under investigation at the time of his death for acting in a similar manner, which may explain Billard's tolerance for Saunière's own indiscretions.

They are all long dead now—Berenger Saunière, Marie Denarnaud, Pierre Plantard, Gerard de Sède, Philippe de Chérisy and Noel Corbu who, having built his La Tour hotel and restaurant into a thriving little business thanks to the myth of the buried treasure, sold it for a pretty price in 1964 and retired. But not for long; he was killed in a motor accident in 1968.

The myth lives on because people want it to survive and even grow, if only to satisfy their love of deep mystery and colorful intrigue. Someone will doubtless claim to see the ghost of Giselle de Razes, beautiful and radiant, strolling the grounds near the Magdalena Tower in her wedding finery, sighing for her lost Dagobert and searching for the buried treasure. If so, only the tower will be real.

FOUR

DRUIDS AND GNOSTICS
KNOWLEDGE AND THE ETERNAL SOUL

IT IS DIFFICULT TO IMAGINE TWO GROUPS WHOSE ORIGINS and interests are in sharper contrast with each other than Druids and Gnostics. One was born in Celtic mysticism, the other in Judeo-Christian theology. One is rooted in naturalism, the other in spiritualism. One sought perfection in this world to match the perfection of the next world, the other saw this world as hopelessly lost and evil.

They are united by misunderstanding and oppression, two qualities that drive individuals and organizations alike into secrecy. They are also, need it be said, shadowy in their origins and activities, and when the shadows are deep enough and the passage of time is long enough, even the most benign groups acquire a veil of suspicion. Especially if they tend to dance in the woods, or are viewed askance by organized religion. Indulging in a little magic, as both Druids and Gnostics tended to do, doesn't help their reputation either.

Each year, approaching the winter solstice in the northern hemisphere, men and women in many Christian nations delight in performing a custom rooted in Druidism. The practice, with its clearly sexual implications, is performed in the presence of a poisonous and

Druids were in many ways soulful precursors to 1960s hippies.

This late-nineteenth-century artist's depiction of a "druidress" holds mistletoe in one hand and a golden sickle in the other.

parasitic life form, suggesting the Druids were a society of subversive deviates who conducted pagan rituals within open-air temples such as Stonehenge, a classic misconception of this shadowy society.

The ritual involves couples kissing beneath mistletoe during the Christmas season, a custom that has no known connection with Druidism beyond the sacred status accorded the plant by its members, and the oak trees that support it. Nor does any confirmed association exist between the Druids and Stonehenge, except for speculation among some contemporary fringe groups.

Admittedly, we know little about Druids because they kept no written records, and because they existed less as an organization and more as a position of status among royalty, especially in Celtic communities of Western Europe. All of our understanding of Druidism is obtained third-hand, filtered through both time and social bias; even their ritualistic use of mistletoe is known to us primarily through the writings of the first-century Roman Pliny the Elder. According to Pliny, and Maxim of Tyre, Druids considered the oak tree a visible representation of the deity, the result of Druids living in intimacy with the natural world. "They hold nothing more sacred than the mistletoe," Pliny wrote, "and the oak tree on which it grows." Druids misread the true behavior of mistletoe. The plant is a parasite, drawing nourishment from the tree's sap; Druids, whose specialty after all was spiritual studies and not botany, believed that mistletoe gave life to the oak. This idea became strengthened in winter when the oak lost its leaves and grew dormant, yet the mistletoe retained its foliage.

"Anything growing on the [oak] trees," Pliny continued, "is regarded as life sent from heaven, a sign that the tree has been chosen by the gods themselves. When [the mistletoe] is found, it is gathered with great ceremony on the sixth day of the moon." According to Pliny, first a feast was held beneath the tree bearing the mistletoe. At the completion of the feast, a Druid priest in white vestments climbed the tree carrying a golden sickle or pruning hook, and gathered the plant in a white cloth. When he returned to the ground with the sacred plant, two white bulls were sacrificed to the gods in exchange for the mistletoe.

The Druids, incidentally, were not the only people to hold mistletoe in such high regard. The Japanese treated it with similar veneration, although they favored a variety that grew on willow trees. Swiss, Slavs, and others considered mistletoe an exceptional plant representing many mystical qualities, most associated with fertility. The fertility connection spawned the custom of couples kissing beneath the mistletoe's fruit during the winter solstice, in hopes of the woman becoming pregnant and bearing a healthy child during the coming year.

Mistletoe, and its winter solstice/Christmas ritual, remains the only tangible link most people maintain with Druidism, yet the movement is considered by some to comprise a secret society working towards shadowy ends.

"Druid" refers not to the member of a religious sect, but to the priestly class of Celtic and Gallic societies, especially in the British Isles. The true origin of the word has been lost in the mists of time. Several theories abound, including one that combines the Greek word *drus*, meaning an oak tree, with the Sanskrit *vid*, meaning knowledge (and the Sanskrit word for timber is *dru*). The Greek word identifying forest gods and tree deities was *Dryades*, another clue. Celtic scholars categorize *Drui* as a term for "the men of the oak trees," and the Gaelic *Druidh* identifies a wise man or a sorcerer. Other clues point to Teutonic and Welsh sources. Whatever the etymology of the word, tracking its origin leads to an endless and unanswerable chicken-or-egg discussion. It is enough, perhaps, to accept that the word suggests one meaning above all: priestly.

While "priestly" implies that Druids performed a religious function, their role extended well beyond that purpose, encompassing philosophy, science, traditions, teaching, judgments, and fulfilling the duties of royal counselor. Perhaps the best way to describe them in today's vernacular is *religious intelligentsia*, with the understanding that "religious" implies a wider meaning than normally assigned to it. The Celts lived as close to nature as any ancient people, and closer than most. Their myths, beliefs and practices reflected their deep woodland environment, a world that simultaneously supported, frightened, and spiritually uplifted them.

Those seeking to become Druids at the height of the movement's influence, generally considered to be between 100 BC and AD 1000, qualified according to three levels of ability. The initial level of Ovates (*Ovydd*) consisted of neophytes needing no special purification or preparation. Dressed in green, they were welcomed into the order according to their naturally acquired knowledge of medicine, astronomy, poetry and music. Ovates wishing to advance in recognition and power studied to become Bards (*Beirdd*). To qualify for this level they were assigned to memorize at least some portion of a reported twenty thousand verses of Druidic poetry. Bards were often portrayed strumming a primitive harp holding as many strings as there are ribs on one side of the body, the strings composed of human hair. Candidates to become Bards wore striped robes of blue, green and white, the three colors identified with the Druids. When they had achieved full status, they changed to a sky blue garment.

The third level marked the highest rank, the *Derwyddon*, distinguished by white robes symbolizing purity. Druids ministered to the religious needs of their people, and within this group were six ascending levels or degrees of wisdom and power, each degree marked by a different color of sash worn over the white robe. In the uppermost position were Arch-Druids, elected by their peers according to their virtue and integrity. There were never more than two Arch-Druids at any one time, the men identified by golden scepters carried in their hands and wreaths of oak leaves crowning their heads.

The training period required for an individual to qualify as a full Druid was apparently extensive, some historians claiming it took twenty years to absorb and understand the teachings. Such a level of acquired wisdom qualified Druids for special privileges, and during royal festivities a Druid always sat to the immediate right of the king, filling the role of the king's conscience. As one prominent Celtic historian puts it, "The Druid *counsels* and the king *acts*." Perhaps the best modern analogy is of a corporation's CEO and its legal adviser; the CEO may deliver bad news to the shareholders, but the phraseology originated with the lawyer.

Incidentally, studies suggest that many Druids were women, fully in keeping with the dominant culture of the time. Celtic women enjoyed more freedom than other females of their time, including the right to join in battle and the right to divorce their husbands. In Ireland and Scotland, at least, it's realistic to believe they played a substantial role in the practice of Druidism. And extending the earlier analogy, it's highly likely that the Celtic world experienced more female Druid priests than our current world contains female CEOs.

Male Druids lived in strict abstinence and celibacy, dedicating their lives to the study of nature, the accumulation of wisdom, the assessment of nominees to the order, and the maintenance of the order's secrets. Many found that a life of solitude best suited their philosophical needs, and while some resided in monastery-like residences, most lived in rough-hewn shacks deep in the forest, entering villages and towns only to perform their religious duties.

Even during the Dark Ages this was considered somewhat eccentric behavior, and unusual qualities began to be attributed to Druids. They became associated with magic and divine events, including an ability to defend their land from invaders by causing great clouds of fog and mist to appear on command. They may also represent the earliest form of peace activism; the

Greek historian Diodorus, who considered Druids as intermediaries between Man and the gods, described the practice of
Druids throwing themselves between threatening armies as a
means of avoiding war.

For centuries, Druidism was the dominant influence on
spiritual beliefs in Europe until diluted and pushed westward by
the arrival of the Roman Empire, followed by the spreading
influence of Christianity. In fact, this paralleled the decline of
Celtic influence generally. From the dominant social structure
of pre-Roman Europe the Celts gave way first to the Romans
and later to the Saxons, reduced to pockets in Wales and Scotland. Only in Ireland did Celts retain their identity through
centuries.

Caesar, as talented at observing and recording social structures as he was at commanding armies, found Druids especially
interesting. He noted that Gallic and Celtic societies maintained three levels of class: plebeians, who were little more than
slaves; equites, the nobility; and Druids, who provided guidance
on holy matters and wisdom. "A great number of young people
search them out for instruction," Caesar wrote, "and [the
Druids] are treated with much respect and veneration. It is they
who judge all public and personal disputes; when a crime is
committed or a murder takes place, or when an inheritance or
land boundary is contested, the Druids determine who is at fault
and who has been harmed, and decide the damages and penalties.... All Druids are under the command of a single Druid
who exercises ultimate authority upon them." Caesar also noted
wryly, considering his reputation and primary occupation, that
Druids did not go to war (they were exempted from military
service of any kind), and did not pay taxes.

The Druids were a remarkably forgiving and supple society
who welcomed into their ranks anyone who successfully pursued a defined course of study focused on the natural world and
the manner in which it represented the deity. This openness
towards new members seeking leadership may not appear
impressive, given our familiarity with contemporary organized

religion, but the prospect of gaining access to a privileged class solely on the basis of education and vocation was almost revolutionary. Their practice of accepting all who qualified by dint of study and dedication influenced Christianity. Instead of demanding that its leaders be selected according to bloodline or some mysterious deity-operated lottery, as previous religions had, Christians agreed with Druidic tenets that anyone who absorbed sufficient knowledge and demonstrated high levels of commitment could fulfill the role, whatever their social origins. This was new, and enormously beneficial. It also followed a Christian tradition—some might prefer "strategy"—of adapting characteristics of the pagan model it sought to displace. And it worked: from about AD 500 forward, Druids and Christians were riding opposite ends of the same teeter-totter; the higher Christianity rose in power, the lower the Druids sank.

So who was most responsible for the decline of the Druids—Romans or Christians? It depends on where you stand, literally and figuratively. In continental Europe, where Roman influence was paramount, the Galls adapted Roman law and customs as a prudent means of self-preservation. Under Roman law, Druidism became so compromised that it essentially ceased to exist until resurrected later, in a highly modified state, as part of Christianity's operative machinery, with Druid high priests replaced by bishops and abbots. In the British Isles, the impact of Romanization proved not nearly as dominant. Here, Druidism managed to survive the onslaught, finally yielding to the Saxons. Ireland avoided invasion by both the Romans and the Saxons, and as a result much of our knowledge of Druidism retains a decidedly Irish flavor. With this awareness in hand, Druidism may well have been broader in scope and more complex in structure than we know.

After the Irish Celts adopted Christianity and became among its most fervent missionaries, Druidism fought a near-hopeless rear-guard battle. Prominent Druids withdrew to remote regions where they secretly spread their doctrine and oral traditions to the few stubborn adherents who sought them out. As time passed, however, the power and influence of

Druids dwindled until they were viewed by common folk as little more than fortunetellers and prophets, descendants of the apocryphal Merlin and his ilk, cursing and conjuring but achieving little beyond a measure of entertainment.

With so little recorded history and such limited achievement, why do Druids occupy any position at all among our grasp of secret societies? The answer lies within the movement's romantic association with installations such as Stonehenge, and the assumption that Druidism encompassed long-forgotten mystical practices and secret occult knowledge. There is, after all, nothing like the scent of lost knowledge to boost a society's status.

The idea that Druids knew something the rest of us do not grew out of an eighteenth-century fascination in England and Scotland with mysticism, often embraced in a playful manner to relieve the tedious restrictions of Calvinism, Lutherism and other movements that assumed anything fun was a sin—or should be. During this period, Freemasonry crystalized as a secret fraternal society, adapting as it did certain elements of the public's erroneous perception of Druid mystical practices. The

Modern Druids bless the rising sun at Stonehenge, which has no connection with Druidism.

Masonic use of exotic headwear, among other rites and costumes, was derived from Druidism and various ancient cultures.

There is more mysticism than fact in the common association of the Druids with Stonehenge. Druids may have conducted some sort of ceremony at Stonehenge from time to time, but they were people of the forest, not prancers and dancers on the windswept Salisbury Plain. Besides, historians have pegged the date of the site's origins around 2000 BC, long before any indication of the Druids' existence. Stonehenge may have functioned as a temple, an observatory, a monument or any of a dozen other purposes. We do not know for certain what it was; we do know that it was surely not Druidic.

Irish culture assimilated many Druid beliefs and values, and their echoes and influences can be found in the poems of William Butler Yeats and the novels and short stories of James Joyce. Several mystical elements of Druidism may indeed represent the stylistic core that distinguishes Irish authors, and mark the reason for their unique impact on English literature. The demise of the sweet-natured Druids at the hands of Romans and Saxons, philistine in comparison, may also represent the wistful root of Celtic literature. Yeats made use of it several times in his poetry, including these lines from "To the Rose Upon the Rood of Time" that sum up all the gentle Celtic sadness as effectively as several choruses of "Danny Boy":

Red Rose, proud Rose, sad Rose of all my days!
Come near me, while I sing the ancient ways:
Cuchulain battling with the bitter tide;
The Druid, grey, wood-nurtured, quiet-eyed,
Who cast round Fergus dreams, and ruin untold;
And thine own sadness, where of stars, grown old
In dancing silver-sandaled on the sea,
Sing in their high and lonely melody.

Druids appear several times in Joyce's *Ulysses*, although with less reverence and more boisterousness than Yeats's melancholy references. When Stephen Dedalus tells Buck Mulligan he had just been paid, Mulligan rejoices.

> Four shining sovereigns, Buck Mulligan cried with delight. We'll have a glorious drunk to astonish the Druidy Druids. Four omnipotent sovereigns. He flung up his hands and tramped down the stone stairs, singing out of tune with a Cockney accent....

These and many other references to Druids in Irish literature and folklore help fuel speculation that Druidic influence extends down through the ages, perhaps even to today. Like the Masons encouraging the concept of a link with the Templars, many of those who claim a connection with Druid beliefs encourage the idea that the ancient movement continues to operate in secrecy, with a vague aura of conspiratorial activities. Their efforts serve to provide a patina of mystique to a faction that has had more influence than substance, and been composed of more fable than fact.

To appreciate the breadth of Gnosticism, imagine a private club whose rules and activities are equally attractive to both Hugh Hefner and Mother Teresa. If you are able to grasp the concept of such an organization, you can begin to plumb the deeper teachings and contradictions of the ancient Gnostics, if not their contemporary supporters.

Their name derived from the Greek *gnosis*, meaning *knowledge*. (The "G" is silent: NO-*sis*.) In this context, the definition is inadequate; *insight* or *enlightenment* are perhaps more accurate. Knowledge suggests a factual, intellectual aspect rejected by adherents of Gnosticism, who believe that our true spiritual nature can be found only by looking within ourselves. Both our bodies and the material world in which we live are evil because they were created by the malicious God of the Old Testament. Our pure inner spirits, in contrast, are the product of a higher and more abstract God, as revealed by Christ. Thus the goal of Gnosticism can be described as a means of freeing our pure spirits from the enclosure of our evil bodies.

Beyond this central core of their conviction, little about the Gnostics can be easily established, including their origins. Some sources claim they pre-date Christ, some claim they were contemporary with the first Christians, and some identify Gnosticism as a reaction against many of Christianity's firmly established tenets. A number of clues and a handful of facts exist to define the group's beliefs, structure and influence over the past 2000 years.

Gnostics, like followers of all religions, believe the world is imperfect; Gnostics go further by insisting it is also evil. Like Buddhism, Gnosticism acknowledges that life is filled with suffering. In fact, suffering is inescapable. All life on earth survives by consuming other life, and mankind consumes more than its share. Beyond its basic needs for survival, mankind inflicts multiple layers of suffering on a grand scale via wars, and on an individual scale through insults and betrayals. Along with suffering come injury and death as a result of natural catastrophes like earthquakes, floods, fires, drought, pestilence and disease.

Yet the human spirit, according to Gnostic teachings, is pure. Only the matter that surrounds it, including the body it occupies, is flawed. By that measure, life is absurd and only by fleeing this imperfect world can the spirit find true contentment.

The concept of pure spirits residing within an evil world represents an about-face from traditional Christian principles, especially as articulated in Genesis. The Old Testament's initial tale describes a perfect paradise in which two near-perfect people dwell in bliss until the arrival of the serpent persuades them to contaminate it and themselves with sin. Gnostics would argue that the world was already evil before the arrival of the serpent, an issue that did not endear them to Christians.

This core concept of an evil world launched a remarkable schism in Gnostic beliefs and practices, producing extremes of both ascetic and licentious sects, leading to that opening analogy of Hugh Hefner and Mother Teresa under the same philosophical umbrella. Surprisingly, a rationale exists for both points of view.

Ascetic Gnostics, which included followers of Saturninus and the Manicheans, considered the human body as evil matter and tried to divorce themselves—or more correctly their pure spirits—from its actions as much as possible. Separating soul from body, in their view, was the first stage in elevating the spirit to ultimate salvation. They believed matter, as exemplified by the body, was sinful, and distancing themselves from all matter strengthened and purified their spirit. As a result, these Gnostics avoided foods that provided anything beyond mere sustenance. Marriage was sanctioned because it united two pure spirits, but nuptial intercourse was forbidden, a decision that no doubt produced much frustration and no offspring, since children were considered merely the reproduction of yet more evil matter.

This same philosophical foundation pointed licentious Gnostics, such as the Ophites and Carpocratians, in the opposite direction. If pure spirits or souls are alien to this evil world, these sects believed, then it didn't matter what they did here on earth. To these Gnostics, the concepts of sin and immorality were rarely addressed; by definition, everything the soul did was pure and everything the body did was evil. Since both were separate entities, why worry about the ramifications?

This led to a few startling tales of Gnostic activities, many of them challenging credulity, and some reminiscent of the scandalous lies spread about early Christians. In the case of the Gnostics, the Christians themselves may have been the instigators instead of the recipients.

Promiscuous intercourse was attributed to this group of Gnostics who, having sanctified each other and been redeemed, were now above the law. "All the earth is earth," they were taught, "and it matters not where one sows, as long as one sows." About 2000 years later this was paraphrased into "If it feels good, do it."

The Ophites, a group of Gnostics whose name honored serpents, based their entire communion service on the presence and activities of a snake. The service began by attracting the reptile from the safety of its *cista mystica* and encouraging it to slither among loaves of bread, which were later eaten. Members were required to kiss the snake, which was either very tame or well drugged, on the mouth before falling to their knees and worshipping the animal.

Followers of the Gnostic sect led by Carpocrates were granted even more license and encouragement. Carpocratians believed that the purity of the soul could not be contaminated and made evil, any more than a pearl could be debased by dropping it in the mud; at its center, the pearl would always remain a pearl. Based on this libertine view, the soul ought to experience everything available to it in this world. Carpocratians shared their sexual partners and took part in massive orgies, although males were instructed to practice *coitus interruptus* not as a method of birth control but as a means of collecting semen to be consumed as the body of Christ, as was menstrual blood. Recruitment methods of the Carpocratians were basic and no doubt successful in attracting male followers. The most beautiful female members were encouraged to offer themselves as bait to draw adherents, and a related group formed a male elite called Levites who practiced open homosexuality.

Should a woman become pregnant as a result of these activities, the fetus would be aborted, pounded to jelly in a mortar, mixed with honey and spices, and eaten by sect members, a practice chillingly reminiscent of the most lurid fables associated with early Christians.

This kind of practice represented an extreme, perhaps even mad, branch of Gnostic belief. Larger and more respectable was the sect led by Simon Magus, a charismatic scholar who fills an interesting role in at least one biblical tale that provided an eponymous definition in English.

Born in the Samarian town of Gitta, Magus was raised in Alexandria, the great intellectual center of the civilized world in its time, where he received a first-rate Greek education and was baptized by Phillip. He also reportedly acquired enough skill in Arabic-Jewish magical medicine to make himself invisible, levitate himself at will, and metamorphose into an animal, or at least persuade his audience that he had.

A follower of John the Baptist, Simon gathered his own disciples around him and was viewed, not surprisingly, as a potential competitor to early Christian leaders. He appears in the New Testament (Acts 8: 9–24) in a less than favorable light when he encounters the apostles Peter and John and attempts to purchase spiritual powers from them, providing the source of our word *simony*, the practice of trafficking in spiritual powers or items.

Peter's rebuke ("Your money will perish with you, because you have thought that the gift of God may be purchased with money. You have neither part nor lot in this matter, for your heart is not right in the sight of God.") may have motivated Simon to launch Gnosticism, as some followers claim. If he didn't actually initiate the religion, he is acknowledged as the inspiration for a faction whose members were labeled, not

surprisingly, Simonians. In Simon's view, shared by most Gnostics, the true God possessed a female aspect, a Mother God sometimes referred to as "Sophia" in recognition of Her wisdom.

This attitude angered early Christians, but it was not quite as revolutionary as it appears today. The Hebrew version of the Old Testament actually identifies the Spirit of God as *Ruwach*, a feminine

Gnostic Simon Magus, who gave his name to an unpopular act, fell to the Roman Forum while attempting to ascend to heaven.

gender. Simon would have been aware of this reference, and perhaps used it as a stepping stone towards new interpretations of the nature of God. As often occurs when freethinkers challenge a dominant authority, it wasn't what Simon proposed as much as the way he proposed it.

He later personified his vision of God's femininity in Helen, a woman from Tyre who some Christians claimed was a prostitute and others described as "a shameless slut" lured by Simon away from the bed of Dositheos, Simon's former mentor. Whatever carnal attraction Helen may have represented to Simon, she apparently inspired him at a somewhat higher level because he claimed to see the Spirit of God within her. While this supported many Gnostic beliefs, including the idea that the Spirit of God existed in all matter, Simon's claim that it took a fallen woman to reveal the deity to him outraged Christians.

Christians may have become his enemies, but Simon had friends as well. One of them was the Roman emperor, Nero, who appointed him court magician and was amused by Simon's skill at causing furniture to move without being touched, and walking through a wall of fire to emerge unscathed on the other side.

Simon's magical skill, according to legend, had its limits, and he met his end in one of two ways, depending upon the source. One account claims that Simon boasted he would be buried alive as Christ had been and after three days he would rise from his grave hale and hearty. The burial took place; the resurrection did not.

In the other account, Simon bragged that he would rise into heaven from the Forum, with the apostles Peter and Paul observing the event as witnesses. Employing his levitation skills, he began to

This stone in the Church of Santa Francesca Romana bears the knee marks of Peter and Paul, who knelt to pray for Simon's fall.

soar into the sky while Peter and Paul fell on their knees, pray-
ing fervently for Simon to fall. Their prayers were answered
and Simon dropped to the Forum, dashed to pieces near the Via
Sacra. Adherents of this version delight in visiting the Church
of Santa Francesca Romana in the Roman Forum, where the
stone on which Peter and Paul knelt to pray remains on display,
the mark of their knees pressed into the marble surface.

The death of Simon Magus and other Gnostic sect leaders
produced neither the collapse of the religion nor its elevation,
as occurred with Christianity. The Gnostic core belief continued to evolve, spurred on by new leaders, and while the creed
did not want for constant renewal over several centuries, the
result was an often bewildering range of variations when it came
to values and practices.

In fact, along with the concept of a true, ultimate and tran-
scendent God and a faulty world in which humans dwell, the
only constant factor among Gnostic sects was the notion of
Aeons, intermediate beings filling the void between humans and
God. Aeons and God comprise the realm of *Pleroma*, or
Fullness, because they enjoy the full potency of divinity. Simon
Magus's Helen, renamed Sophia in honor of her wisdom, was
an Aeon in Gnostic teachings. Humans, as long as the spirit
remains trapped within its flawed and evil body, are merely exis-
tential according to Gnostics. Instead of the Fullness we are
promised, we live in Emptiness.

The spirit's most valuable ingredient is a Divine Spark, the
element that separates us from other forms of life and remains
trapped within the prison of the body. Unless the required degree
of Gnosis is gathered during life, the spark will be re-embodied
upon death in another flawed and evil form of earthly life.

Not every human is capable of achieving the goal of retaining the spiritual element beyond earthly existence. Those
whose spirituality is strong enough to make the transformation
are called *pneumatics*; they will achieve Gnosis and liberation. A
second group, identified as *psychics*, have little awareness of the
spiritual world beyond matter and mind; they may, through suf-

ficient effort and insight, rise to the level of pneumatics. Most people, labeled *hyletics*, are earthbound and materialistic. Their dedication to physical reality, and their inability to achieve gnosis, dooms them to remain forever in a flawed and evil existence.

As Christianity grew in strength it became less tolerant of Gnosticism. In the Christian view, Gnostics were basically Christians who had wandered so far from the path that their beliefs became heretical. Whether or not Gnostics suffered abuse at the hands of Christians, their numbers shrank and they began to exhibit classic behavior associated with secret societies, including the use of initiations, passwords, secret handshakes and communication via codes and symbols. By the end of the third century AD, Gnosticism ceased to be an influential movement, although segments of its central teachings can be found among the dualist religion Manichaeism as well as medieval religious groups like the Albigenses, Bogomils and Paulicians. Students of the Kabbalah perceive kernels of Gnosticism within that philosophy, and a small non-Christian sect, the Mandaeans, reportedly exist in some corners of Iraq and Iran. Otherwise, for almost 1700 years, Gnosticism became something of a shadowy footnote to the rise and domination of Christianity in the Western world, its near-anonymity broken only by efforts by people such as Jakob Boehme (1575–1624) to revive the movement, and echoes of its philosophy in the writings of William Blake.

Gnosticism received two injections of renewed interest during the twentieth century. The first occurred in 1945 near the Egyptian village of Nag Hammadi when twelve codices containing over fifty writings on Gnosticism were discovered by a peasant digging an irrigation ditch, their origins traced

The Gnostic texts, retrieved in 1945 from their desert hiding place near Nag Hammadi in Egypt.

back to the fourth century AD. Likely prepared by monks at the nearby monastery of St. Pachomius, and hidden to escape destruction by the emerging Orthodox Church, the scriptures provided a wealth of information on Gnostic teachings and values.

Meanwhile, psychologist Carl Jung was evaluating Gnosticism as a source of inspiration for his ground-breaking experiments and writings on the workings of the mind. On that subject, he found traditional Christianity lacking in insight compared with Gnosticism. "In the ancient world," Jung wrote, "the Gnostics, whose arguments were very much influenced by psychic experience, tackled the problem of evil on a broader basis than the Church Fathers."

These events, plus the drug-induced frenzy to explore mystical practices and beliefs that swept North America during the 1960s, restored another wave of interest in Gnosticism. For the most part, however, the Gnostics represent bit players in an ecclesiastical drama extending over 2000 years, their secrecy more a means of protection from attacks from Christians than a means of carrying out acts against society.

FIVE

KABBALAH
ORIGINS OF THE APOCALYPSE

HERE IS THE FABLE:

A man in search of universal truths travels to Israel, where he studies an ancient school of mysticism based on the same Hebrew texts from which the Bible evolved. Absorbing this wisdom of the ages from an elderly Jewish scholar, the man achieves a degree of enlightenment he had not been able to attain through other systems of belief. With each revelation of this ancient knowledge he feels his soul elevated, his powers expanded, his insight honed and his horizons broadened.

Upon the death of his mentor, the man vows to carry his acquired wisdom to a select group of people who are prepared to engage in the sacrifices necessary to absorb the knowledge and benefit from the teachings. He will spread his message to the ends of the earth, providing humanity with secrets hidden for several millennia. He will convey this power as a means of alerting humanity to its destiny. He will become the new source of the ancient wisdom known as the Kabbalah.

Neither a religion nor an organization, Kabbalah is a system of thought drawn from Jewish theosophy, philosophy, science and mysticism. Various interpretations (and spellings) of the word exist, but they all relate to the notion of a secret oral tradition handed down through generations to a select few students by scholars and wise men. The exclusivity of knowledge and closed structure of Kabbalah gave rise to the English word *cabal*, meaning a private intrigue of a sinister nature. Over time, this definition reversed its flow to the point where these traits are now applied to the root word regardless of its original intent. Kabbalah, many believe, functions according to the definition of *cabal*, suggesting a group of Semitic conspirators working in the shadows to achieve devious ends through secretive means.

Kabbalah began as an oral tradition, an interpretation of the word of God as expressed in the first five chapters of the Old Testament: Genesis, Exodus, Leviticus, Numbers and Deuteronomy. In the Torah, also known as The Five Books of Moses, these books represent a general philosophical basis for Kabbalah, including historical descriptions of the origin of Judaism and over 600 specific laws.

Those familiar with the Old Testament chapters will recognize that laws are almost nonexistent in them, with the exception of Deuteronomy. The other books, especially Genesis and Numbers, consist primarily of stories and analogies as a means of presenting ideas that could be translated into laws.

Where laws were concerned, ancient Hebrew theology was divided into three sections. First was general Biblical law, taught to all children of Israel. Next was *Mishna*, the soul of the law, granted to rabbis and teachers. Finally came *the soul of the soul of the law*—the Kabbalah—concealed from all but the most perceptive and worthy Jews.

Beyond this definition, things become confusing to the uninitiated. On the one hand, followers of Kabbalah and Jews generally believe that every word and every letter of every word in the Torah conveys special significance, requiring wisdom and insight to decode its true meaning. On the other hand, stories in the Torah do not follow strict chronological order; the location of one story versus the other may have more to do with the concept of the belief structure than its relationship to tales preceding and following it. With such an enormous range of interpretations, it's not surprising that various factions have seized on their own explanation of messages supposedly hidden within the Torah. One faction even suggests that the entire content of the Torah represents the true name of God, broken into stories in order that mortals, lacking divine discernment, can absorb it.

It's a challenging, confusing and inhibiting task, this attempt at knowing the unknowable, and in one sense Kabbalah represents a technique of by-passing logic to fathom these meanings with a transformation of consciousness. Other disciplines that employ similar techniques to achieve similar results include Hinduism, Buddhism, Taoism, Zen and some forms of yoga. Originally, extensive training was required to elevate the searcher's consciousness to the necessary level, a process involving a sequence of experiences, each more radical and demanding in its methods.

With time Kabbalah became a label encompassing the entire range of Jewish philosophy, designed to probe the mysteries of life and death by discovering the essence of God. As evidence, Kabbalah scholars point to elements of this search in the Bible, including portions of the opening chapter of Ezekiel:

> The heavens opened and I saw visions of God....I looked and lo, a stormy wind came sweeping out of the north—a huge cloud and flashing fire surrounded by a radiance; and in the center of the fire, a gleam of ember. (Ezekiel 1: 1,4)

The mystical study of the Creator may have been important, but in the opinion of many rabbis it was also dangerous. According to a well-known Talmudic story, four rabbis once gathered to immerse themselves in mystical studies, vowing to remain in deep contemplation of the Torah's meaning until they reached an understanding. Over time one went mad, another died a premature death, and a third became a heretic, abandoning the faith of his fathers. Only the fourth entered the discussion in peace and left it in peace. This tale, and stories of others who became mentally unbalanced while engaged in deep contemplation of Kabbalah teachings, served for centuries as a warning that these deep mystical secrets are not to be trifled with.

Whatever the true meaning of the Torah, Kabbalists generally agree that it is best viewed as a practical tool, not an intellectual exercise. Like all tools, it should be applied for the

constructive purpose of enlightening humanity and not practiced in solitude with the selfish goal of enriching the reader
materially or intellectually. Ultimately, Kabbalists share similar
goals with traditional religions, especially with Gnostics. Both
seek answers to vexing questions: *Why did a good and merciful
God introduce evil into the world He created? How could an infinite
God create a finite world? How is it possible for humans to know the
Unknowable?*

Kabbalah deals with the mystery in two ways, one logical
and the other allegorical. The logical explanation states that
every idea contains its own contradiction, and since God is the sum
of all ideas, He contains all contradictions. Good and evil, justice and injustice, mercy and cruelty, limits and infinity, and
other opposites are all united into a greater whole that is God.

The allegorical version suggests God is a mirror that shines
a brilliant light towards the world. Before the light reaches us,
it is directed through a series of several mirrors; each time His
light is reflected towards us, it loses brilliance until, by the time
it reaches earth, much of the radiance has been absorbed and
the pure light is blemished. Among the blemishes are elements
of evil and pain, and humans must either see beyond these
blemishes or move closer to the source of light and its original
holy brilliance.

If followers of Kabbalah merely sought knowledge of questions that have vexed every culture through the ages, why were
they considered secretive and sinister? And how effective is the
movement in dealing with these mysteries today?

To simplify an understanding of Kabbalah and its followers,
the movement can be divided into three eras or phases: ancient,
medieval and modern. Each is distinct from the other to the point
where the differences are more prevalent than the similarities.

Depending on the shade of your religious belief, Kabbalah
reaches back to the desecration of Eden when angels, who
acquired the wisdom of Kabbalah directly from God, brought
its lessons to Adam in an effort to help him and Eve return to
the embrace of the Creator. Subscribers to this tale believe the

same knowledge was passed to Noah, Abraham and finally Moses, who included the first four books of the Bible into Kabbalistic teachings.

In addition to these biblical writings, three other books dominate ancient Kabbalah philosophy: The Book of Creation (*Sepher Yetzirah*); the Book of Splendor (*Sepher ha Zohar*); and *Apocalypse*, the Book of Revelation. Some followers of Kabbalah claim Abraham authored the Book of Creation, although modern scholars date its writing from AD 12. The Book of Splendor originated around AD 160, authored by Rabbi Shimeon bar Yochai who, sentenced to death by the coregent of Roman Emperor Aurelius Antoninus, hid in a cave for twelve years while he wrote the text.

The author of the Apocalypse may or may not have been St. John the Divine, and its role within both Kabbalah and Christian society continues to be controversial. A few scholars label it "pagan writing," born from the scheming mind of someone steeped in Egyptian and Greek mysticism, and composed as a counterattack on the efforts of Christians to convert pagans. According to this theory, Apocalypse was meant to serve as a means of converting Christians back to pagans. In a corollary to this idea, popular in the early part of the twentieth century, the "pagans" may well have been Jews seeking to satirize Christianity for their own amusement and ends. Whatever its origins and intent, the scenes of death, destruction and selective salvation in Apocalypse are difficult for modern readers to comprehend, especially identities linked to its many allegories. To readers more than 1500 years ago, for example, the allegory of the Great Whore that appears in Apocalypse refers to Babylon, and the beast with seven heads that she rode would be understood to represent Rome and its seven hills.

Ignoring these coded interpretations, contemporary readers, especially those in fundamentalist/evangelistic branches of the faith, appear to delight in the visions of Apocalypse, discovering prophecies and foreseeing myths that two millennia of Hebrew scholars appear to have overlooked.

More relevant and intriguing than the question of authorship or even the specific aim of the ancient books is the Sephiroth or Tree of Life, derived from the allegory of God's perfect light blemished during its reflected journey to earth. Out of this concept of an emanation from the Creator came nine more, producing ten linked centers joined by pathways. The result was a device which, with all due respect to sincere followers of Kabbalah, resembles a cosmic board game.

The Sephiroth has been traced back at least as far as the tenth century, with some Hebrew scholars suggesting it originated as early as the third century, first presented in the *Sepher Yetzirah*, or Book of Creation. According to the Sepher Yetzirah, God employed thirty-two secret paths of knowledge when creating the world, consisting of the ten emanations of the Sephiroth (each emanation is called a *sephirot*) plus the twenty-two letters of the Hebrew alphabet. Together, all thirty-two components represent the Tree of Life and are the central image of Kabbalistic meditation. In addition to the path that God used to descend into the material world—and the route mortals must take in their ascension to God—the elements of the Sephiroth actually spell the sacred name of God.

At this point, things become dense and complex.

The base of the Sephiroth (Malkut) represents the world, with all of its flaws and perfections. The pinnacle (Keter) represents God, or the Supreme Crown. The rest are identified in this fashion:

Chokma	Wisdom
Binah	Understanding
Chesed	Mercy
Gevurah	Strength
Tiferet	Beauty
Netzach	Victory
Hod	Splendor
Yesod	Foundation

The ancient Sephiroth or Tree of Life, tracing the path from earth to heaven's perfection.

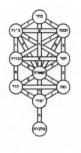

Three triangles are formed by the nine sephirots and connecting pathways above the Malkut. These symbolize the human body; the topmost represents the head, the middle represents the trunk and arms, and the bottom represents legs and the reproductive organs.

Employing the Sephiroth, mankind can ascend to God by moving upwards through one sephirot at a time, gaining the wisdom of each before moving to the next. Each sephirot is divided into four sections, with each section representing one of Four Worlds: the world of Archetypes (Aziluth); the world of Creation (Briah); the world of Form (Yetzirah); and the Material world (Assirah). Each sephirot also holds the sacred unknowable and unspeakable name of God, Yahweh or the Tetragrammaton, a word so hallowed that other words, including Elohim, Adonai and Jehovah, are substituted for it in scriptures employed by the Kabbalah.

Adding a fillip of gamesmanship to the concept of the Sephiroth as a religio-philosophical puzzle or ecclesiastical Ouija board was the principle that angels guard every sephirot. Their role is to prevent climbers from ascending closer to God unless they possess the acquired wisdom, purity of soul, and determination to continue their climb to the next sephirot.

Everyone familiar with Kabbalah knows and understands the Sephiroth, but few completely agree on its purpose or application. Some believe it represents stages of the creative process used by God to create a succession of realms that eventually produced the universe. Others suggest that it signifies fundamental laws of physics such as gravity and magnetism.

To ancient mystics, the Sephiroth provided unlimited opportunities to explore, intellectually and spiritually, the primary mystery of life. Tracing its paths, assessing its components and exchanging views on its meanings generated as much cultural diversion for them as any twenty-first-century electronic entertainment device produces for ourselves, although the Sephiroth's aims are infinitely higher, of course. This explains why Kabbalah and the use of the Sephiroth spread across Europe into Germany and Italy, and how it spawned multiple offshoots and interpretations. These varying meanings were either staunchly defended by its adherents or discussed only in code at secret meetings.

The complexity of the Sephiroth's design, the density of its interpretation, its role as a code-breaking device available exclusively to Kabbalah's devotees, and latent anti-Semitism all bred fear and suspicion among outsiders, many of whom suspected that Kabbalah devotees were members of a secret society bent on overthrowing Christianity.

In the thirteenth century, a Spanish Jew named Moses de Leon injected new layers of mystique into Kabbalah, and new sources of paranoia among outsiders who considered the movement a threat. Depending upon your point of view, de Leon was either a brilliant religious mystic with the good fortune to stumble upon an ancient Kabbalah document, or a medieval P. T. Barnum.

Born in 1250, Moses de Leon could use colorful phrases devoid of any well-defined thought to pontificate on almost any subject, like today's ebullient pitchmen selling kitchen gadgets on late-night television. He wrote several manuscripts dealing with Kabbalistic principles, some of them intentionally provocative, but his *Midrash de R. Shimeon bar Yochai*, better known as the Zohar ("Splendor"), essentially revitalized and redirected Kabbalah.

Written in Aramaic, the language of the Talmud, the Zohar is an extended commentary on the Torah, the first five works of the Bible, seeking to explore the mystical aspects of its familiar stories. The Zohar defines the human soul as comprising three elements: *nefesh*, or lower animal part, linked to instincts and bodily cravings; *ruach*, or middle soul, containing moral virtues; and *neshamah*, the highest measure of the soul. Besides separating man from animals, the neshamah enables humankind to share in an afterlife. De Leon, who claimed he had come into possession of the original document drafted by Rabbi bar Yochai, produced and sold several copies.

From the outset, readers of the Zohar were split about its meaning and authenticity. The most ardent followers of Kabbalah and many eminent scholars of the Talmud accepted de Leon's claim that the Zohar's contents were revelations from God handed down through Rabbi bar Yochai to his devoted disciples more than 1000 years earlier. Others were less certain, and more than a few suspected de Leon of fraud. This latter opinion is supported by the story of a wealthy man who, following de Leon's death in 1305, approached de Leon's widow and offered a large sum of money in exchange for the original ancient document of the Zohar. The widow, left destitute, confessed there was no original: her husband had been the sole author. "When I asked him many times why he put his teachings in the mouths of others," she explained, "he always answered that doctrines placed in the mouth of the miracle-working Shimeon would be a better source of profit."

The wealthy man who sought the original Zohar copy may have been disillusioned by this story but other, more fanatic followers were not. "If de Leon indeed wrote these words," they countered, "then he wrote them aided by the magic power of the Holy Name, and it does not matter into whose mouth he meant to place them—they emanated from the mouth of God, and that is all we need."

The fanatics won out, based in part on de Leon's attractive writing style that convinced many followers only God could have spoken with such eloquence. Soon the Zohar was being quoted with as much veneration as was the Bible, and even Talmudic scholars began to regard it as a sacred book, turning to it as an authority when dealing with various theological questions.

Success begets success, in both publishing and theology. Soon a later addition to the Zohar appeared. Titled the *Raaya Meheimna*, its unknown author added two more parts of the soul

to the Zohar's description: the *chayyah*, which provides mankind
with an awareness of the divine life force; and the *yehidah*, the
highest plane of the soul, where union with God becomes
attainable.

The Zohar, Talmud and Sephiroth may provide both a
source of rich inspiration and a fount of endless speculation for
its followers, but how could such arcane viewpoints propel
Kabbalah into the realm of secret societies and the whirlwinds
of threats and conspiracies they share?

Anti-Semitism played its usual role, aided from time to time
by infallible self-fulfilling speculation. From the thirteenth to
the seventeenth centuries, it was acknowledged in Britain with
some distress that Jews held secret religious ceremonies, where
elements of Kabbalah were discussed. And it was no doubt true.
The British alarmists conveniently forgot, or overlooked the
fact, that Edward I had expelled Jews from England in 1290.
Those who ventured back, along with their descendants, were
forced to hold clandestine services while denying their own
existence, meeting the classic prerequisites of a secret society.

Kabbalah, with all of its complexities and mysticism, provided conspiracy proponents with everything needed to brand
the movement subversive and dangerous. In her well-researched
but outrageously racist *Secret Societies and Subversive Movements*,
author Nesta H. Webster proposed two Kabbalahs. The ancient
version, i.e., before the appearance of the Zohar was the Good
Kabbalah, filled with wisdom handed down over generations by
Jewish patriarchs. The modern Kabbalah, including the Zohar
and its spin-offs, was simply evil. According to Webster, the
Zohar's original wise counsel had been "mingled by the Rabbis
with barbaric superstitions, combined with their own imaginings
and henceforth marked with their seal," qualifying it in
Webster's judgment as "false, condemnable and condemned by
the Holy See, the work of Rabbis who have also falsified and per-
verted the Talmudic tradition."

Whenever the opportunity arose, the antics of one individual or another served to personify Kabbalah and its subversive

nature for people who chose to see it in that light. None was better suited for the task in the mid-1700s than Hayyim Samuel Jacob Falk, a well-known London eccentric. In addition to promoting an association with Kabbalah, Falk claimed to perform miracles, a talent he drew from the wisdom of Kabbalah. Falk could burn a small candle for weeks, fill his cellar with coal by repeating a special incantation, and exchange an expensive dinner plate with a pawnbroker for cash only to have the plate mysteriously appear in his home before he returned. Or so the stories went. When London's Great Synagogue was threatened by fire, Falk reportedly averted disaster by writing four Hebrew letters on the door, causing the fire to by-pass the building even as it consumed other structures.

Falk appears to have reveled in the sense of mystery and occult practices that enveloped him. He also enjoyed living well—asceticism had no place in Falk's lifestyle. A letter written by a contemporary of Falk to a friend described an encounter with the Kabbalah mystic:

> His chamber is lighted up by a silver candlestick on the wall, with a central eight-branched lamp made of pure silver of beaten work. And albeit it contained oil to burn a day and a night, it remained enkindled for three weeks. On one occasion he remained secluded in his room for six weeks without meat or drink. When at the conclusion of this period ten persons were summoned to enter, they found him seated on a sort of throne, his head covered with a golden turban, a golden chain round his neck with a pendent silver star on which sacred names were inscribed. Verily this man

Hayyim Samuel Jacob Falk and the "proof"
of a Kabbalah-Freemason connection.

stands alone in his generation by reason of his knowledge of holy mysteries. I cannot recount to you all the wonders he accomplishes. I am grateful in that I have been found worthy to be received among those who dwell within the shadow of his wisdom.

Falk's wealth and the power of his personality attracted the equally rich and famous to his side, including dukes, princes, diplomats and bankers. When he died, Falk was one of the wealthiest men in London, bequeathing enormous sums of money to charities and synagogues; more than a century later, annual payments from his estate were still being paid to the poor.

All of this might have served as the innocent antics of a colorful character except for his Kabbalah connection and a portrait, widely circulated after his death, in which Falk is posed with a compass and Star of David. With an "Aha!" that must have echoed from London to Lisbon, conspiracy theorists claimed the star was *not* a symbol of Judaism, but two interlocked triangles, emblematic of Freemasons—a proposal made obvious, they insisted, by the presence of a compass.

The claimed linkage with Freemasons was enough to vault the Kabbalah back onto the secret societies horse, which immediately galloped off in all directions. The first stop was the Sephiroth, where the conspiracy buffs beheld a fascinating assortment of concealed messages. *Tiferet* (Beauty) occupies the central position within the Sephiroth. Later interpretations suggested that the *Tiferet* experience required the individual to pass from human form into a "formless" condition, a process Freudians might call "transcending the ego," leading to rebirth or resurrection, and eventually metamorphosing into a symbol of Christ. From there it was a small step to associate this with the Holy Grail, supposedly possessed by Templars and later Masons, inspiring fresh connections to new galaxies of secret conspiracies. These revised interpretations, limited only by the instigator's imagination, produced a herd of unrestricted, uninhibited and often unfathomable organizations that treated the various occult philosophies like a smorgasbord of mystiques waiting to be sampled.

One of these groups was the *Hermetic Order of the Golden Dawn*, which employed Kabbalah philosophy as the foundation of an exotic stew combining the Sephiroth with various Greek and Egyptian deities. For added flavor, Hindu and Buddhist theories were added, the potage served on dishes borrowed from the Freemasons and Rosicrucians.

Riding a wave of interest in the occult, the Golden Dawn attracted members of the British elite whose lives needed an injection of mystery regardless of origin or validity. Perhaps the most admired and celebrated of the Golden Dawn members was the poet William Butler Yeats who, we have seen, also plumbed Druidic thought for inspiration. The most reviled and infamous member was undoubtedly Aleister Crowley.

Born in 1875 in a family that had inherited substantial wealth from his grandfather, Crowley became fixated on sex in the midst of strict high-Victorian values, a contradiction that may explain his bizarre life. At age fourteen, he impregnated one of the family housemaids and was tossed from various schools for similar behavior; one school expelled him when it was discovered he had contracted gonorrhea from a prostitute. Still, he was intelligent (and wealthy) enough to be enrolled at Cambridge University, where he spent much of his time composing sexually explicit poetry. On the day he turned twenty-one, having claim to his portion of the family inheritance, Crowley left Cambridge with little regret on either side, and launched a life of sexual excess, narcotics addiction, extensive travel and mystical curiosity. He even found time to write several books.

Joining Golden Dawn exposed Crowley to the Sephiroth. Inspired by the idea of a mechanical means for

The notorious Aleister Crowley as a youth. Between orgies and opium parties, he discovered Kabbalah.

exploring inner mysteries of the soul, he launched his own organ-ization, the *Astrum Argenium*, or Silver Star, and assumed control of the *Ordo Templi Orientis* (Order of Oriental Templars), or OTO. Both employed aspects of Kabbalah in their teachings. Thanks to his over-the-top sexuality ("I rave and I rape and I rip and I rend" is from one of his more prosaic works) and his extensive writings, absorbed with relish by late-Edwardian readers even while being condemned for their amorality, Crowley became a figure of note throughout Europe. He resided for many years in Italy and Egypt where, between orgies and opium parties, he managed to com-plete several manuscripts. Two of his best-known books, *Diary of a Drug Fiend* and *Magick in Theory and Practice*, make sidelong ref-erences to his study of Kabbalah and the Sephiroth. Another publication, *Liber 777*, consists of a set of tables connecting cere-monial magic and religious tenets from both eastern and western religions with 32 numbers, representing the 10 sepherots and the 22 paths within the Sephiroth. His notoriety and his association with Kabbalah, as contrived as it was, strengthened the convic-tion in some quarters that the Jewish mystical philosophy represented a serious danger to Christian values, and was part of some unarticulated global conspiracy.

Crowley died penniless in 1947. His personal influence may have waned over the years, but he succeeded in establishing Kabbalah in the minds of many people as a secret organization with connections to the Templars and Freemasons, among others.

Remember the fable of the man who ventured to Israel in search of universal truths and ancient wisdom, returning with hidden secrets of the Kabbalah? His name was Feivel Gruberger. He

made his trip to Israel in 1968, not in search of understanding but in search of people to buy insur-ance policies he was peddling, and to avoid paying support to the wife and eight children he left

Brooklyn insurance agent Feivel Gruberger morphed into Philip Berg, modern Kabbalah guru.

behind in Brooklyn. To soften any loneliness he might experience in his new land, Gruberger was accompanied by his former office secretary, a divorcee named Karen.

Whatever opportunities may have arisen to sell insurance in Israel were abandoned when Gruberger encountered Rabbi Yehuda Brandwein, an eminent scholar of Kabbalah. According to widely dispensed lore, Gruberger absorbed all of Rabbi Brandwein's deep knowledge of Kabbalah, exceeding his mentor's insight and understanding of the complex religious philosophy, or so he claimed. Calling Gruberger a quick study is something of an understatement because, when the rabbi died within a year of encountering Gruberger, the former insurance salesman assumed directorship of Brandwein's organization.

Soon after Rabbi Brandwein's passing, Gruberger transformed himself into a direct descendant of Moses named Philip Berg, the world's leading authority on Kabbalah, and converted the rabbi's long-established seminary into The Kabbalah Center, moving its headquarters to Los Angeles, California. Gone was any reference to Feivel Gruberger, the philandering insurance salesman, or his family in Brooklyn. Gone too was the insurance office secretary who had accompanied Gruberger to Israel. The divorced mother of two who previously had demonstrated neither interest nor aptitude in religion and spirituality was now Karen Berg, author of several distinguished books on Kabbalah.

The appearance of a California-based mystical religious assembly, promising everything from spiritual comfort to better sex, attracted converts from the beginning, not an unusual event. Such groups in California are almost as prolific as the state's orange groves, and the shelf life of both products is often similar. But the Kabbalah Center proved different in many ways.

First, its structure and appeal were unique. No other sect could boast 2000 years of acquired wisdom, plus a road map to spiritual knowledge in the form of the Sephiroth. Also, access was as easy as a McDonald's drive-through window. Instead of parsing philosophical dogma written in an ancient style, peppered with vague references and thickened with allegories, neophytes need only follow a visual ten-step process with various pathways to explore at their own pace. For an extra measure of fun, they could attempt to decipher various clues appearing as letters of the Hebrew alphabet, but this was optional and unnecessary, according to Kabbalah Center leaders.

It was a strange adaptation of an ancient faith structure. Medieval scholars once believed the Sephiroth represented a corridor towards enlightenment. Now many Californians eager to sample the Creed of the Month considered it a fashionable diversion, a claim to inner peace and understanding that others had yet to embrace.

Berg and his staff, which included Karen's sons Yehuda and Michael, proved to be brilliant marketers. After serving for two millennia as a mystical solution to the deepest questions of spiritual life, Kabbalah was transformed into a supermarket of pious accoutrements, a Wal-Mart of fashion-of-the-day spiritual trinkets and treatises. By 2005, more than twenty books and CDs, all authored by Karen Berg and her sons, had been cranked out. With titles like *God Wears Lipstick*, and a twenty-two-volume version of the Zohar, the collection represented at best a successful marketing exploitation of gullible dilettantes and at worst a mockery of an ancient tradition. As though to test the credulity of their followers, the Bergs added products ranging from scented candles and Kabbalah baby clothing to blessed mineral water and boxes of seventy-two stones, each invisibly imprinted with a different name for God. It is, of course, a test of faith to believe that anything is on the stones. But perhaps that's the point.

The height (or depth) of its marketing scheme was reached with its most successful and profitable gimmick: a short piece of red string cut, it is claimed, from a strand once wrapped around the tomb of the Hebrew matriarch Rachel. Kabbalah believers are assured when the string is tied around the left wrist in the prescribed manner

we can receive a vital connection to the protective energies surrounding the tomb of Rachel. It also allows us to take Rachel's powerful protective energy with us and draw from it anytime. By seeking the Light of holy persons, such as Rachel, we can use their powerful influence to assist us. According to Kabbalah, Rachel represents the physical world in which we live.

Shipped complete with Operating Manual, the two-foot length of string sells for $26.

Tying the string may be the most difficult action Kabbalah members need perform to achieve wisdom. While it is important for followers to purchase books from the Kabbalah Center, it is not necessary to read their contents. Berg and his instructors assure everyone that simply passing your fingertips over the text, in a process called "speed meditation," enables you to absorb their wisdom. This technique will undoubtedly prove popular among college students cramming for exams.

Devout Jews were appalled and cynics were amused over the concept of a blessed piece of string and other Kabbalah items being priced so outrageously, and being taken so seriously. Their reactions changed to dismay when many show business stars began praising the Kabbalah Centers, paying homage to ex-insurance salesman Berg and wearing the blessed red string on their wrists. Among the most vocal and influential celebrity members were Madonna, Britney Spears, Demi Moore, Paris Hilton, Barbra Streisand, Elizabeth Taylor, Diane Keaton, and David and Victoria Beckham. As a result of the public embrace of Berg and his Kabbalah Centers by these and other notable characters, weavers around the world began dying string red to be sold for $1 per inch.

Mick Jagger, David Beckham, Madonna and Paris Hilton are among the celebrities who turn to Kabbalah for strength and solace.

The Kabbalah red string comes with its own operating manual.

An empire was born. Soon more than two dozen Kabbalah Centers were in operation around the world, in locations from Russia and Poland to Brazil and Canada, each with ballooning membership lists. The appeal was obvious. How else could an ordinary person belong to the same club as Madonna and Sarah Ferguson, the Duchess of York? Or wear a bracelet identical to the one clinging to Liz Taylor's left wrist?

Psychologists were not surprised at the enthusiasm of high-profile celebrities to embrace Berg's materialistic-based pseudo-religion. The appeal, they suggest, is not one of seeking the wisdom of the ages but of finding a way to deal with acquired guilt. Many celebrities are enormously insecure over their success, knowing that thousands of others with equal talent but less luck remain unknown and unheralded. Why do the stars bask in glory and wealth while others struggle through anonymity and near-poverty? They crave an explanation to assuage their guilt, and flock around any system of belief that preaches their success was preordained or stage-managed in some manner. With baffling irony, those who were rejected mimic the actions of their celebrity heroes.

Membership in the Kabbalah Centers, along with sales of Kabbalah-branded items and a 10 percent tithe from its followers, unleashed a flood of money into the pockets of the Bergs. Karen and her sons reside in side-by-side Beverly Hills mansions, while Philip Berg, a.k.a. Feivel Gruberger, occupies an apartment in New York's Waldorf-Astoria Hotel. The Kabbalah Center, of course, is registered as a religious non-profit organization.

Kabbalah's covert nature over thousands of years resulted from racism and religious bigotry rather than from conscious efforts by its members to lurk in the shadows, and the "secret society" identity it acquired is at the heart of its recent commercial success. Its near-indecipherable doctrine may have been a barrier to many who sought its reputed wisdom, but it proved an incentive to the Bergs, who persuaded potential followers that they alone held the key to that particular code. The rest was salesmanship.

But what is the future of a creed that claims a pathway to God, a system of belief forged over twenty centuries by some of the finest spiritual minds of their age, when its name appears in flashing lights on Sunset Strip billboards, its leaders promise absorption of deep wisdom through the fingertips, and its most visible symbol is a length of colored string?

SIX

ROSICRUCIANS
THE PURSUIT OF ESOTERIC WISDOM

ROSICRUCIANS OWE THE ORIGIN OF THEIR SOCIETY TO TWO men, only one of whom actually lived. He was a trickster whose youthful fraud developed into a global organization claiming to do good works yet functioning in curious secrecy.

The order began, or so the legend persists, with a young man born into a noble Germanic family in 1378. Possessed of a spiritual bent, Christian Rosenkreuz entered a monastery, determined to dedicate his life to deep reflection and service to God. When the monastic life failed to satisfy his spiritual needs, Rosenkreuz set off for the Holy Land, visiting Damascus and Jerusalem. At some point in his journeys he encountered Arab mystics, who taught him principles of alchemy and suggested a non-papal form of Christianity a hundred years before Martin Luther.

Returning home, Rosenkreuz and a number of followers launched a secret organization dedicated to exploring the powers of the occult, operating beyond the bounds of the papal church, and providing aid and comfort to the sick and needy. The members would travel widely in performance of their duties, achieving anonymity by dressing in the manner and style of the country whose citizens they were serving. Vowing to maintain the secrecy of their order for one hundred years, they would identify each other via symbols incorporating the rose and the cross, and meet annually at the order's secret headquarters, the *Sancti Spiritus*, Edifice of the Holy Spirit. To ensure the order's continuity, every member was instructed to name his successor, whose identity would become known only upon the death of the brother who nominated him.

The choice of the rose and cross as symbols launched the first of many debates about the movement. Were they a play on the founder's name, or were they chosen with a deeper purpose in mind? The rose symbolized a need for silence and secrecy; carved in the ceilings of rooms where clandestine meetings were held, its presence dictated that all conversation within that space must remain confidential—thus the term *subrosa*, meaning in secrecy or confidence. The cross, drawn with arms of equal length, was used by medieval alchemists to symbolize the material world. In combination, both symbols suggested that the order was engaged in trading secrets of alchemy and other magical activities, and their nomadic claim of helping the sick was actually a means of exchanging information in a furtive manner. A suspicious few connected the symbols with those used by early Gnostics, and later others pointed out that both the rose and cross appeared in the family coat of arms of Martin Luther. Still others saw the rose and cross as an adaptation of the red cross of the banished Templars, suggesting that Rosenkreuz and his followers were resurrecting that movement while introducing elements of the ancient Kabbalah into its teachings.

None of these discussions took place during the remarkably long life Rosenkreuz led, surviving to 106 years of age. Nothing else about Christian Rosenkreuz was notable to his contemporaries. There is no record of his existence, or of the brothers who followed him and shared his Christian mysticism. Until 130 years after his death, no record existed either of the man or the organization he founded. Had the movement he launched proved so successful at concealing its existence and true purpose?

The world first learned of Rosenkreuz and his organization in 1614, when a manuscript titled *Fama Fraternitatis, des Loblichen Ordens des Rosenkreutzes* (The Declaration of the Worthy Order of the

Cover of the *Fama Fraternitatis*.

Rosy Cross) began circulating in Germany. The following year, a second pamphlet appeared, expanding on the contents of the first publication and describing the discovery of Rosenkreuz's tomb in 1604. After 120 years, the manuscript noted, the body of the order's founder remained "whole and unconsumed," surrounded by several books and ornaments interred with him.

Like a Boy's Club annual, a third publication on the same subject appeared the next year, published in Strasbourg and bearing the provocative title *Di Chymische Hochzeti Christiani Rosenkreuz* (The Chemical Wedding of Christian Rosenkreuz). Filled with so many references to the Templars that it was immediately condemned by the Catholic Church, *The Chemical Wedding* is written in Rosenkreuz's voice, describing his attendance at the marriage of a king and queen. Within their magnificent castle, the regal bride and groom celebrate the event with a strange ceremony involving the killing and restoring to life again of selected guests, using mysterious techniques of ancient alchemists.

While the earlier two publications had generated limited curiosity among readers, *The Chemical Wedding* launched a flood of interest. Soon Rosicrucian groups were appearing everywhere in Europe with many illustrious names among their membership lists, including prominent Englishmen Sir Francis Bacon, Robert Boyle and mathematician and mystic John Dee. The common interests of these three men led to their founding of The Royal Society, whose presidents over the years have included Christopher Wren, Samuel Pepys and Isaac Newton. The society exists to this day as Britain's national academy of science.

Bacon's identification with the Rosicrucians has inspired some surprising claims regarding his life and the influence of Rosicrucians on literature. Born in 1561, the precocious Englishman became a brilliant scholar and statesman, was appointed attorney-general under King James 1, and was later selected to be Lord Chancellor. The king even assigned Bacon the responsibility of performing the final edit on the English-language version of the Holy Bible, the same King James translation so widely used today.

Two aspects of Bacon's life have fascinated students of secret societies. Charges of indulging in the bribery of public officials forced him from office. In retrospect, it's widely agreed that the charges were unfounded, and that Bacon was caught in a power struggle between King James I and the Commons. The uncertainty of Bacon's guilt and speculation that he had been a martyr to political intrigue adds an extra veneer of mystery to the plot. In any case, forced to retire in 1621, Bacon spent the remainder of his years paralleling the efforts of his contemporary Galileo by trying to break the hold of Aristotelian logic on scientific study and replace it with deductive reasoning. This was a man, apparently, whose intellect knew no bounds.

The second, more fascinating facet linking him with Rosicrucianism in the minds of many is his supposed association with Shakespeare. A small but obstinate cluster of scholars insists that Shakespeare could not have produced all the works attributed to him without assistance from a colleague more prolific, more skilled and more educated than himself. Stratford-on-Avon, they claim, could not have yielded the store of culture Shakespeare drew upon for his plays and poems. Moreover, they add, Shakespeare's parents were illiterate and their son had demonstrated no aptitude for study. "Where did Shakespeare acquire his knowledge of French, Italian, Spanish and Danish, to say nothing of classical Latin and Greek?" the skeptics demand, noting that his contemporary, Ben Jonson, claimed Shakespeare knew "small Latin and even less Greek." They point to the few examples of his penmanship, all of them signatures, suggesting the man was "unfamiliar with the use of a pen, and it is obvious either that he copied the signature or that his hand was guided while he wrote."

This is not the place for a to-and-fro discussion about the true source of the plays and sonnets that represent the core of English literature, but it demonstrates the degree to which many people search for, and find, evidence of covert incursion into everyday life. It also illustrates the far-fetched convictions of individuals who insist that our lives are manipulated by clandestine groups.

Were the works of Shakespeare composed by the erudite Sir Francis Bacon, prominent Rosicrucian?

Literary scholars have their own explanations for many of the unanswered questions about Shakespeare's life and works, but conspiracy theorists focus on a subversive explanation. Building on the secrecy aspect of Rosicrucian philosophy, they insist not only that Bacon created all the works attributed to Shakespeare but that the greatest body of work produced by a single author in English literature is, in reality, an extended proselytization on behalf of Rosicrucianism.

Shakespeare, they contend, acted as a front for Bacon, a gullible or perhaps collaborative partner in a scheme to imbed Rosicrucian beliefs and principles into English culture. Bacon's immense library, they point out, contained all the sources for quotations and anecdotes that inspired the Bard of Avon's plays, many of which did not exist in English translations during his lifetime. The plays were created and performed not for their entertainment or commercial value, but as vehicles to communicate with other Rosicrucians. Or so the story goes.

Is it possible that the greatest single fount of English literature is merely a series of envelopes containing clandestine messages in murky codes? Consider a handful of the claims:

- Sir Francis Bacon's cipher number—his identity as a Rosicrucian—was 33. In Henry IV, Part One, the word "Francis" appears 33 times on one page.
- Acrostic signatures indicating Bacon's identity show up frequently in the plays. Note how Miranda's speech in act I, scene II of *The Tempest* appears (italics added):
  You have often
    *B*egun to tell me what I am, but stopt,

*A*nd left me to a bootless inquisition,
*Con*cluding, 'Stay: not yet.'

- The word *hog* frequently appears on page 33 of various port-folios of Shakespeare's plays.
- Watermarks on works by Shakespeare illustrate Rosicrucian or Masonic symbols, including the Rose Cross, urns and grapes.
- Mispaginations in many Shakespearian folios, consistent among various printers, represent keys to Baconian ciphers. These usually involve pages ending in 50, 51, 52, 53 and 54. Example: Both editions of the First and Second folios identify page 153 as 151, and pages 249 and 250 respectively as 250 and 251.
- Decorative designs on Shakespearian publications incorporate Rosicrucian symbols.

And many more.

But why, assuming there is any veracity to the suggestion, would Bacon and his colleagues undertake such a complex and obscure chore, using the (supposedly) undereducated and untalented Shakespeare as a beard, and for what nefarious motives? And how could Bacon create all the plays and poems attributed to Shakespeare while simultaneously producing his own vast body of work, including the final edit of the King James Bible? Manly P. Hall, author of a codex to ancient occult traditions and the wisdom of antiquity, suggests an explanation:

> Bacon is not to be regarded solely as a man but rather as the focal point between an invisible institution and a world which was never able to distinguish between the messenger and the message which he promulgated. This secret society, having rediscovered the lost wisdom of the ages and fearing that the knowledge might be lost again, perpetuated it in two ways: (1) by an organization (Freemasonry) to the initiates of which it revealed its wisdom in the form of symbols; (2) by embodying its arcana in the literature of the day by means of cunningly contrived ciphers and enigmas.

Why be so secretive and complex? Hall has a reason:

> Evidence points to the existence of a group of wise and illustri-
> ous Fratres who assumed the responsibility of publishing and
> preserving for future generations the choicest of secret books of
> the ancients, together with certain other documents which they
> themselves had prepared. That future members of their frater-
> nity might not only identify these volumes but also immediately
> note the significant passages, words, chapters, or sections
> therein, they created a symbolic alphabet of hieroglyphic
> designs. By means of a certain key and order, the discerning few
> were thus enabled to find that wisdom by which man is "raised"
> to an illumined life.

Perhaps. But there remains a small problem of the origin of
the Rosicrucian writings, and their author.

In the midst of all the early excitement over the Rosenkreuz
books and the society that everyone wanted to join, establish, or
resurrect when they first appeared, a Lutheran pastor named
Johann Valentin Andreae made a startling confession: *he* had
written *The Chemical Wedding* as well as the two preceding pamphlets. The entire tale of the Rosicrucians was a hoax, Andreae
admitted, a mockery of alchemy and its zealous adherents that
had spun out of control.

Christian Rosenkreuz had never lived, had never traveled to
Palestine for ancient Arabic secrets, had never founded a secret
order, and had obviously never been buried after his death at
106, only to be found 120 years later as whole as the day he had
died. He and his adventures were the product
of Andreae's imagination, nothing more. He
had written the *Fama* as a prank, adding the
second pamphlet and *The Chemical Wedding*
when many people took the *Fama* seriously.

The family crest of Johann Valentin Andreae, with roses
and a cross on the shield.

It bore the ring of truth. Andreae had a reputation as a prankster; in his youth, he had been refused the right to complete his final examination after he was caught nailing a libelous note to the chancellor's door. With no degree, he spent the next few years hiking through Europe, returning to his studies and successfully writing his liturgical examinations at age twenty-eight. After Andreae's admission that he had conceived the character of Rosenkreuz and his organization like a modern-day mystery writer concocting the plot, setting and characters of a whodunit, people began to notice that his family's coat of arms was composed of roses and a cross. Could there be any doubt?

There was, among the most fervent members of the new order. If Andreae could claim that he wrote the Rosicrucian stories as a prank, some wondered, how do we know this so-called confession isn't the real prank? Or perhaps he wrote the books as a means of galvanizing people into doing good works and pursuing esoteric interests. Even if Rosenkreuz's life were entirely fictional, the argument went, it inspired an idea that could benefit the world, and a philosophy that could reward mankind with insight and spiritual value. Perhaps, it was proposed, Andreae declared that the league existed with the expectation that those who believed in its principles would create it. And they had. So what did it matter?

The debate continues. If, as seems likely, the tale of Christian Rosenkreuz and his secretive followers sprang entirely from Andreae's imagination, it was an idea whose time had come. But what inspired him to conceive of this tale in the first place? The answer may have been incinerated in Rome's Campo de Fiori on a February morning in 1600 when, after eight years' imprisonment and torture, the mystic and former Dominican priest Giordano Bruno was burned at the stake on charges of heresy.

Bruno, one of history's most intriguing and mysterious characters, was the ultimate ecclesiastical rebel, a man who insisted on being free to ponder questions of spirituality and

The father of Rosicrucianism may be Giordano Bruno, whose dark statue broods over the Campo di Fiori in Rome.

existence unbound by Church restrictions. Traveling widely in Europe and England, where he was received by the court of Queen Elizabeth 1, Bruno's imagination and perception carried him into territory that was both uncharted by lesser beings and denied by papal authority. Rejecting beliefs in alchemy and supposed powers of the occult, Bruno trusted only his own deductive reasoning and focused insight. He perceived the universe as infinite space harboring other forms of life, and sharpened the concepts of Copernicus in understanding how the earth moved about the sun. He also pioneered the study and evaluation of statistics, proposed social assistance for the needy, and explored notions that in the sixteenth century were unfathomable by scientists and blasphemous to clerics, yet today are easily articulated by schoolchildren.

Bruno's writings became widely circulated after his martyrdom, especially in Protestant countries where the Copernican theory and other concepts were being proposed without fear of punishment from the Inquisition. Andreae, an admirer of Bruno, may well have been inspired by the Dominican's rejection of alchemy as a serious subject for consideration, and his proposal of performing good deeds on behalf of the poor, free of oversight by the church. If *The Chemical Wedding* is seen as a reflection of Bruno's mockery of alchemy, and Rosenkreuz's directive to dispense charity without acknowledgment or Church involvement as an expression of Bruno's philosophy, this could answer the question of Andreae's inspiration.

Inspired by Bruno or not, the concept of Rosicrucianism continued to gain momentum well past Andreae's death in 1654, thanks to a combination of an old mystical attraction and a new mechanical contraption—the printing press.

Christians, Templars, Gnostics, Druids and early Kabbalah advocates had spread their word in the ancient oral tradition, supported by limited distribution of hand-copied manuscripts. Rosicrucianism was the first society of its kind to take advantage of Gutenberg's invention and its ability to produce thousands of copies of its tracts cheaply and quickly. Within a few years after the appearance of *The Chemical Wedding*, copies were being distributed, translated, and reprinted all across Europe with an impact far beyond that of similar philosophies distributed prior to Gutenberg. It had been one thing to hear a tale of magic whispered by a passing stranger; it was quite another to read the same tale, unsullied by new interpretations or ornamentations, on the printed page.

Exclusivity added another boost to the sudden spurt of growth. The ability to read was restricted to the best educated and most privileged class of society, and their embrace of Rosicrucian principles added veracity to a movement rooted in a hoax.

The wave of new adherents to the loosely established philosophy grew so fast and wide that the movement began simultaneously absorbing beliefs of other groups and splintering into competing factions, each division claiming to be the "true" fraternity of the *Fama*. Hermetists, Gnostics, Pythagoreans, Magi, Platonists, Alchemists and Paracelsians, minor coteries all, huddled beneath the Rosicrucian umbrella even as mainstream members began to be absorbed within larger, more tightly constructed groups. With a philosophical interbreeding between Rosicrucianism and Freemasonry around 1750, the splinters became slivers when factions such as St. Germaine, Cagliostro, Schropfer, Wollner and others spun off from the mainstream. Within a century, certain Master Masons in the U.K. and U.S. had created "colleges" of a Masonic Rosicrucian society. Meanwhile, Rosicrucian members not associated with the Masons began referring to their organization as "The Brethren of Light."

The dilution and fragmentation might seem to dim the prospects of the Rosicrucians' survival, but the organization managed to widen its geographical reach if not its membership numbers. Most of the growth through the years from 1850 to 2000 came from supporters in the U.S., inspired by individuals such as George Lippard, who employed their often-bizarre backgrounds to create colorful and charismatic personas as Rosicrucians.

If you believe Rosicrucian claims, "precocious" fails to describe the man. After graduating from Wesleyan College at age fifteen, the Philadelphia-born Lippard determined that any preacher who failed to live under the same conditions as Christ was a charlatan. Not wishing to be associated with charlatans, Lippard became a law student under the tutelage of a future Pennsylvanian attorney-general. Four years of associating with lawyers seems to have persuaded Lippard to categorize that profession with men of the cloth. With that much cynicism in hand, Lippard believed the only pastime that suited him was journalism, and he began writing romances and nonfiction historical features for the prestigious *Saturday Evening Post*.

He still retained the adolescent ideas of an unbending morality, and in 1847 at age twenty-five he became a Rosicrucian as a means of combating the evil he encountered in life, including the American policy of slavery. Later, he launched the Brotherhood of the Union, a secret arm of the movement whose objective was to spread the basic principles of the Rosicrucians to a wider public.

Lippard published over a dozen books in his short life—he died at age thirty-four—and moved in exalted circles, claiming friendship with men such as Horace Greeley and Edgar Allan Poe, whom he might have influenced in the development of the mystery novel. Something of a romantic, Lippard spent much of his time in solitary walks along the banks of the Wissahickon River; he was even married on the river's banks at sunrise. Romantic notions aside, however, Lippard's greatest achievement lay in his embrace of Rosicrucian teachings and his impact on U.S. history.

According to Rosicrucian documents, Lippard met future U.S. president Abraham Lincoln soon after subscribing to

Rosicrucian principles, and claimed he was responsible for arousing Lincoln's interest in abolishing slavery. If this is true—while Lincoln and Lippard appear to have met each other, no one except the Rosicrucians claim Lippard influenced the future president's actions—Andreae's prank had indeed changed the world.

A contemporary of Lippard, Paschal Beverly Randolph, was also acquainted with Lincoln and had an even greater influence on Rosicrucian activities in the U.S. Randolph's life story has all the drama of a nineteenth-century romantic novel awaiting its conversion into a Hollywood drama. Claiming a mixture of Spanish, East Indian, French, Oriental and "Royal Madagascar" blood (he vehemently denied rumors that he was descended from a dalliance between an Afro-American slave and white plantation owner), Randolph spent time in a New York poor-house before being informally adopted by a failed actress and her husband. Like Lippard's disillusionment with religion and lawyers, this experience scarred Randolph, who claimed he witnessed the husband forcing his wife into prostitution as a means of earning household income. "Thus, at less than ten years old," Randolph wrote, "I had become proficient in knowledge of the shady side of human nature.... Up to my fifteenth year, I was cuffed and kicked about the world."

After wandering the globe for several years, during which he became an accomplished journalist, Randolph grew interested in the Rosicrucian movement. He first joined the organization in Germany before returning to the U.S. in 1851

where he, like Lippard, was also introduced to Lincoln. Unlike Lippard, Randolph never claimed to having persuaded Lincoln to take a stand against slavery, but the two men established a

Paschal Beverly Randolph. His close relationship with Abraham Lincoln did not qualify him to ride on the funeral train.

close relationship. In fact, Randolph had been invited to travel with the train carrying the president's body back to Illinois following Lincoln's assassination, but he was ordered off because of his Afro-American appearance.

Soon after, Randolph was awarded the title of Rosicrucian Supreme Grand Master for the Western World at a German conclave. He founded the Fraternitas Rosae Crucis as the true center of Rosicrucianism in America, and dedicated the rest of his life to promoting Rosicrucian ideas of achieving ultimate wisdom via ancient mystical means, and writing books—many books. Rosicrucian historians claim he wrote and published over two dozen books and pamphlets, most of them proselytizing the Rosicrucian association with love, health, mysticism and the occult. Boasting titles such as *Dealing with the Dead* (1861), *Love and Its Hidden History* (1869) and *The Evils of the Tobacco Habit* (1872), Randolph managed to attract a number of readers who normally might pass up the opportunity to absorb thoughts of oriental mysticism and medieval occult practices.

In the end, Randolph's life proved to be almost as tragic as Lincoln's. In 1872, he was arrested and charged with the crime of promoting "free love" and immorality, a charge, court documents revealed, that had been trumped up by former business associates seeking copyright privileges of his books. Although eventually acquitted, Randolph never overcame the humiliation of defending himself, and was found dead of a self-inflicted gunshot wound. Just 49 years old, Randolph had managed to elevate the awareness and power of the Rosicrucian movement throughout the U.S., and the momentum of his work carried it well into the next century.

Randolph may have helped improve the state of the Rosicrucians, to the point where it ranked second in membership numbers to the Freemasons, but he couldn't overcome the splinter effect that plagued the group from the beginning. Each offshoot imposed its own beliefs and restrictions on members. These variations were often the result of cultural differences between nations, and by the early 1900s American

Rosicrucianism had evolved into a branch distinct from other countries.

Each of the various organizations claimed to be the true home of the movement. The most prominent included Randolph's Fraternitas Rosae Crucis; the Societas Rosicruciana in Civitatibus Foederatis (SRICF), a smallish group that originated with British and Scottish Masons and required Masonic membership prior to acceptance; the Societas Rosicruciana in America (SRIA), a sliver from the splinter SRICF that accepted non-Masons as members; The Rosicrucian Fellowship, launched in Oceanside, California, to promote mail order courses in astrology and the occult; the Rosicrucian Anthroposophic League, dedicated to investigating the occult laws of nature and helping mankind "attain self-conscious immortality, which is the crowning feat of evolution"; Lectorium Rosicrucianum, an American cousin of a branch originating in the Netherlands whose objective is to disseminate the teachings of its founder, J. Van Rijckenborgh; the Ausar Auset Society, created to foster Rosicrucian values exclusively to Afro-Americans; and the Ancient and Mystical Rosae Crucis (AMORC).

Of these, AMORC claims the largest, most active membership, the only "true believers" in principles extending back to the organization's roots. Its founder, a man named Harvey Spencer Lewis, spent much of his life moving back and forth both spiritually and geographically. Born in New York City in 1883, Lewis pursued occult interests there and in France and Florida before settling in San Jose, near San Francisco. The AMORC's San Jose headquarters complex includes Rose-Croix University, a planetarium, the Rosicrucian Research Library and, most prominent of all, the Egyptian Museum, which has become a prominent local tourist attraction in its own right.

On the basis of facilities alone, AMORC rightfully calls itself the world's largest Rosicrucian order. Although the organization refuses to divulge the size of its membership, it lists lodges in ninety countries, holds annual conventions, and publishes two magazines, one for the general public (*The Rosicrucian Digest*) and one restricted to members only (*The Rosicrucian Forum*).

AMORC takes great pains to identify itself not as a religious order but as "a non-profit educational charitable organization," helping its members "find a greater appreciation of the mystical principles underlying their individual religions and philosophical beliefs." The order claims its members "are practical men who believe in progress, law and order and self-development.... [They] frown...on all wrong-doing, seek...to elevate man in his own esteem [and] teach...due and loyal respect to woman, the laws, society and the world." This is a club John Wayne might have been proud to join.

The description grows even more righteous. Its spiritually minded members must possess three virtues: a pure life, "virile and strong but unsullied"; a desire "to penetrate the mysteries of nature"; and a willingness "to sacrifice for one's development while helping others along the path."

Amid all this righteousness and splintering, the belief system of Rosicrucianism appears to be overlooked. In fact it is, for a simple reason: it does not exist.

Rosicrucians are quick to identify their ideal personality characteristics and values, but they refuse to document anything as inflexible as a creed or doctrine, claiming they offer not a formula but a search. As AMORC puts it:

> We do not propose a belief system, nor a dogmatic decree, but a personal, practical approach to living that each student must learn and master through their own experiences. Our teachings do not attempt to dictate what you should think—we want you to think for yourself. What we provide are simply the tools to enable you to accomplish this.

One unusual aspect of Rosicrucianism is its emphasis on modesty. Other organizations may delight in attracting attention—consider the Shriners—but Rosicrucians prefer anonymity. According to Reuben Swinburne Clymer, who became a Rosicrucian Grand Master at the tender age of 27 and published several books that amount to a Rosicrucian manifesto:

"A true Rose Cross does not indulge in secret hand signs or shakes, celebrations, vain displays of wealth…or meaningless rituals. Rather, a Rose Cross is a person (male or female) who is silent in his work and discreet in his speech (no bragging, 'I am a Rose Cross'). He also performs good works, is a servant to all, and remembers that 'goodness, not knowledge, is power.'"

And for those who may confuse Rosicrucian values with those of the Masons, Clymer scolded: "Unlike Masons, Rosicrucians have no special rings, nor do they (like some clandestine orders) wear rose crosses or possess any items which stand out in society. True Rosicrucians do not care to be known as such. They prefer to study and work, rather than be paraded before the curious mass." Then Clymer adds an effective analogy: "A gold coin passes very quietly through the world, but your counterfeit makes a great noise wherever it may chance to be; so with pseudo-Rosicrucians."

Without doubt, doing good work for society and concealing it within a cloak of modesty is a commendable quality. It does, however, introduce a serious flaw. If your good works are all done in secrecy, the outside world sees no evidence of your charity. And, given the public's inclination to equate secrecy with evil, the opposite effect may occur: instead of admiration, you create suspicion.

As much as the Rosicrucians may assure everyone that all members represent the highest moral quality, seek the purest spiritual achievements, and act in the most modest manner regarding their good works, they are prone to secrecy in a manner that appears to contradict many of their esteemed qualities.

In a 2005 issue of *Rosicrucian Digest*, a writer named Sven Johansson, identified as Grand Master Grand Lodge of the English Language Jurisdiction for Europe and Africa, identifies the Seven Elements of Mystical Development. (The elements themselves are not all that mystical. According to Johansson, they include Imagination, Concentration, Visualization, Meditation, Contemplation, Psychic Participation, and Cultivating the Experience of God, with "God" defined as "the greatest and most all-inclusive reality there is.")

Johansson's lengthy and meandering article, readers are informed, was drawn "from discourses presented by the Grand Masters and the Imperator at the World Peace Conference." The discourses were originally planned to be published as a book, but "because some of the discourses include information from upper degree monographs," it was decided not to reveal their contents.

Why the secrecy? Are "upper degree monographs" too difficult for the average individual to comprehend? Or do the various Grand Masters gather to discuss aspects of life, in and out of Rosicrucianism, that they prefer remain concealed?

SEVEN

TRIADS
CULTURAL CRIMINALS

MOST SECRET SOCIETIES DERIVED FROM A NEED EITHER TO promulgate or defend their religious beliefs. As a means of avoiding the internecine battles that often occur between different faiths, it became necessary to conceal the group's true principles. But this appears to be primarily a Western phenomenon, rooted perhaps in the splintering of a single religious foundation into multiple interpretations, whose adherents consider any dissension an expression of heresy. The most obvious example has been the Christian Reformation, especially the fragmentation of Protestant sects into a multitude of interpretations. As we saw with the Assassins, Islam has suffered its own splintering into hostile factions resulting in deep suspicion and violent confrontations. Nothing breeds concerns about secrecy (and a need for it among persecuted minorities) like suspicion.

For the most part, Eastern societies have avoided the bitterness generated by conflicting sects, perhaps as a result of the pervasiveness of Buddhism and the generally accepted premise that, among most Eastern cultures, religion is considered primarily a personal matter. If no dominant religious organization threatens to infiltrate one's life, religion fails to become a locus of unease about personal security. Chinese triads reflect this distinction between Eastern and Western cultures where secret societies are concerned. Their roots lie almost entirely in ancient nationalist and cultural differences; only in recent years have they deviated into raw criminal activity.

The assessment of triads by Westerners is done through a racist lens. While violence is not unknown among triads, it occurs less often than it does in comparable organizations such as the Mafia or the Japanese Yakuza. It is also restricted almost exclusively to Chinese communities; Westerners who fall victim to triad activities represent collateral damage and not prime targets. In other respects, triads fulfill many classic secret society characteristics; they are as closed and ritualistic as any, and more active than most.

Westerners also mistakenly interchange the labels "triad" and "tong" or "Asian gangs" generally. Tongs (the word "tong" means "meeting hall") were created in the nineteenth century as social organizations for Chinese immigrants brought to the U.S. and Canada as laborers. The life of these laborers, and their treatment at the hands of Westerners through the nineteenth and early twentieth centuries, is more than a smudge on history. It is a disgrace. In Canada, 17,000 Chinese men were brought to Canada as laborers, building the roughest stretches of the transcontinental railroad. All were paid barely half the wages earned by white laborers, and more than 700 coolies (from *kuli*, meaning *bitter strength*) died in the process. In the U.S., Chinese played the role of cheap labor following the ban on slavery, and many of the old wooden slave ships altered their course between bringing Africans across the Atlantic to bringing Chinese across the Pacific.

Once in North America, they were pressed into service performing work that European-descended men avoided. Much of this was categorized as "women's work," including cooking and laundering, and for generations North American Chinese identified with these two activities almost exclusively. For practical and perhaps racist reasons—most whites feared the idea of the Chinese population expanding and settling among them—only male Chinese were permitted entry into North America, and intermarriage with the white race was as prohibited and dangerous as similar activities were for Afro-American males. In desperation, the Chinese turned to tongs.

Widespread throughout southern China, where families in many villages shared a common ancestry, tongs proved a vital source of assistance and comfort to unmarried male immigrants who felt isolated, both socially and culturally. Providing services and advice that was unavailable or unreliable from other sources, the tongs acted as a source of financial assistance, legal counsel and social services while protecting the Chinese men from exploitation.

The exploiters were originally white bosses, but as the number of Chinese immigrants grew over the years, tongs helped protect individual Chinese citizens from sources familiar in their homeland. These included members of powerful and prestigious families like the Lees, Tams and the Toishanese, Chinese from the area near Canton (now Guangzhou) who owed allegiance to each other through blood or tradition. In place of blood and tradition as a bond, tong members pledged an oath of secrecy and loyalty, adding mystical rituals, private code words, and secret signs as a means of recognizing and communicating with each other.

For a time in the nineteenth century, the tongs proved effective in lending comfort and security to a seriously exploited race. By 1900, however, criminal elements from within Chinese society had taken charge of the larger, more effective tongs, using them as a means of controlling gambling, prostitution, drugs, tax collection and other illegal activities. The tongs grew larger, more powerful and more ruthless in protecting and expanding their territories, launching "tong wars" involving dozens of members clashing in the streets of Chinatowns in New York and San Francisco. Armed with swords and axes, the tong gangs would hack and slash at each other until the streets ran with blood and unfortunate victims lay writhing on the pavement.

In reality, these confrontations were less frequent and violent than portrayed by the sensationalist newspapers of the time. Late Victorian and Edwardian readers shuddered in delight at the racist descriptions of Chinese engaged in riots that were likely no more bloodthirsty than mob battles in mining communities and docklands throughout the U.S. Perhaps the most enduring legacy of the tong battles was the description of a tong member waving a meat cleaver over his head, his weapon and determination leading to the designation of "hatchet man," more common today in corporate boardrooms than they ever were in Chinatown streets.

Tongs continue to operate in North America, their power and influence severely diluted by the arrival of later immigrants and later generations, to whom the original premise and function of the groups is neither heeded nor needed. Triads, however, are another matter.

China has a long tradition of secret societies linked to the culture's veneration of emperors who, like popes of the Catholic Church, once were assumed infallible. Tradition dictated that Chinese emperors possess special qualities including absolute virtue, honesty and benevolence. In many respects, early Chinese emperors were regarded by their subjects in the same manner that Christians regard Christ, as the Son of Heaven on earth.

Unlike the Christian attitude towards Christ, however, the Chinese acknowledged that the Son of Heaven remained a mortal, and if he were to lose the attributes that qualified him as Emperor, he would "forfeit the mandate of Heaven," and the people had a duty to rise up and depose him.

This occurred in AD 9 when Emperor Han Ai was deposed by Wang Mang after Han attempted to name his male lover as his successor. When Wang succeeded in occupying the imperial throne, a group of citizens banded together to restore the Han dynasty. Identifying themselves in battle by applying red makeup to their eyes and calling themselves the Red Eyebrows, they assassinated Wang and installed a new member of the Han family on the throne. Then, in a development that has proved all too familiar, instead of disbanding, the Red Eyebrows turned their battle skills against ordinary citizens, becoming bandits who roamed and terrorized the country.

Flag of the Ch'ing dynasty. Attempts to overthrow its leaders inspired early triad groups.

Five hundred years later, a new group appeared. Calling themselves the White Lotus Society, persecuted and pious Buddhists overthrew the Mongol Yuan dynasty and installed one of their own, a monk named Chu Yuan-Chang, on the imperial throne. Assuming the name Hung Wu, he became the first Ming emperor of China, "Ming" derived from two revered Buddhist figures, Big and Little Ming Wang, who had been sent from heaven to restore peace to the world. Many historians consider the White Lotus Society the first of the true triads, although the actual term was not applied to these groups for another thousand years.

The first appearance of an actual triad society occurred in 1644 when Manchu invaders overthrew the Ming emperor and launched the Ch'ing dynasty. A group of 133 Buddhist monks, united by a blood oath to restore the Ming dynasty, fought a guerrilla war against the Manchu for many years, but their resistance proved futile. In 1674, all but five of the fighters were captured and brutally murdered, and the monastery that served as their headquarters was destroyed.

The term triad is derived from the three-sided symbol used by the Hung Mun. The sides signify Heaven, Earth and Man.

The remaining monks, united in hatred of the invaders, vowed revenge. Forming a secret group dedicated to annihilating the Manchu, they chose a triangle as their emblem, with the three sides representing Heaven, Earth and Man, the essential elements of the Chinese universe. The choice of a triangle carried other implications as well. Chinese culture pays special attention to the significance of numbers, and the numeral 3 is assumed to hold special powers, especially among the criminal element. Extortion rates, for example, are often calculated by three. While the surviving five monks, known today as the Five Ancestors, called their organization the Hung Mun, or Heaven and Earth Society, its more familiar title (in the West) was based on the three-sided symbol. Thus the term *triad*, used almost exclusively by Westerners. Resident Chinese usually refer to the organizations as *hei she hui*, literally translated as "black (or secret, sinister or wicked) society."

While the Hung Mun failed to depose the Ch'ing dynasty, it remained active for many years, joining forces with White Lotus members to harass the emperor's forces and provoke citizen uprisings against injustices. Reflecting Buddhist principles, its members were instructed to respect the rights and concerns of the peasants, a tactic employed with enormous success almost 300 years later by Mao-led communists, and inspiring an aphorism that "the armies protect the emperor, but the secret societies protect the people."

Triads wielded power and influence, although they were unsuccessful at their primary goal of overthrowing the Ch'ing emperors, who continued to alienate the people with repressive measures. The organization's members were seen in a positive light until 1842 and the arrival of British rule in Hong Kong. Although the triads remained focused on political and cultural goals, Britain was uncomfortable with their presence and declared the societies "incompatible with the maintenance of good order," claiming they increased "the facilities for the commission of crime and the escape of offenders." Following the pattern of nineteenth-century imperialist powers in China, British authorities declared not only was it a crime to belong to a triad, it was also a crime to even *pretend* to be a member. The punishment: up to three years in prison. If the triads had no overt criminal intent at this stage, this heavy-handed edict undoubtedly drove them towards it.

In 1848, the Hung Mun allied itself with a new secret society from the Canton area, the Society of God Worshippers. Together, they launched the Taiping Rebellion, laying siege to Canton and launching revolts in Shanghai and other cities. To this point, triad rituals still emphasized positive social qualities; Taiping is translated as "universal peace and social harmony," and as China became oppressed by Britain, the United States and France, the triads represented the country's only organized resistance to foreign exploitation and abuse.

The Boxer Rebellion of 1900 marks the transformation of the triads into groups devoted exclusively to criminal activities. The rebellion, so-named because it was led by the secret Society of Righteous and Harmonious Fists, attempted to drive foreigners from the country through murder and intimidation directed towards enclaves and missions in Peking (now Beijing) and Shanghai. When besieged diplomats and trade representatives in these cities appealed to their home governments for aid, an eight-nation expeditionary force was dispatched.

Over 2000 military personnel from Great Britain, Germany, Russia, France, the United States, Japan, Italy and Austria, all under the command of British Admiral Sir Edward Seymour, arrived in June 1900. Strong opposition from the Boxers and the Imperial Chinese forces caused Seymour to retreat and call for reinforcements, and in August an additional

Boxers, rebels like this one seeking to drive foreign-ers out of China, drove the triads towards full-scale criminal operations.

20,000 men arrived. After seizing con-trol of Tianjin, the foreign armies battled their way to Peking, reaching the capital on August 14.

The size of the forces occupying China grew over the next several months, completing their occupation of Peking and spreading into the countryside in pursuit of the rebellious Boxers. In February 1901, Chinese authorities agreed to abolish the Boxer Society, and later that year they signed a peace protocol with the allied nations, officially ending the Boxer Rebellion. The country had suffered a demoralizing blow to its prestige and power, made even more humiliating when the foreign nations were permitted to consoli-date their interests and continue their exploitive activities. The ripple effects of this event spread through the balance of the twentieth century.

From that point forward, it was clear to the triads that they would have little impact on determining China's national inter-ests. The Boxers, as secretive in their manner as any of the triads, had not only failed to protect the nation, they had been crushed, and foreign enemies of China were now stationed throughout the country, heavily armed and resolved to quash any internal revolt.

At this point, the societies turned inward. If they could not win against foreign abuse, they would win by exploiting their own people, growing in strength and disassociating themselves from any non-Chinese influence or threat, although they retained interest in, and influence on, political issues for some time. Their most significant move was to provide support for Dr. Sun Yat-sen's overthrow of the Manchu Ch'ing dynasty, replacing the emperor with a republican system of government. Sun may have actively recruited the triads to ensure his revolution's success, an obvious move if he had been, as many observers suggest, an enforcer in the triad Green Gang/Three Harmonies Society (San Ho-Hui) during his youth.

There is little doubt that Sun's successor as leader of Sun's Kuomintang party, Chiang Kai-shek, was a triad member. When the Chinese republic began to collapse from in-fighting and the pressures of Mao's communists, Chiang recruited triad support, but nothing could save Chiang's corrupt group. Mao's victory in 1949 drove Chiang and his followers to Formosa (now Taiwan), and triad leaders who chose to remain in mainland China were hunted down and executed. A few escaped to Portuguese-controlled Macau or to Hong Kong where the British government, weakened by the recent war with Japan and more tolerant than a century earlier, continued to declare the triads illegal but failed to enforce the laws with the same draconian fervor.

For the last half of the twentieth century, Hong Kong represented the hub of triad activity, serving as the nerve center for many of their global enterprises. Among the largest and most notorious organizations was 14K, named for the address (number 14 Po Wah Road in Canton) and the initial of its founder, Kuomintang Lieutenant-General Kot Siu-wong, who founded the triad in the 1940s. By the 1980s, membership in 14K was estimated at more than 25,000 in Hong Kong alone, and the 14K group was singled out as a prime participant in heroin trafficking, with branches in the Netherlands, Britain, Canada and the U.S. Royal Canadian Mounted Police investigators claim 14K and other triads maintain a presence in every Chinese community of substance across North America, engaging in almost any criminal activity that promises a profit, from extortion and loan sharking to credit card fraud and video piracy.

The more the triads moved away from cultural and political objectives towards criminal activities, the more they refined their secret rituals, adding new complex ceremonies. The core of the initiation procedure remained rooted in historical aspects of the groups, including elaborate ceremonies that require up to eight hours to complete. Among the rites initiates perform is "the passing of the mountain of swords," in which they walk slowly beneath threatening swords held just above their heads.

New triad members are taught secret handshakes and subtle signals, long a distinctive feature of the society. The way chopsticks are held or set down, and the number of fingers used to grasp a goblet while drinking, communicates important signals among triad members. Certain phrases are used to signify information not to be shared with others. According to the RCMP, who infiltrated and assessed the triads more effectively than any other Western police force, "bite clouds" meant "smoke opium," and "black dog" was code for a gun. (The past tense is used because, after an extended list of code words was published in a 1987 issue of the RCMP *Gazette* and later in several other journals, it is unlikely that the triads retain the same definitions today.)

Initiation into the more potent triads may include the ceremonial decapitation of a live chicken. Blood from the still-writhing bird is poured into a bowl and mixed with the blood of the initiate, followed by a goodly measure of wine, and the concoction is shared by everyone in attendance. After the blood-and-wine mixture has been consumed, the bowl is broken to signify the fate of any members who might break faith with the triad.

The new triad member must pledge that his allegiance to the group will surpass the loyalty he owes to his family and loved ones, a pledge involving thirty-six oaths extending back to the seventeenth-century origins of the triads. The oaths are specific, demanding and inflexible. In the first oath, the initiate vows that he "must treat parents and relatives of sworn brothers" as his own kin, and "I shall suffer death by five thunderbolts if I do not keep this oath." In oath number four, he swears: "I shall always acknowledge my Hung brothers when they identify themselves. If I ignore them, I will be killed by a multitude of swords." With many of the oaths, the new member acknowledges that he must "be loyal or be killed."

Oath number 36, a reflection of the original triad objective, is common to all Hung societies: "After entering the Hung gates, I shall be loyal and faithful, and shall endeavor to overthrow Ch'ing and restore Ming....Our common aim is to avenge our Five Ancestors." This pledge is at least 100 years out of date, yet it continues to be delivered as part of the organization's tradition, adding an element of mysticism to the act, always a desired component for secret societies.

Titles granted to triad members extend the mysticism by connecting it with numerology. All triad members are identified two ways: by a job description that explains, in a tangential manner, their responsibilities within the organization; and by a number.

The leader of the society is the Dragon Head (*Shan Chou* or *Chu Chi*) and is referred to as 489. These three digits add up to 21; the Chinese-language characters for 21 are very similar to the characters representing *Hung*. In addition, 21 is also 3 (the three elements making up the triad symbol—Heaven, Earth and Man) multiplied by 7, a number revered as much in Chinese culture as in Western society. In this manner, 489 manages to sum up the life cycle of the society.

The organization's financial adviser, filling a role similar to the *consigliore* in Cosa Nostra circles, is called the White Paper Fan (*Bak Tse Sin* or *Pak Tse Sin*) and identified as 415. Enforcers, trained in kung fu, are called Red Poles (*Hung Kwan*) with the numeral designation 426. Other operatives include the Straw Sandal (*Cho Hai*), number 426, who handle communications; and the *Fu Shan Chu*, number 438, a deputy of sorts to the Dragon Head. The number 438 is also attached to the Incense Master (*Heung Chu*), in charge of rituals. The lowest rank in the triad, a soldier or *Sey Kow Jai*, is assigned number 49.

While it is tempting to draw comparisons between the triads and the Italian Cosa Nostra, the differences between the two are substantial. The Cosa Nostra may be Italian at its core, but in the past it has strategically partnered with other ethnic groups, particularly Jewish and Irish criminals. Triads, in contrast, remain defiantly Chinese in membership and culture; unlike Italian-based criminals, who make no distinction among the individuals and organizations they may target, triads select only Chinese as their prime source of income. While some collusion between triads and both the Cosa Nostra and Japanese Yakuza has occurred, triads have retained the most independence and secrecy of the three secret criminal elements.

Another key difference between triads and the Mafia concerns structure and discipline. As anyone exposed to *The Godfather* movies or an episode of *The Sopranos* can attest, the Italian organized gangs are as rigidly structured and tightly controlled as any corporation (or were, as we shall see in the next chapter). Mafia members must receive approval from the authority level directly above before engaging in any money-making activity, and agree to forfeit a portion of the profits to the same authority. Neglecting or defying this rule can lead to severe punishment.

Triads are not nearly as rigid, and the concept of passing approval down the line to workers and passing profits back up the line to bosses is totally absent. Here's how one member of Hong Kong's notorious 14K triad described his arrangement to an Australian parliamentary crime investigator during an interrogation procedure:

> I was not required to pay any percentage of profits to the 14K leadership. Triads do not work that way. Triad members do favors for each other, provide introductions and assistance to each other, engage in criminal schemes with each other, but triads generally do not have the kind of strictly disciplined organizational structure that other groups like the Italian Mafia have. For example, a triad member would not necessarily be required to get permission from the dragonhead of his triad to engage in a particular criminal job.... On the other hand, on...traditional Chinese holidays, such as Chinese New Year, triad members traditionally give gifts to their "big brothers" or "uncles" who often are officers in the triads.

An argument can be made that triads practice greater finesse than Mafia members, whose penchant for brutality is legendary. Triad enforcers may be just as direct, but they often couch their threats in subtle warnings before taking murderous actions. One Hong Kong businessman who chose to defy triad threats was sent the severed head of a dog, perhaps by enforcers impressed with the celebrated scene, incorporating the severed head of a horse, from *The Godfather*. Only when he failed to heed this threat was he stabbed to death several days later.

Their restricted association makes the triads doubly difficult for Western law enforcement groups to penetrate. Chinese communities in North America are among the most insular of all ethnic groups, with justifiable suspicion of outsiders probing into their culture. As a result, reaching triad leaders involves penetrating two layers of defense: the general cultural barrier erected by all Chinese against foreigners, and the secrecy veil drawn over the triads themselves.

Another complication for law enforcement officers has been the ability of the triads to compromise local police forces, especially in Hong Kong. For many years prior to the handover of Hong Kong to the mainland government in 1997, the Royal Hong Kong Police lacked any form of criminal intelligence system, and appeared to play down the size and impact of triads in the colony. Only a detailed study in 1983 revealed the true extent of the secret groups. The report also disclosed an enormous level of corruption in the RHKP, including long-term collusion between senior police officials and triad leaders with regard to drug trafficking. Many RHKP officers grew enormously wealthy through their triad connections and, according to RCMP sources, more than a few emigrated from the colony to Britain and Canada in advance of the communist takeover in 1997, bringing their riches with them and settling down as respectable affluent businessmen.

The arrival of mainland rule in July 1997 also sent triad members abroad to avoid the inevitable crackdown, but many observers familiar with the level of corruption under the communist regime expect that the triads have since achieved their old levels of influence. One difference is critical, however. Under British rule, the few triad leaders who were caught and convicted faced prison terms. If the Beijing government applies the same policy in Hong Kong as it applies on the mainland, senior triad members can expect to be punished with a bullet in the back of the head.

The Hong Kong triads may now be Beijing's responsibility, but their influence extends literally around the world, although with varying impact. In Britain, the National Criminal Intelligence Service conducted a study of triad activities in that country under the unimaginative code name Project Chopstick. While the 1996 NCIS report noted that four triad societies were operating in Britain, it concluded that none was controlled from Hong Kong, and thus the groups were not part of an international criminal conspiracy. Victims of the triads, the study reported, were usually small businesses operated by Chinese immigrants who often avoided reporting crime to British authorities. Nor, the study claimed, did triads play a significant role in the country's drug trafficking, contrary to situations in Australia, Canada and the U.S.

In 1988, an Australian government study estimated that 85 to 95 percent of all heroin entering that country was controlled by Chinese triads. Ten years later, however, a U.S. investigation indicated that triad dominance had been reduced by competition from Southeast Asian countries and their organizations, primarily Vietnam, Cambodia, Burma (Myanmar) and the Philippines.

During the 1970s and 1980s, most high-quality heroin entering North America originated in Turkey and was shipped to Marseilles for processing before being routed to the U.S. (the famed French Connection), with distribution controlled by the Mafia. The emigration of triad leaders from Hong Kong in the 1990s enabled the Chinese to assume control of the networks. By-passing Marseilles, which had once handled the bulk of the material, the triads established routes either through

Amsterdam or directly to Toronto, Montreal and Vancouver before importing the drug to its ultimate market, the U.S. Most investigators identify the 14K triad as the primary source of the drug.

In the end, however, the triads' methods may be their undoing. In the North American drug market, their dominance has been challenged by violent new Vietnamese gangs who dismiss tradition and mystique in favor of raw physical intimidation. The Vietnamese have long been considered more ruthless and aggressive than other Asian groups, a tradition that began with their first infiltration of North America during the 1980s. As one former RCMP drug squad officer explained: "The leaders of the early gangs came out of the aftermath of the Vietnam war. These guys were already hardened. They might have been army-trained or street criminals, but when (North Vietnam) took over, first they settled in refugee camps, then they had to fight and survive long enough to get to Canada or the U.S. without a penny to their names. They had already seen death and violence on a grand scale and they figured they were lucky to live through that experience, so they really had little to lose."

In many cities, triads actually withdrew from some criminal activities rather than clash with the more violent Vietnamese, preferring to focus on Chinese businesses and individuals exclusively and leave the rest of the market to the newcomers.

The future of the Chinese triad secret societies remains cloudy. Some speculate that the rising economic power and continuing high levels of corruption in China will produce a corresponding increase in triad activity there, in spite of that country's policy of conducting swift executions of high-level criminals. Others suggest that triads have flourished, to some degree, as a result of China's historical subservience to foreign powers, and with its growing economic clout and international influence, the triads may return to their historical emphasis on cultural concerns.

Whichever way the triads evolve, they will retain the secrecy and structure built over 2000 years since the Red

Eyebrows banded together to overthrow a domineering emperor. Of all the secret societies active in the world, the triads remain engaged in a cultural and linguistic environment that few Westerners can begin to fathom.

EIGHT

THE MAFIA
AND COSA NOSTRA
WISE GUYS AND BUSINESSMEN

NOTHING DISTINGUISHES THE MAFIA FROM OTHER SECRET societies more than *omerta*, its rigid code of silence. And nothing more clearly tracks the decline in the Mafia's discipline and status, in America at least, than the contrasting actions of two high-level members: Louis (Lepke) Buchalter, head of a notorious gang of hired killers, and 400-pound Joseph (Big Joey) Massino, don of New York's once-powerful Bonanno crime family. Buchalter died in 1944, seated stolidly in an electric chair. Sixty years later Massino dealt his own organization a potential death blow in a manner that would have driven the short-fused Buchalter into a state of apoplexy.

Between them, they trace the fall of one of the world's most powerful secret societies from a zenith of authority and dominance down to a band of disorganized thugs, many of whose exploits would be humorous if they were not so deadly.

Omerta, like the Mafia itself, was born not from the machinations of a criminal mastermind but out of the desperate necessity of middle-class Sicilian families seeking control over their own lives. Like triads and Templars, the appalling behavior of the Mafia and its various progeny is actually rooted in good intentions.

The most easily recognized country in any atlas of the Mediterranean region is Italy and its boot-shaped peninsula. The toe of the Italian boot ends barely twenty kilometers from the shores of Sicily, making the island appear as a distended soccer ball being eternally kicked across the sea. The image is apt;

due to its strategic location, Sicily was the object of invasion, colonization and exploitation by powerful outside interests for hundreds of years. Sicily proved vital to Mediterranean trade and colonization, an important port for merchants and military expeditions traveling to and from North Africa, the Middle East, Europe and the Adriatic.

Following the collapse of the Roman Empire, Sicily endured a chain of invasions, each leaving an indelible mark on its people and culture. The spread of Islam brought Arab raiders to its shores in AD 826. The Muslims proved relatively tolerant of the existing society, permitting non-Muslims to practice their own religion, and their influence on Sicilian culture lies at the root of two Mafia qualities maintained to this day.

One was the position of women in society. Until the arrival of the Muslims, Sicilian society functioned much like others living under Judeo-Christian influence, with women playing a relatively important role in family decision making. In comparison, Islamic law subordinated women. After their arrival, decisions within the family and within the culture generally were made by men, an attitude that took deeper root in Sicily than in other Christian nations that experienced Islamic influence, and one that continues down to this day.

The Arabs also brought a sense of internal justice. Lacking a system of enforcement to deal with criminal acts, Islamic forces depended upon personal responsibility to avenge crimes. These two qualities—limited rights for women and an obligation to seek vengeance for personal redress—remained imbedded in Sicilian society long after the departure of the Islamic invaders.

In AD 1000, a wave of invasions brought Normans, who replaced Islamic influence with an imposed feudal system in which vassals owed their allegiance and lives to their landlord. Each lord dispensed justice in his own manner, producing a patchwork system that left native Sicilians angry and confused. Out of control of their own destiny, and subject to the whims of outsiders, the Sicilians turned inward, embracing the assumption that nothing and no one was to be trusted except immediate family. Only family provided hope for security and justice, and a man could commit no more outrageous crime than to break his loyalty to his own family. With this presumption, the seeds of the Mafia were sown onto fertile ground.

For hundreds of years Sicily remained a pawn of foreign powers. In 1265 Pope Clement IV, acting in his own interests, declared Charles of Anjou, brother of French king Louis IX, the new king of Sicily. Arriving with a large, powerful army and intent on totally dominating the Sicilians, Charles followed the pope's dictates faithfully, becoming among the most arrogant and brutal of all medieval monarchs.

With the passage of time, seething hatred towards Charles and his French administrators produced a fable that supposedly explains the origins of the term "Mafia." According to the tale, Sicilian loathing of the French was expressed in a slogan whispered among rebellious Sicilians, who would greet each other with *Morte ala Francia Italia anelia!* (Death to the French is Italy's cry!). To prevent the phrase from being overheard by French soldiers, it was shortened to the acronym *Mafia!* The story is considered apocryphal at best; most dictionaries attribute the word to a Sicilian dialect, meaning "bragging" or "manly," and in Sicily it does not necessarily imply a criminal identity. Whatever its origins, "Mafia" came to symbolize the secretive and distrustful nature commonly associated with Sicilians.

Charles and his army brutalized Sicilians to the point where the island nation's entire population developed into a massive bomb waiting for a detonator, which arrived on Easter Sunday, 1282, in classic "Mafioso" manner. On that day, a young Sicilian woman in Palermo on her way to vespers was accosted and insulted by a group of French soldiers. Without warning, several outraged Sicilian men attacked the soldiers, killing them on the spot. When word of their assault spread, first to neighboring towns and eventually across the island, other Sicilian men joined the revolt, overwhelming and annihilating the French garrison in an explosive uprising that became known as the Sicilian Vespers.

Sicilian leaders knew it was only a matter of time before Charles gathered an army and returned to Sicily with massacre on his mind. In a strategic move, they appealed to Peter III of Aragon, a sworn enemy of Charles and possessor of extensive lands in Spain. Peter was naturally pleased to oblige, proclaiming his sovereignty over Sicily and preventing Charles from wreaking terrible vengeance on the Sicilians as he planned. With Peter's death, however, Sicily's fortunes were now in the hands of Spanish rulers, where they remained for 500 years.

The Spaniards, in contrast with the Muslims who opened Sicilian life to other cultures, exerted tight control by imposing strict censorship on the country. Sicily remained isolated from the rest of the world for the next several hundred years, a period when all the rest of Western Europe was caught up in the artistic and scientific advances of the Renaissance. As a result, the intellectual and cultural eruption that changed the character of European civilization by-passed Sicily entirely. Developments in music, painting, sculpture, philosophy, agriculture, science, architecture and other miracles of the period passed unknown to people living literally within sight of the Italian boot, where many of these advances were taking place.

The Spanish preserved the feudal system imposed by the Normans long after it had crumbled in mainland Europe. The Sicilians suffered more under Spain's rule than under the Normans' because the Spanish were even more discriminatory and brutal in dispensing justice. Some powerful Spanish lords living in Sicily, for example, were exempted from paying any tax at all. To fill the quota, other lords had to impose higher demands on their own vassals and peasants, increasing the inequality of Sicilian life.

Sicilians who dared object to Spanish dictums risked execution by either their lord or representatives of the Spanish government. The other long arm of Spanish reckoning, the dreaded Inquisition, added hideous torture to the hazard of speaking out or defying authority in any manner.

Other cultures were subjugated in a like manner through history. Only in Sicily, however, were injustices imposed so heavily on a people who had learned to turn inward as a means of defense and self-preservation. Only in Sicily was the population removed for so long from the positive influences of the Renaissance and the increasingly enlightened views of the Catholic Church. And only in Sicily did anything like the Mafia rise in direct response to this long litany of violence and humiliation.

Around 1500, one aspect of contemporary European life arrived in Sicily when the island's tradesmen began forming guilds. In other countries, the guilds functioned as a means for the tradesmen to train personnel and establish standards, just as the Freemasons began in England. Sicilian trade guilds added a unique aspect to their operations when they assumed a judicial role as well, dispensing punishment to their members without any involvement from local officials who, of course, could not be trusted.

The rise of the guilds coincided with the rise of bandit gangs. Reminiscent of the legendary (and highly fictional) bandits led by Robin Hood in England 500 years earlier, the gangs targeted Spanish lords and nobles, robbing and murdering them, and represented the only means available for most Sicilians to strike back at their oppressors. They also distributed food to starving families in the villages beyond Palermo. To ensure their fair share, families would choose someone to represent them and distribute the food among brothers, sisters and cousins. These men, many of them members of bandit gangs, were called *capodecina*, shortened to *capos*.

Like Sherwood Forest outlaws, the Sicilian bandits created their own folk heroes, lauding their bravery and exploits as examples of gallantry. The most celebrated of them, a man named Saponara, was captured and imprisoned in 1578. According to Sicilian lore, Saponara was tortured by his Spanish captors in an effort to learn the names of his cohorts but Saponara chose to die in agony rather than betray others. His bravery became a symbol for every Sicilian who believed their salvation could be achieved only through loyalty.

Driven by the actions of the bandit gangs that grew steadily in strength and daring, many Spanish landowners abandoned the countryside to relocate in Palermo, Sicily's largest city. By the early 1600s, most of the largest estates were being administered by *gabelloti*, managers chosen by the Spanish landowners for the prominence and respect they commanded among local citizens. The most important function of the *gabelloti* was tax collection, carried out by *uomo di fiducia*, men appointed to visit personally every citizen and pocket the tax payable. The collectors were often accompanied by *campieri*, armed and mounted men assigned to maintain peace and command respect.

To anyone familiar with the modern Mafia, the *gabelloti*, *uomo di fiducia* and *campieri* portray an early Mafia organizational chart. Even the management technique is recognizable. From a distant and luxurious setting, the order to collect stipends from the common people would go out to a series of bosses (*capos*). On instructions from the capos, low-level workers would pay personal visits to the targeted sources of money, accompanied by armed men to enforce the command. Neither Al Capone nor Tony Soprano could have drawn up a more appropriate model for the system that enriched them.

The withdrawal from the countryside of the Spanish lords, and their replacement by appointed bosses, served as inspiration for Sicilians to begin to assume control of their own destinies. Coinciding with the belated rise of the middle class, who sought affluence through the new (to Sicily) role of playing middleman, the mould to achieve wealth and power had been created, and it remained in place after the Spanish withdrew in the mid-nineteenth century.

The Spanish departure created a vacuum of authority. For a thousand years, Sicily had no effective governing body, and with the withdrawal of the Spanish only one organization existed to fill that role: the Mafia. The Italian nation-builder and liberator Garibaldi arrived in 1860 to bring Sicily into the

Italian kingdom, but those hundreds of years of secrecy and independence could not be undone overnight. In fact, as history has proven, they were not undone at all. The Mafia continued to exert its power and influence over government institutions imposed on Sicily by Rome, and within a few years virtually every Sicilian political office and court was infiltrated and controlled by Mafia elements.

Centuries of dominance by outside powers had carved a scar across the face of Sicily that prevented most of the island's citizens from trusting any imposed authority, no matter how legitimate its power or how even-handed its approach. The law, as enforced by government, could not be trusted to deliver justice. To most Sicilians only a vendetta was effective, because all crimes were personal and all vengeance was to be meted out by the oppressed victim and his family, as dictated by *omerta*.

The code of *omerta* decreed that any man who appealed for law enforcers to right a wrong was either a fool or a coward, and any wounded or offended man who would name his assailant was beneath contempt. The classic response of a wounded man to his assailant, spoken aloud or silently, was "If I live, I will kill you. If I die, you are forgiven."

The Mafia's strength originated with, and continues to be drawn from, its organizational structure. Primitive in terms of other, more beneficent institutions such as governments and the Catholic Church, the Mafia nevertheless managed to develop a configuration that exerted discipline and control over its members. Over time, it crafted the group into an effective power in the same manner that disorganized guerrillas are transformed into an effective fighting force by adapting the techniques of a regimented and motivated army.

Ranked from the top down, the organization of the Sicilian Mafia included the following:

Capo Crimini/Capo de tutti capi (Super Boss/Boss of bosses)
Capo Bastone (Underboss, or second-in-command)
Contabile (Financial adviser)

Caporegime or Capodecima (Head of a crew consisting of ten
sgarristas)
Sgarrista (Foot-soldier carrying out daily business of the family;
in the U.S., referred to as a "made" member)
Piciotto (Low-ranking soldiers; enforcers, "button men")
Giovane D'Honore (Non-Sicilian or non-Italian associate)

Italians correctly maintain that the Mafia's existence has created offensive stereotypes. Not every Italian is a Mafia
member, of course, just as not every Chinese is a triad member
or every Muslim a supporter of Al Qaeda. But even the most
vociferous Italian patriot must agree that the Mafia is not
unique among Italian secret societies bent on crime and violence. While criminal gangs exist in virtually every large urban
center the world over, the Italian breed remains distinctive in
its fixed structure and reliance on violence as a means of
achieving its goals.

Nor does the Mafia represent the only Italian secret criminal society. In reality, at least three other extensive
organizations with Italian roots remain active, their existence
inspired, if not nurtured, by the Mafia.

Of these, the 'Ndrangheta is most closely associated with
the Mafia, both geographically and historically. Operating in
the rugged rural regions of Calabria, the southernmost part of
the Italian "boot," the 'Ndrangheta resulted from the Italian
government's ill-fated efforts to break up the Mafia by banish-
ing its most violent and powerful leaders and their families from
Sicily in the 1860s.

It was a foolish move. The families simply relocated on the
mainland directly across the Straits of Messina where, in remote
Calabrian villages, they formed a secret society that differed
from the Mafia in two distinct ways: it became even more secretive, and arguably more violent. A high-ranking Italian
government official recently described 'Ndrangheta as "the
most powerful and dangerous criminal organization in Italy
because of its viciousness."

The organization derives its name from the Greek word *andragathes*, meaning a noble and courageous man worthy of respect. Reflecting its origins—those violent families banished from their ancestral Sicilian homes—the 'Ndrangheta is organized exclusively along family lines, which produces a profound difference between it and the Sicilian Mafia. The Sicilians are bound by oaths, the 'Ndrangheta by blood. In addition, the 'Ndrangheta reportedly uses women in active roles from time to time, although its structure remains clearly male-dominated.

Unlike the classic pyramid structure of the Mafia, the 'Ndrangheta is organized on a horizontal basis and divided into clearly defined family segments or *'ndrinas*. No overlap occurs between the activities or geographic region of two neighboring families; each has full control within its own territory and a monopoly on all activity there. The combination of tight structure and family blood provides the 'Ndrangheta with an enormous ability to maintain both secrecy and loyalty, consolidated through carefully arranged marriages between 'ndrinas. Nothing in Sicilian and Calabrian culture is more sacrosanct than family, and where linkages exist through marriage it would be an act of serious dishonor for one family to perform any act that would threaten the security of a related family. As one Sicilian parish priest explained: "There is strength in the sacred and impregnable structure of the family, the only secure place. *Only blood does not betray.*" (italics added).

Compared with 'Ndrangheta, the Mafia appears almost lax and sloppy in its internal discipline. Sons of Mafia members may choose to follow their fathers into the organization or not; sons of the *'ndranghettisti* have no choice. To become a member of the criminal family is their *diritto di sangue* (right of blood), assigned at birth. While being groomed for their life's work, a process that begins shortly after puberty, male children are *giovani d'onore*, or "boys of honor." At maturity, they become *picciotti d'onore*, soldiers expected to carry out orders from their superiors without question and without fail. The best of these are chosen as *cammorista*, in charge of groups of *picciottis*. When they have risen to the next level as a *santista*, they can finally claim a fixed share of the spoils instead of the small stipend paid to the lower ranks.

Through exceptional work, and after solemnly swearing his dedication on a Bible, a *santista* may be promoted to the level of *vengelista*, perhaps later to join the *quintino*, five privileged sub-bosses with direct linkage to the *capobastone*, the highest power within the 'Ndrangheta family. Members of the *quintino* are permitted to identify themselves with a tattoo of a five-pointed star.

Tight secrecy, together with a reputation for extreme violence, has been the 'Ndrangheta's strength in maintaining its power and expanding its influence. Unlike the Mafia, no one can confidently estimate the size and global extent of its criminal activities, although in 2004 the Italian government suggested the 'Ndrangheta consisted of 155 family clans and a total membership of over 6000.

Either as a result of honest ignorance, the organization's extreme secrecy, or an effort to downplay the 'Ndrangheta's power, some observers suggest the group is harmless to non-Italians, and Italians themselves are quick to endorse this perception. Promoting the region as a holiday destination, the Calabrian tourism office admits "you will find no Florences or Venices in Calabria." Instead, in an act of remarkable candor, the tourism office notes, "Calabrian roads can be brutal, and occasionally they are obstructed by police roadblocks." The office, which organizes tours of Calabria, promises: "We have avoided planning itineraries in certain inland areas which are virtual strongholds of the 'Ndrangheta, the local Mafia, whose main source of revenue is kidnapping the children of wealthy northern industrialists and hiding them in inaccessible caves in the Aspromonte until astronomical ransoms are paid for their release. It should be said that tourists are never the object of this type of crime and indeed, if you travel to Calabria, you will probably never encounter any of these dangers."

Reassuring. Of course, you may also enter a Calabrian village and encounter a sight similar to that witnessed by the citizens of Taurianova, a town not far from Reggio di Calabria, where local 'ndrina first beheaded a councilor who opposed their control of the region, then used his severed head for target practice in the town square. This was not a medieval era act, nor even an event that took place 100 years ago. It occurred in 1995.

In the 1860s, a traveler to Naples arriving by sea noticed that, moments after he handed his boatman the fare, a man appeared at the boatman's side, muttered a word, and received a portion of the traveler's payment before vanishing into the shadows. The same traveler, stepping from the carriage that brought him to his hotel that day, observed a similar incident—a man appeared at the driver's side and inspected the fare before claiming a portion of it. Reaching the door to his hotel room, the traveler paused to watch the porter, whom he had just tipped for carrying his luggage to his room, stop to hand part of the gratuity to another man, as furtive and silent as the first two. That evening, the tourist attended the opera to find men of a similar dress and demeanor, carefully counting the money that changed hands from patrons to ticket seller. When the tourist described these events to an Italian acquaintance the next day, anticipating an explanation, the friend closed his eyes, shook his head slightly, and said simply, "*Camorra*."

Camorra—the word's origins may lie in the Spanish term for dispute, although today it's more simply translated as "gang"—sprang up as a Neapolitan strain of the same breed of secret society as the Mafia and 'Ndrangheta. Unlike these two criminal branches, Camorra was spawned not within blood-related families but from prison gangs who, released from custody, carried their talent for organization and intimidation to the streets.

Camorra established itself in and around Naples as a paternal organization, dedicated to providing assurance to the citizens and businesses of Naples that they would not be harassed by anyone except, of course, Camorra members in the event that its payments were not received. Mafia families in the

U.S. adapted this ploy during the 1920s, where it became known as "the protection racket." Members were also ready to settle disputes and offer assistance to poorer families or victims of accidents and disease.

The organization proved as vicious in handling its own members as in intimidating the public, whose income it siphoned. Admission into the order required that newcomers commit a major crime to prove their courage and dedication. The very act of being asked to qualify for Camorra membership represented a crisis, because any man who refused the opportunity to join the group by committing the crime risked signing his own death warrant if his killing became the task assigned to a more courageous and less scrupulous candidate.

Whether they considered it futile to battle the Camorristi or to fulfill its own Machiavellian strategies, Neapolitan government officials not only tolerated the group but reportedly employed it for the government's own ends. For years, Neapolitan jails and prisons were administered and disciplined by the Camorra, and the organization reportedly worked with local police to track down and punish criminal acts carried out by anyone who was not Camorristi.

The group's structure reflects the Mafia's for the most part, with a *capo di Camorra* collecting and distributing payments to several smaller groups made up of second-tier leaders and their soldiers. Unlike the Mafia, however, it appears to shun mystical initiations and procedures.

Like other secret organizations engaged in criminal activities, the fortunes of Camorra ebb and flow. From time to time, crusading politicians claim it has been laid to rest, or so weakened that it is no longer a serious factor. Recent assessments suggest the Camorra consist of over 100 different clans with about 7000 members.

Through much of the twentieth century, the Camorra's principal source of income was cigarette smuggling throughout Italy and neighboring countries, performed with such efficiency that Camorra combined forces with the Mafia to handle that organization's European drug distribution, an immensely profitable move. This led to a series of territorial battles within the Camorra resulting in an estimated 400 violent deaths and driving as many as 200 Camorra members to the U.S., where they quickly set up gangs to deal in money laundering, extortion, robbery, blackmail, kidnapping and counterfeiting. Despite that flurry of expansion, Camorra remains primarily a Naples-based operation, lacking the mystique and historical fascination of the Mafia.

Yet another Mafia-oriented group germinated in southern Italy, this one in Puglia (often called Apulia in English), the peninsula that forms the heel of the "boot." Sacra Corona Unita, or United Sacred Crown, began like the Camorra with prison gangs who gathered in remote regions where they could be free from surveillance by central authorities. Headquartered in the port city of Brindisi, the Sacra Corona earned much of its income by smuggling travelers to and from Croatia, Albania, and other countries across the Adriatic. It has never achieved the scale of operations of the Mafia or Camorra, either in Italy or in the U.S.

Had the Mafia remained in Italy, it would hardly have registered on any books other than those dealing exclusively with criminal organizations. Its arrival in the U.S. on the cusp of the twentieth century, and its metamorphosis into a purely American strain of secret society, vaulted it into the public consciousness and secured it a place in popular culture. Everyone in the U.S. knows "Mafia"; few, however, fully understand its structure, operations and influence.

For example, the term "Mafia" is not entirely correct when referring to the U.S. counterparts, whose members refer to their organization as Cosa Nostra, "this thing of ours."[10] And while *omerta* and other tools to ensure secrecy remain in place,

---

[10] Journalists often write La Cosa Nostra, which is grammatically incorrect.

the American branch has attempted to structure itself as a reflection of U.S. business principles rather than an extension of mystical medieval vows. In the Americas at least, the perceived values of Wall Street carry more authority than thousand-year-old rituals of Sicily.

The first recorded incident of Mafia-based crime occurred in New Orleans in 1891, when a Sicilian crime family murdered the local chief of police, who had been pressuring them with arrests and harassment. The family leaders were tried for murder, but thanks to some witnesses being bribed and others being threatened with death, they were all acquitted. Before they could be released, however, an angry lynch mob shouting anti-Italian slogans stormed the jailhouse, dragged the culprits into the street, and shot or hanged sixteen of them. A lesson may have been learned; while New Orleans has one of the highest crime rates of any city its size in the country, the influence of Cosa Nostra there has never reached the level of other communities, notwithstanding Oliver Stone's claims in his movie *JFK*.

While Cosa Nostra's roots were well established by the end of World War 1, two events—one in Italy and the other in the U.S.—propelled the organization into a major force.

The introduction of Prohibition in 1919 created a low-cost, high-demand and high-profit opportunity for criminals, especially those operating within an organization that could manufacture, import and distribute its products under the noses (or with the collaboration) of law enforcement. No other criminal activity promised such enormous profits.

Meanwhile, the dictator Benito Mussolini was rising to power in Italy with the promise of eradicating crime and ensuring that the trains ran on time, among other pledges. He succeeded at both. His fascist administration was the only one brutal enough to threaten Mafia control, and soon many Mafia families were emigrating across the Atlantic, where they joined families reaping massive amounts of money from illegal alcohol.

Northern cities like New York, Chicago, Cleveland and Detroit are most closely identified with Cosa Nostra activities but more than two dozen communities, as bucolic in nature as Des Moines, Iowa, and San Jose, California, also became operational centers. The repeal of Prohibition in 1933 left an intact organization that turned its attention to other illegal means of making a profit. Again, timing was fortuitous for the criminals and disastrous for the public. Two years before Prohibition, the state of Nevada legalized gambling, and on the brink of World War II, America developed a taste for narcotics. Both events were quickly and efficiently exploited by Cosa Nostra families. By the 1950s, Cosa Nostra was a dominant factor in almost every criminal activity in the U.S., and the major milker of the Las Vegas cash cow, reaping tens of millions of dollars annually from gambling, prostitution, narcotics and the age-old protection racket.

Reflecting strategies perfected by 'Ndrangheta, Cosa Nostra maintained the family structure, although it waived the Calabrian organization's requirement for a blood connection. In fact, it easily overlooked any prerequisite for Italian heritage among its partners, welcoming Jewish and Irish criminals on an associate basis.

While every U.S. city center was placed under the aegis of one or more families, the five families in New York and adjacent New Jersey became the most celebrated due to their power and to the media that covered their activities. The five included these:

BONANNO: Founded by Joseph (Joe Bananas) Bonanno, the family once was a presence in the garment trade but became deeply infiltrated by the FBI, as told in the movie *Donnie Brasco*. As we'll see, its most recent boss, Joe Massino, has caused the family even more grief than Brasco did.

COLOMBO: The original boss was Joe Profaci, who ran the family from 1930 until his death in 1963 when Joe Colombo assumed leadership. Colombo was an effective boss right up to the day in 1971 when he was shot at an Italo-American rally. He survived, although he remained in a coma for seven years before expiring. An extended war developed within the family, with Carmine Persico emerging as the victor until he was sentenced to 139 years in prison for murder and racketeering.

His son, Alphonse (Allie Boy) Persico, is one of the few Cosa Nostra family bosses to secure a college education, where he appears to have majored in wardrobe selection. Allie Boy likes to dress well, even when tooling around the waters of the Florida Keys in his fifty-foot speedboat christened *Lookin' Good*. One day the U.S. Coast Guard, taking a good look at Persico and his boat, found a hand gun and a shotgun on board. They ordered the guns to be unloaded, inspected the boat, found everything in order, and went on their way.

Allie Boy had lucked out because no one on the coast guard boat checked his criminal record. Only when the coast guard crew returned to port did they learn that Persico had served time for federal racketeering and, banned from owning any firearms, was subject to a ten-year prison term upon conviction. Most college graduates would have tossed the guns overboard as soon as the coast guard was out of sight, but Persico apparently skipped his college classes on logic because, a few hours later when the coast guard cutter pulled alongside the *Lookin' Good* at dock in Key West, the weapons were still on board and Persico was lookin' at a decade in the slammer. Lapses in judgment like that one have made Allie Boy such an ineffective boss that other New York families no longer acknowledge the Colombo group.

GAMBINO: This was the infamous John Gotti's family, dating back to the 1920s and named for Carlo Gambino, who ran the family from 1956 to 1976. Gambino, considered one of the most effective family heads ("dons") in Cosa Nostra, kept a low profile, avoided publicity, stayed in touch with family members, and built the family into a financial powerhouse through narcotics and gambling. In the 1970s he added car theft to the operations, sending stolen luxury automobiles to the Middle East via Kuwait. Gambino's successor, his cousin Paul

Paul (Big Paulie) Castellano at the height of his powers and notoriety.

(Big Paulie) Castellano, alienated various capos including John Gotti and his underboss Salvatore (Sammy the Bull) Gravano, who orchestrated Castellano's murder in 1985. Gotti died in prison, where he was serving a life sentence, in 2001, and Gravano, responsible for a reported twenty murders, entered the witness protection program. Through a series of successions, Gotti's son John Jr. now heads the family.

GENOVESE: Another New York family dating back to the 1920s, the Genovese gang was originally associated with Charles (Lucky) Luciano and Frank Costello. More than 50 years before John Gotti smirked and strutted across the newspaper pages and TV news like an escapee from a Saks Fifth Avenue window display, Frank Costello set the mark for class, or as much class as a Cosa Nostra boss can display.

Costello, possessed of political smarts and a talent for strategic planning, acquired the title "Prime Minister" among gang leaders, a man who preferred smooth talk and bribes over revolvers and shotguns, although he often resorted to the latter when necessary. For several years mayors, governors, judges and police officers throughout the northeast United States smiled at the sight or even the mention of Frank Costello because both tended to be accompanied by an envelope of cash. Costello was the original dapper don, sporting thousand-dollar tailored suits, custom-made shoes, perfect manicures and a bullet-proof haircut.

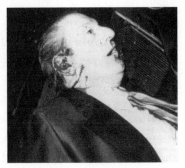

Big Paulie Castellano in a New York gutter, murdered on the orders of John Gotti.

Frank Costello chose good grooming over beating the rap.

Appearances were everything to Frank. Facing charges of tax evasion, Costello was advised by his lawyer not to appear in court dressed so elegantly because it appeared to be alienating the working-class jury. "Start wearing cheap suits, old shoes, a lousy tie," the lawyer said. "You'll do better with the jury."

Frank disagreed. "I'd rather lose the goddamn case," he replied.

And he did. While serving his time, Costello tried managing the family from behind bars but Vito Genovese, the family's ruthless namesake, had other ideas. Genovese wanted to replace Costello at the top and he followed the most widely employed method of succession. While walking down a New York street soon after being released from prison, Costello heard someone shout, "This is for you, Frank!" At the sound of his name, Costello turned his head, and the bullet from the talkative hitman's gun merely grazed his scalp.

Frank could take a hint. Recovering in hospital, Costello spread the word that he was retiring from the family business and he handed leadership over to Albert Anastasia who, lacking both Luciano's and Costello's good fortune, was gunned down in October 1957 while lying back in a barber's chair awaiting a shave. Genovese assumed leadership and gave his name to the family, but he had little time to enjoy the notoriety; within a few years he received a fifteen-year sentence for racketeering and died of cancer in a federal penitentiary. The current boss is Dominick (Quiet Dom) Cirillo, a man out of the Gambino mould who has made this family the most powerful and cohesive group in New York.

As for Frank Costello, he spent the last few years of his life socializing among New York's elite, hosting parties in his Manhattan apartment and his Long Island estate. His guest list included some of the most famous society and political figures of their time, including FBI boss J. Edgar Hoover, whose closet homosexuality and preference for cross-dressing Costello exploited for his own gain. When the Cosa Nostra "Prime Minister" died in his sleep in 1973, his most prominent legacy perhaps was the raspy voice borrowed directly from Costello's manner of speaking, adapted by Marlon Brando as Vito Corleone in *The Godfather*.

LUCHESE: Gaetano (Thomas) Luchese was active in New York's garment industry during his tenure from 1953 to 1967. Among his capos was a man named Paul Vario, the model for the character Paul Cicero in the movie *Goodfellas*. The family has been weakened in recent years with the turning of three key members—Alfonse (Little Al) D'Arco, underboss Anthony (Gas Pipe) Casso and Peter (Fat Pete) Chiodo—into government witnesses.

As Cosa Nostra's public profile grew in the minds of the public, an aura of glamour rose around the gangsters, fueled by celebrity associations. Frank Sinatra was often seen in the company of Cosa Nostra bosses throughout his career as were many of his cronies, including Dean Martin, Al Martino, George Raft and, supposedly, Bing Crosby and Jimmy Durante. Sinatra's heritage—his paternal grandparents were Sicilian—lent at least a blood linkage. The singer vehemently denied any association with crime families, but a famous photograph showing Sinatra arm-in-arm with crime bosses Carlo Gambino and Paul Castellano, and hit-man Jimmy Fratianno, suggests they were

Despite his objections, Frank Sinatra was linked with Mafia bosses such as his buddies Paul Castellano (*far left*) and Carlo Gambino (*third from right*).

all close buddies. Whether the singer was attracted to the gangsters or the gangsters to the Sicilian-rooted singer remains debatable.

Much of the glamour and intrigue that outsiders associate with Cosa Nostra flowed from *omerta*, the code of honor sealed in a secret induction ceremony that pressed the sanctity of the code upon new members. The secrecy was broken, along with other mystiques of the group, in 1990 when the FBI recorded an induction ritual admitting Robert (Bobby Dee) Deluca into Boston's Patriarca family. Gathered in a small Bedford, Massachusetts, house, the head of the family began by stating loudly, in a Sicilian dialect, "*In onore della Famiglia, la Famiglia e abbraccio*" (In honor of the Family, the Family is open).

FBI lurkers heard Deluca instructed to repeat an oath spoken by the boss: "I, Robert Deluca, want to enter this organization to protect my family and to protect my friends. I swear not to divulge this secret and to obey, with love and *omerta*."

Next, each of the eight men pricked their index finger and dropped their blood onto a holy card bearing an image of the Patriarca family saint. The card was set afire, and as it burned Deluca repeated the second oath: "As burns this saint, so will burn my soul. I enter alive into this organization and leave it dead."

The allure of a secret society, the macho posturing of its leaders, and the immense wealth at the fingertips of its most successful members attracted women to the Cosa Nostra men almost from the beginning. Of course, the reverse was true as well: many ambitious young Italian men wanted to join because Cosa Nostra members had no trouble attracting good-looking women. Any woman who associates herself with Cosa Nostra quickly learns that the lessons imprinted on Sicilian society by Muslims 1000 years earlier remain embedded in the attitudes of Cosa Nostra men. To them, women fulfill one of two available roles: angel or whore, wife or mistress.

Wives of Cosa Nostra men enjoy attractive benefits at a price. The benefits include the prospect that her man will rise high enough in the ranks to generate an impressive flow of income, permitting her and her family to enjoy the perks of wealth—a large home, expensive clothes, luxury cars and first-class vacations. Another perk is respect from her husband and his cohorts. The family remains a powerful unifying force among Sicilians and especially among Cosa Nostra members. You don't embarrass your wife, and you don't abuse her either. Exceptions exist, but any Cosa Nostra man known to beat his wife or act disdainful of her loses a measure of respect.

The price paid by the wives is substantial and acknowledged. Male promiscuity within the group is considered a sign of manliness, and the sexuality of any "wise guy" who is without a mistress or two may be suspect. Wives are expected to understand and accept this, just as they understand that they are to maintain a level of decorum. Any woman who swears risks being labeled a *puttana*, a prostitute, and cheating on a husband who happens to be a "made" man is a capital crime.

To avoid embarrassing their wives, Cosa Nostra men set Friday nights aside for their girlfriends; Saturday nights are for wives. The arrangement is strictly observed, avoiding the possibility of a Cosa Nostra man and his spouse encountering an acquaintance with a woman to whom he is not married. In other situations, the tradition becomes flexible—more than one Cosa Nostra wise guy has taken both his wife and mistress on a luxury cruise, the spouse staying with him in a suite and the mistress closeted in a lower stateroom.

Sex and murder collide in the Mafia environment with unique consequences. Vito Genovese reportedly had a man killed because Vito wanted the victim's wife for himself. The murder was excused by Genovese's confreres because a man of passion knows that rules and honor cannot always control his heart's desire. And while a Cosa Nostra man's excessive heterosexual activity elevates his status, the smallest degree of homosexual interest can be lethal regardless of his standing within the organization, as the fate of John (Johnny Boy) D'Amato proved.

D'Amato was head of the DeCavalcante family, the largest in New Jersey and reputed to be the basis of the popular *Sopranos* television series. He had also been a confidante of the notorious John Gotti, a relationship that might have protected him in other times and other circumstances. With his girlfriend Kelly, D'Amato began frequenting clubs where men and women swapped partners and engaged in group sex. At more than one of these events, D'Amato's girlfriend witnessed him performing oral sex on other men, and she tearfully confessed it to one of D'Amato's wise-guy friends. When the friend reported the incident to Mafia heavyweight Vincent (Vinnie Ocean) Palermo, the mob boss ordered D'Amato's murder. The motive was clear. "Nobody's gonna respect us if we have a gay homosexual boss sitting down discussing business," D'Amato's killer testified in court.

A millennium of secrecy and ruthless activity may appear to ensure the Mafia's survival in Italy, where its future seems assured despite periodic claims by that country's law enforcement groups that they have "broken" the society. In the U.S., however, the future of Cosa Nostra is not nearly as certain. Unlike Italian Mafia, the American Cosa Nostra faces wider competition from rivals often more ruthless than themselves, including Colombian drug lords, Vietnamese street gangs and Russian mobsters.

Even more critical to Cosa Nostra's survival, respect for the long-standing code of *omerta* is breaking down just when the society needs it most, a situation best demonstrated with a comparison between the actions of the two Mafia members we met earlier: Louis (Lepke) Buchalter and Joseph (Big Joey) Massino.

Buchalter rose through the ranks during the Mafia's glory days of the 1920s and 30s as a muscle-man in New York's garment district, where he became notorious for his callous, violent

The late Johnny D'Amato. All the sex you want, as long as it's hetero.

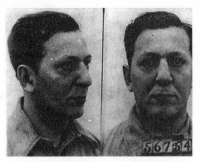

Louis (Lepke) Buchalter. He sat in the electric chair as though riding the subway to work.

ways. Any manufacturer or shopkeeper who failed to pay his allotted protection money was not merely warned or risked having his legs broken. He was simply killed, usually on the site of his business. Buchalter's standard *modus operandi* after each killing was to ransack the premises and torch the business, burning the evidence.

Thanks to his notoriety and a few traitorous colleagues, Buchalter was convicted of murder and sentenced to die in the electric chair on March 4, 1944. In spite of appeals by his lawyers for a commutation, Lepke's death sentence was carried out, and he was executed along with two associates. Buchalter was the last of the three to die, and while the first two men had stumbled quivering with fear into the execution chamber, Lepke strode in confidently, plopped himself into the electric chair, and sat as impassively as though he were riding the subway to work. Five minutes after being strapped in, he was pronounced dead.

The next day, Buchalter's widow hosted a press conference at a hotel near the prison in Ossining, New York, where her husband had been executed. "My husband dictated this statement in his death cell," she told reporters, "and I wrote it down, word for word." According to Beatrice Buchalter, Lepke had insisted that his statement receive the widest possible coverage, and reporters wrote down every word that Beatrice read from his note.

"I am anxious to have it clearly understood," Lepke dictated, "that I did not offer to talk and give information in exchange for any promise of commutation of my death sentence. I did not ask for that!" According to his widow, Lepke insisted on the exclamation point.

Buchalter, everyone agreed, was providing a clear signal to Mafia cohorts that he had not broken *omerta*. Some observers believed he did this to prevent reprisals against his family, but others suggested his motive was less practical and more emotional. Even in death, it was important that others understood he had acted in an honorable fashion towards his colleagues, if not towards his victims. This was a matter of personal pride that the prospect of having 5000 volts of electricity blasting through his body within a few hours could not divert.

Sixty years later, Big Joey Massino was boss of New York's Bonanno family, the top man of one of Manhattan's five most powerful Mafia. But the 400-pound leader of a group that practiced extortion among the same garment district that Lepke Buchalter terrorized proved to be a very different kind of man. *Omerta* may have meant honor to Buchalter but it meant nothing to Big Joey—not when he was looking at a hard-time life sentence after being convicted of murder and racketeering. Out on bail in September 2004, the Mafia boss did the unthinkable for a man of his stature in the world's most powerful criminal society: he agreed to wear an FBI microphone and record a colleague discussing the slaying of an associate and the planned murder of a federal prosecutor. Through his cooperation, dozens of his family members were brought to justice, and Massino avoided a potential life sentence.

When news of Massino's turncoat behavior became known, it hit Cosa Nostra members with the impact of an express train. Massino was hardly the first to break the *omerta* code; Joe Valachi set that mark back in 1963 when he testified to the U.S. Congress about the Mafia's presence, using the term "Cosa Nostra" in public for the first time. Since then, dozens of members have sought lighter sentences by cooperating with prosecutors. In every previous case, however, these were lower-level wise guys, with limited knowledge of the family's operations, no hope of reaching the higher levels where the big money was earned, and perhaps with a grudge or two against the men above them. The turning of a family boss was unprecedented and foreshadowed the possibility of a total breakdown of discipline within the organization. How can any Cosa Nostra family generate respect and loyalty, and exert discipline among the lower levels, when a family head betrays the entire organization?

The future of secrecy within the American branch of the Mafia/Cosa Nostra is in doubt. The prospect of its continued existence, and the strength of its control over criminal activities long associated with it, are even less certain.

NINE

YAKUZA
TRADITIONS AND AMPUTATIONS

TOKYO'S GINZA DISTRICT REMAINS THE SAME GLITZY ENTER-
tainment area it has been since the end of World War II, a
Japanese blend of New York's Broadway and London's Soho,
with a dash of Las Vegas. One recent night on a main Ginza
thoroughfare, several dozen Japanese businessmen sat mesmerized in front of pinball-like machines, watching small shiny balls
meander their way down through a maze of metal pins. This is
pachinko, a national craze among Japanese men, its name derived
from the sound of the chrome balls as they bounce among the
pins, over and over.

The atmosphere in a private men's club located directly
above the parlor was very different. Here the lights were
dimmed, the furniture was plush, and soft music, played on traditional Japanese instruments, floated through the smoky air.
In a far corner, a man in his 60s sat in front of a low table,
flanked by two young women who giggled at the orders he
gave in a harsh and guttural manner to several young men hov-
ering nearby. The men approached at his command, nodded at
his instructions, then bowed and withdrew, sent on errands
elsewhere in the club or onto the busy street below. A simple
nod from the older man brought a drink or a serving of tem-
pura from an attentive waitress; a similar gesture silenced one
of the younger men in mid-sentence. From time to time, the
older man smiled at the young women, one in a short cocktail
dress, the other in a schoolgirl's pleated plaid skirt and starched
white blouse. When he slipped his hand up the leg of the
woman in the cocktail dress or stroked the blouse of the

woman in the schoolgirl uniform, they laughed nervously and covered their mouths.

To a Westerner, the scene appeared to be a Japanese version of a Mafia godfather dispensing orders, retribution and rewards to his underlings. In some ways, it was. In other ways, it differed, especially when a young man appeared at the entrance to the club and stood waiting for his presence to be acknowledged. Dressed in the same slim-fitting suits as the other men his age, his hair shiny and his white shirt perfectly starched, he lingered nervously shifting his weight from one foot to the other, his face pale. His left hand was bandaged. His right hand held a small, carefully wrapped object.

Finally, responding to a curt nod from the older man and keeping his head down and his eyes lowered, the young man approached the older man in the corner. The girls ceased their giggles. The other young men stepped aside, permitting him to pass. The room grew silent.

Standing in front of the older man, the newcomer, his eyes and head still lowered, set the small parcel, using both hands in a gesture of solemn ceremony, onto the table. The older man looked at the young man's bandaged hand, nodded, and waved his own hand over the package in a signal to remove it. One of the other young men approached and whisked it away.

Inside the package was the severed last joint of the newly arrived man's pinkie finger, removed and submitted as an act of contrition and a plea for forgiveness. Something the younger man had done offended the older man, his boss. Apparently, other men in the room had offended him in a similar fashion, for many of them were also lacking a portion of their smallest finger. Some had no small finger on one hand at all, suggesting multiple affronts committed in the past. This was the Japanese Yakuza, a secret crime society tracing its origins back to the days of samurai warriors, and enforcing discipline in the same traditional and terrible manner.

Like chivalrous knights defending a lady's honor and flint-eyed sheriffs of the American Wild West, samurai warriors are

The samurai may be hailed as great and noble warriors, but their exploits belie their reputation. They also inspired the Yakuza.

viewed by many as guardians of medieval Japanese moral standards. Once again, the reality falls far short of the legend.

The samurai rose out of coalitions of warrior-chiefs in twelfth-century Japan, which was evolving into a feudal society much like the one already established in Europe. As with European feudalism, weaker leaders and groups pledged allegiance to larger and more powerful forces in return for protection. These groups, bonded by personal and family loyalties, began selecting the best fighters among them to serve as "gentlemen warriors," men skilled in combat and prepared at any moment to defend their personal chiefs. (Samurai is translated as "one who serves.")

Along with their fighting ability, the samurai were marked by a fanatical dedication to loyalty. Over time, this loyalty aspect grew to override other aspects of the warrior's life. Love of wife and children, duty to one's parents and fear of death were all secondary to the samurai's obligation of absolute loyalty and ferocity when encountering an adversary. Battles between warring factions became chilling events marked by samurai fighters boasting of their prowess and the exploits of their illustrious ancestors as they swung their swords at the bodies of their enemies.

Such ferocity and dedication set the samurai apart from the rest of Japanese society and earned them special privileges. Only recognized samurai, for example, were permitted to own *katana*, the long two-handed swords that the samurai revered like sacred objects. If a samurai believed he had been insulted by someone of a lower birth status, he could cut the offender in two with his sword and suffer no punishment. Samurai weapons evolved into the central object of an elaborate code of honor. Swords used to slay many opponents in battle were believed to possess spiritual powers, and new swords were tested on human bodies, usually the corpses of beheaded criminals.

Like medieval knights, wealthy samurai fought on horse-back clad in helmet and flexible armor while less affluent warriors functioned as foot-soldiers. Unlike their European counterparts, however, samurai were motivated not by religious fervor or motives of chivalry but by simple dedication to the orders of their warlords. In this sense, they resembled mafia *capos* more than heroic battlers.

Nor, contrary to the aura often associated with the samurai, was there much heroism exhibited during battles. Consider this account of a thirteenth-century raid on an emperor's palace:

> The nobles, courtiers and even the ladies in waiting of the women's quarters were slashed to death.... The palace was set ablaze and when the occupants rushed out, so as not to be burned by the fire, they were met by warriors. When they turned back... they were consumed by the flames.... [Some] even jumped into wells in large numbers and of these, too, the bottom ones in a short time had drowned, those in the middle were crushed to death by their fellows, and those on top had been cut to pieces or burned by the flames....

Inevitably, admirable samurai standards grew corrupted with time, and eventually even their noble causes began to crumble. In the seventeenth century the *hatamoto-yakko* (servants of the shogun), an extravagant branch of independent samurai, found their services unneeded during an extended period of peace. Unable to function in ordinary society, they veered from performing service on behalf of their warlords to creating mayhem among the populace. In some cases, they acted like Robin Hood-inspired folk heroes, defending the poor and defenseless, and sharing stolen booty with starving peasants. In most instances, however, they grew as ruthless and exploitive as any mob of hoodlums, despite their claimed penchant for ceremony and honor.

This evolution of samurai from warrior-heroes to organized thugs generated a response from the victims of their plundering, common folk, who shrugged off their veneration of samurai and responded by forming a citizen militia known as the *machi-yokko*. Within a few years, the tables had turned against the samurai; the machi-yokko were now viewed as protectors of the ordinary Japanese, and they acquired a mantle of respect and reverence while operating beyond the reach of the law, a direct parallel with the rise of the Sicilian Mafia. When the samurai were subdued, the machi-yokko remained as defenders of the common folk, even after modern-day Japanese culture arrived with centralized authority and law enforcement, leaving the machi-yokko outside the law.

By this time the various machi-yokko branches began referring to themselves as *yakuza*, a name derived from the organizations' fondness for gambling. One of their favored games, *hana-fuda* (flower cards), was played with three cards in which the worst possible hand totaled 20 points. "Ya" in spoken Japanese means 8, "ku" means 9, and "sa" means 3, yielding the dreaded 20-point hand and implying that Yakuza members are the "bad hands" of society.

As the Freemasons did with the Templar legend, the Yakuza fostered an association with the more noble aspects of the samurai, and their practice of severing a pinkie finger as punishment relates directly back to the ancient warrior class. When wielding a *katana*, the swordsman's pinkie finger exerted greater control over the weapon than any other part of his hand. A samurai with an injured or missing pinkie was at a distinct disadvantage in battle and relied heavily on his master for protection. Thus the punishment exerted by Yakuza bosses on errant members.

Removal of a pinkie, known as *yubizeum*, represents punishment for displeasing or disappointing a Yakuza master and symbolizes both the member's error and courage. The offending

Yakuza is alerted to the need for the amputation when his superior hands him two items: a knife, and a length of string to staunch the bleeding. No words are spoken. None is necessary. The offender must have no connection with the group until he carries out his own punishment, confirms its completion, and receives forgiveness from the master.

In addition to incomplete pinkies, Yakuza members may be identified by their extensive tattoos, often applied not as individual symbols like those favored in the West, but as extensive murals depicting dragons, flowers, landscapes and abstract designs applied to parts of their bodies normally covered with everyday clothing. With his face, neck, lower arms, ankles and feet left free of tattoos, a naked Yakuza appears to be wearing long underwear. The meticulous application of the designs takes hundreds of hours and costs thousands of dollars, yet remains hidden from view to all but his most intimate partners. Its purpose is to demonstrate, to those who witness the body art, that its owner has both the wealth and the courage to absorb the cost and pain.

Westerners who encounter a group of Yakuza without knowing their identity may see them as unintentionally comic. The

members favor tight-fitting silk suits, pointed-toe shoes, slicked long hair in a pompadour style, and a swagger more reminiscent of the sitcom TV character The Fonz than of butchers like Vito Genovese and Lepke Buchalter. The gangster cliché is strengthened by

Naked Yakuza are obviously a chilling sight. The overall-body tattoos signify wealth and resistance to pain.

the preference, among Yakuza members, for American Cadillac and Lincoln automobiles, oversized and ostentatious in the land of Toyotas and Hondas.

Reflecting the classic pyramid structure of the Mafia/Cosa Nostra, the Yakuza organization is somewhat more complex and multi-layered, based on an *oyabun-kobun* relationship. *Oyabun* means "father role," and *kobun* means "child role." Unquestioned loyalty to the boss is demanded of every Yakuza member. A Yakuza doctrine dictates "When your boss says the passing crow is white, you must agree that it is white," and underlings filling the child role must never differ from the "father's" opinion. The *oyabun*, in turn, is obligated to offer protection and wise counsel to all of his children.

At the summit of each Yakuza organization is the *kumicho*, or Supreme Boss. Immediately beneath him are the *saiko koman*, his senior adviser, and the *so-honbucho*, or headquarters chief. The *wakagashira* are regional bosses who manage several gangs, each assisted by a *fuku-honbucho*, who may have several gangs of his own. Lesser regional bosses are *shateigashira*, with a *shateigashira-hosa* assisting them. Within each gang family are several *shatei*, or younger brothers, and *wakashu*, junior leaders.

Initiation into a Yakuza gang is filled with symbolism but surprisingly passive in nature. The candidate and his *oyabun* sit facing each other while cups of sake are prepared for the ceremony by adding salt and fish scales to the heated liquor, which is poured into each man's cup. The cups are identical in size but the oyabun's cup is always filled to the brim while the candidate receives much less. When the oyabun raises his cup to drink from it, the candidate does the same. Then the two men exchange cups, drinking from each other's. This sharing of the drink seals the entry of the young man into the group.

Yakuza existed in Japan for 300 years without making a major impact on society, although its members were major participants in the widespread corruption that marked Japanese society in the 1920s and 1930s. In the years following World War II, however, greater freedom and prosperity saw Yakuza numbers grow spectacularly. One recent estimate, suggesting that 5200 Yakuza gangs were operating throughout the country, placed the total number of Yakuza members at 184,000, making them larger in numbers than the Japanese army at the time.

Japanese police pressure in recent years has shrunk Yakuza, but they remain a potent force in Japan and, through intermediaries and political connections, in Korea, China and the Philippines as well. They tend to favor sex-related activities, running prostitution rings often consisting of young girls purchased from poor Chinese and Philippine families. Other young women may be attracted to Japan with promises of high-paying jobs as waitresses, receptionists and models. Once in Japan, they are put to work first as strippers and later as prostitutes.

In recent years, the Yakuza have branched into smuggling banned automatic weapons and drugs into the country, although traditional narcotics like heroin and cocaine are less popular these days than methamphetamine. They are also reputed to be deeply involved in casino operations throughout the world, preying on Japanese gamblers who are offered large cash loans in Las Vegas, Atlantic City, Monte Carlo and elsewhere. The wealthy gamblers, assuming the loans will be uncollectible back in Japan, are enticed to borrow substantially. If they lose—and most do, of course—they return to Japan to discover that Yakuza partners of the loan sharks are determined to collect the debt along with a murderous rate of interest.

Perhaps the group's most lucrative and profitable diversification has been in the corporate field, where its leaders have grown adept at a uniquely Japanese form of extortion. After acquiring a few shares in a large publicly traded company, the Yakuza gathers scandalous information about the firm's top executives. Some of the executives' activities, such as dalliances with prostitutes or drug habits, the Yakuza themselves may have fostered. Evidence of other practices such as tax evasion, maintaining unsafe factory conditions, and ignoring environmental laws are obtained through bribery.

Like the Mafia, the Yakuza has been glamorized in films.

When enough dirt has been accumulated, Yakuza members approach the top members of the corporation's executive committee shortly before the annual shareholders' meeting and deliver an ultimatum: either the Yakuza are well compensated for destroying the evidence or the group's *sokaiya* (meeting men) will disclose the information at the annual shareholders' meeting. The *sokaiya* are chosen for their vehement style, capable of shouting down anyone who tries to silence them and describing the executives' misbehavior in colorful, provocative language.

Japanese society is sensitive to revelations causing shame and embarrassment, and corporate CEOS and others quickly pay whatever the Yakuza demand. According to Japanese sources, the Yakuza have made millions of dollars from this technique.

Still, the glory days of the Yakuza may be fading. Many Japanese citizens refuse to be cowed by the gangsters, and have driven the organizations from some neighborhoods in spite of threats, beatings and killings. The organizations may also be breaking up from the inside because, unlike the Mafia/Cosa Nostra, Yakuza members do not dedicate their lives to the group. Many Yakuza thugs, having joined while impressionable young men, choose to leave in their mid-30s, having perhaps salted away their earnings or being attracted to the less strenuous corporate life. In some instances, these Yakuza drop-outs have discovered that the managerial skills acquired during their years as Yakuza members are highly valued in the corporate world, and many apparently occupy executive suites in corporations they may have targeted at one time for attack by *sokaiya*.

How they manage to explain a missing pinkie or their elaborate body tattoo art remains a mystery.

TEN

WICCA
THE GREAT GODDESS AND THE HORNED GOD

AMONG THE WORLD'S MANY SECRET SOCIETIES, MOST CHOSE their covert nature as a means of avoiding harassment from groups and individuals who felt threatened by the society's existence. Perhaps no faction in history was more severely persecuted, in Europe and elsewhere, than witches. From the early medieval period through the Renaissance, untold thousands died, often under horrific circumstances, on the basis of nothing more than mere suspicion or empty accusation. With few exceptions, the victims were women; and in many instances, their persecutors were male members of the Christian Church.

While we think of the medieval and Reformation periods in Europe as the era of persecution against witches, the practice of witchcraft predates Christianity. Originally, the term referred to anyone who practiced magic, and both the pre-Christian Greeks and Romans made a distinction between "white" and "black" witchcraft. White magic was positive, and included the ability to bring good fortune or cure illnesses, while black witchcraft was any mystical action that caused harm against others. The Romans declared that any witch or magician who caused the death of another through spells or potions was subject to the same capital punishment as someone who committed murder with a sword or poison, a reasonable rule at the time.

In reality, witchcraft was usually little more than an extension of pagan religions that believed their gods were embodiments of natural powers, similar to the Druids. Some of these belief cultures assigned powers not to plant life such as the oak and mistletoe, revered by Druids, but to animals—goats, cattle and, especially in Europe, cats. A good deal of witchcraft in this period was as harmless as any personal spiritual practice. A few practitioners, however, recognized the power that accrued to anyone who could make a plausible claim to casting spells and mixing potions, activities that generated fear and income among credible neighbors. In this environment, witchcraft was viewed as simply another trade, like the practice of medicine, likely with an equal measure of success and failure.

The advent of Christianity changed everything. Clear distinctions were made between mystical practices in praise of the Christian God and similar activities not sanctioned by the Church. In an ecclesiastical version of the "You're either with us or against us" doctrine, unsanctioned mystical activities were associated with Satan and condemned accordingly.

Of all the sins defined by Christianity, the ones most often linked with satanic practices involved sex, and since power within the Church resided exclusively with men, who frequently found themselves tempted by the sight or the passive activities of women, females became the target of persecution against witches. What better method, after all, did Satan have for tempting a God-fearing man towards sin than through the wiles of a nubile female?

Women were perceived as tools of the devil in his crusade to garner the souls of Christian men and, as much as any other factor, this contributed to hundreds of years of persecution. The hanging, drowning, burning, imprisonment and mutilation of untold thousands of women over the past two millennia had nothing to do with subversive ideology, religious deviation or racial discrimination. It had everything to do with gender, and with the centuries-old dominance of men over women, a dominance that extends beyond sexuality and economic influence to include spiritual authority.

And while we may be more tolerant, and even amused, by claims of witchcraft and its practitioners, Christian fundamentalists need look no further than the Bible for justification to abuse anyone suspected of being a witch. "For rebellion is the sin of witchcraft," they'll read in I Sam. 15:23, proof that the major failing of witches is a refusal to follow orders. In search of more direct instruction, Christians might examine Exod. 22:18: "Thou shalt not suffer a witch to live."

Modern theologians may argue about the true interpretation of these admonitions, but as recently as the nineteenth century European and American civilizations accepted them as explicit authority to burn, hang and drown women on the basis of their witch-like behavior. The leading oppressors of uncounted thousands of women who suffered this fate through the centuries were always men, and the root of their charges against the victim was still associated with one sin above all: sex.

The most devastating charge that could be brought against witches in Christian mythology was that they engaged in sexual acts with the devil. Perhaps as a means of rewarding those who gave in to his lust, Satan was believed to grant his partners occult powers such as controlling the minds of others, casting evil spells, and having the ability to move solid items with a mere thought or gesture.

Through history, the Roman Catholic Church assumed a leading role in demonizing witches, especially in 1450 when it recycled many of its old charges against pagans. Making no distinction between those who chose to identify themselves as witches performing magical acts and earth-based religions that were usually forms of Druidism, the Church's only goal was to convert the "pagans" to Catholicism. As was often the case, its motives and methods were both heavy-handed and reckless with facts. Claiming that pagans "worshipped the devil," for example, conveniently ignored the fact that the devil is a Judeo-Christian creation. How could pagans "worship" a being whose existence was unknown to them?

Such realities failed to deter Church officials. Witches, they decreed, kidnapped babies, killed and ate their victims, raised hailstorms and tempests, caused horses to go mad beneath their riders, sold their soul to Satan (or at least their bodies, apparently) and, in a remarkable charge coming from men sworn to

The fabled broomstick-riding habits of witches evolved from stimulating either crops or orgasms.

a life of celibacy, not only caused male impotence and fertility but could make male genitals vanish, the ultimate act of castration.

Even the clichéd image of a broom-riding witch was linked with sex. Witches might fly, their accusers charged, but riding a broom had more to do with the broom handle's function, in the minds of puritanical Christians, as a dildo to stimulate orgasm rather than an implement for flight. The actual origins may be less sexual; in some medieval cultures, women ran across fields while astride their broom in an effort to coax the grain to grow, or jumped over the broom handle while imploring the grain to grow as high as they could leap.

Protestants were no more enlightened about witches than Catholics. Luther, in his Commentary on St. Paul's Epistle to the Galatians, wrote: "I should have no compassion on these witches; I would burn all of them." (He also wrote: "If a woman grows weary and at last dies from childbearing, it matters not. Let her die from bearing; she is there to do it.") And Calvin preached: "The Bible teaches us that there are witches and they must be slain.... This law of God is a universal law." John Wesley, founder of the Methodist Church, lectured that anyone who denied the reality of witchcraft opposed not only the Bible but the collected wisdom of "the wisest and best of men in all ages and nations."

Theologians and psychologists both speculate that the true motive behind the persecution of women suspected to be witches was to assist skeptics in resolving their own doubts about Christian doctrine and strengthen their faith in God. The existence of women receiving evil powers from Satan would be proof of a spiritual world which, extending the idea further, provided proof of the existence of God. Satan could not exist without the presence of God, *ergo* God exists. One qualified observer of this theory says, "Without witches, some late medieval theologians were left facing their questions as to why bad things happen. In their pre-scientific biblically-based world view, the logical alternative to witches and demons as an explanation of misfortune was a God [either] not powerful enough to stop bad things from happening, or not good enough to try."

Organized religions have long assigned women the role of ideal scapegoats for events or aspects of life that Church leaders could not explain. Witches were not the only victims of this problem of theodicy, nor were Catholics and Protestants the only groups wrestling with the dilemma of an all-good and all-powerful God coexisting with evil in our world. But throughout Western Europe and America between AD 1000 and 1800, both factions absorbed the Bible's directive regarding witches with totally literal meaning, and while their means of eradicating the world of witchcraft-derived evil differed—in Catholic countries, execution was conducted by burning at the stake; in Protestant countries, the preferred method was hanging—the results were the same.

Evidence was needed to prove that accused women were indeed witches, and their persecutors discovered a remarkable number of ways to obtain it—remarkable because the verdict was almost always Guilty. Consider the means used:

Trial by boiling water consisted of heating a deep container of water until it boiled, and instructing the accused person to remove a stone or ring from the bottom. The scalded hand was bandaged, and the bandages sealed. If a blister half as large as a walnut appeared when the bandages were removed, the verdict was guilt, leading to a sentence of death. The accused were advised to pray and fast the day before the trial was conducted. Most apparently did. Few apparently benefited.

Trial by fire was a simple variation, requiring the accused to walk barefooted across a row of metal ploughshares heated to a red-hot glow. An absence of burns on the soles of her feet indicated innocence.

Trial by drowning represented a historical apex in no-win situations. After throwing the accused into the river, the judges watched to see if she surfaced. If the victim sank to the bottom and drowned, she was declared innocent; if she managed to stay afloat, she was pronounced guilty and immediately hanged or burned at the stake, unless she was tortured first in the usually fruitful expectation that she would implicate others.

The ordeal of the cross placed the accused and her accuser in a church, usually during a regular service. Both were ordered to stand with arms outstretched, simulating Christ on the cross. The person whose arms dropped first was considered wrong.

Oppression against accused witches rose and fell in waves, linked to various influences ranging from natural disasters to religious in-fighting. The hundred years from 1550 to 1650, when relations between Catholics and Protestants were particularly virulent, saw so many trials and executions of accused witches in France, Germany and Switzerland that the period became known as the Burning Times. During the seventeenth century, attitudes towards accused witches began to soften. In 1610, the Netherlands banned the execution of witches, and 1684 marked the last execution of a witch in England. By the time of the Salem witch trials in New England, when dozens of women and a handful of men were executed or died in prison on charges of witchcraft, the wave had crested in Europe.

The lasting effect of the Catholic and Protestant attacks on people who chose to explore their earth-based spirituality, thus associating them with Satan, was to drive the movement underground, and much of the knowledge and tradition acquired over the centuries before bishops rode in search of devil-worshippers has been lost forever. Practices that were once considered open and free, such as paying homage to nature, could be sustained only at the risk of torture and agonizing death. Many found solace in these actions in spite of the risk; others suffered horribly when they had never considered performing such acts, simply on the accusations of neighbors.

THE GREAT GODDESS AND THE HORNED GO

The core beliefs of witchcraft survived because those who observed the rituals and clung to the creed remained secretive. Their spiritual descendants emerged in the mid-twentieth century as members of Wicca, a term used by modern-day practitioners to separate themselves from their persecuted forebears.

The appearance of Wicca as a somewhat cohesive system of principle grew equally from both ancient and recent origins. They include a revulsion against many corporate practices in North America and Europe deemed injurious to the environment, the destruction of rain forests and wilderness, the eradication of native species and the avaricious consumption of limited resources. Bearing many labels, these scattered movements eventually began making their voices heard and attracting various adherents, especially among young people. From an appreciation of the need for conservation and environmental responsibility, it was a short step for these devotees to explore and assume many beliefs of Wicca.

The other driving force behind the re-emergence of Wicca was a revived reverence for shamanism, which was actually the origin of pre-Christian witchcraft. "Shaman" is believed derived from a Siberian native word meaning *he* (or *she*) *who knows*, although the concept of a tribal or village member possessing knowledge to cure ailments and provide spiritual guidance predates every organized religion. Performing as a shaman was one method for a woman in male-dominated tribal societies to achieve power and status, an attribute that continues to influence Wicca, which boasts substantially more female than male followers. Ancient Greek literature identifies shamanistic rites and practices during the early Hellenic period, many of them later adopted by Roman spiritual leaders. Tibetan Buddhism has remained strongly associated with shamanistic principles for millennia, and every American native band from Arctic Inuit to Patagonian tribes practiced their variations of the same beliefs.

The determination of Christian campaigners to spread their creed universally had the same devastating impact on shamanism in the Americas as elsewhere, propelled first by Spanish colonialists. Catholic missionaries and priests denounced shamans and their followers as devil-worshippers, executing them by the thousands. Although the bulk of this devastation occurred from the sixteenth to the nineteenth centuries, as recently as the 1970s missionaries in the Amazon region routinely defaced ancient petroglyphs representing shamanistic beliefs or legends.

Things were no better in the north, where Native American shamans were tagged with labels such as *witch doctor*, and claims of healing ailments with naturally occurring ingredients were broadly derided. Later, scientists noted that many universal treatments, such as chewing the bark of willow trees to cure headache and fever, had a basis in fact, because the willow is a natural source of salicylic acid, the primary ingredient in Aspirin. Only after a positive reassessment of shamanistic practices became widespread did shamans receive respect from other cultures. When many of their teachings were assimilated into the growing concern about the environment, Wicca revived those tenets that managed to survive a thousand years of attempts to eradicate it.

Still, old habits are not easily abandoned. Much of the civilized world remains hostile to the Wicca movement on the basis of religious/moral grounds, fear that it represents a seditious philosophy, and its record of secretive behavior, or simply because its adherents refuse to conform. As a result, Wicca in the twenty-first century remains unknown and often feared, viewed as a secret society by those mired among images of cackling witches and evil spells.

"Wicca" is derived from the medieval *wicce*, meaning "to bend," although most dictionaries make no distinction between *Wicca* and *witch*. This etymology suggests that the practice may be bent or shaped to meet the needs of the practitioner, an interesting contrast with the inflexible dogma of most organized religions. In fact, the core ethical doctrine of Wicca, known as the *Wiccan Rede*, is *An ye harm none, do what ye will*, which echoes to some degree the Golden Rule so warmly embraced by Judeo-Christian teachings. This moral flexibility disturbs conventional religions because it appears to promote situational ethics, anathema to those who preach fixed codes of ethical guidelines from sources such as the Ten Commandments and the Koran. How can such flexibility and adaptability provide firm moral direction? In response, Wicca believers submit the Law of Three.

Along with the Wiccan Rede, the Law of Three serves as a moral direction for members of Wicca. According to this law, all energy dispensed by individuals returns to them threefold in a mystical interpretation of Newton's law regarding action and reaction. In this instance, positive healing energy—love, support, prayers for good health and success—return to the sender with three times the power. Similarly, harmful energy will return to the sender, in one form or another, with three times the effect its sender originally wished to have on the target.

Is Wicca a religion? Perhaps. Its followers identify it as a "paganist religion," which sounds too much like an oxymoron for some to accept. Other members of Wicca prefer to identify it as a "personal, positive celebration of life," something many people would like to see reflected in the goals and activities of conventional religions.

All religions worship some entity or another, and Wicca qualifies to at least this extent, worshipping not one god but two. The most significant deity is known simply as the Great Goddess, although she has several parallel or secondary identities, including the Earth Mother, the Lady of the Moon and the Star Goddess. She may also be called Queen of the Underworld and the Triple Goddess. In this latter role, she represents three personas: the Virgin, the Bride and the Hag; or, if you prefer, the Maiden or the Mother, and the Crone.

In her role as the Virgin she is the Creatrix, the Giver of Inspiration, and the eternal virgin for the goat-god Pan, which suggests some serious questions about their relationship. She is, in Wiccan lore, the lover of all, yet she is wed to none, and her sacred color is white. She is identified with the waxing moon and with Venus as the morning and evening star. Echoes of the Virgin Mary resonate in this description although Wicca followers claim that this persona predates Christianity. Of course, if the later religion has borrowed from the earlier one, this would not be an unusual event.

Next, the Bride identity of the Great Goddess springs from her function as Preserver. She is the Goddess of flocks and herds, the Lady of Love and Fruitfulness and Fertility, represented by the full moon and by fields of sheep and lush plants. The Bride's sacred color is red.

In her third and final role, the Great Goddess becomes Hag the Destroyer, Goddess of the Night and the Underworld, the realm of the cave and the tomb. This is where the warm-and-fuzzy soul of Wicca grows dark and ominous. Hag the Destroyer is the sow who eats her young, a participant in the circle of death and decay that ultimately yields new life. For Hag the Destroyer, Wicca believers look to the waning moon, a crossroads at midnight and silence in shadows. Her sacred color, of course, is black.

Partner to the Great Goddess is the Horned God, and his title generates negative reaction among fundamentalist religions, which interpret the description as either Satan or Satyr. The Horned God clearly is associated with excessive and extramarital sexual activity, although Wicca teachings identify him in this role through various secondary titles: the Ancient God of Fertility, the Lord of Life, the Giver of Life, and especially the Horned Consort to the Great Goddess. Beyond these titles, definitions grow more complex and confusing. The Horned God is both the hunter and the hunted; he is Lord of Light and Lord of Darkness, the sun by day and the sun at midnight.

Here, the pagan traditions underlying Wicca grow more apparent. The Horned God's destiny is to die with the harvest, be buried as seed, and be resurrected in spring out of the womb of the Earth Mother. Like gods in pre-Christian religions and traditions, he is often depicted wearing the horns of a bull, goat, ram or stag, an appearance that persuaded critics of Wicca that his actual identity is Satan, regardless of the Wiccan statement that the devil plays no role in its dogma.

This supposed satanic connection, along with some practices inherited from shamanism, echoes centuries of persecution and prejudice from well before "the burning times" down to our present day. Like the shamans, practitioners of Wicca seek to transcend the physical world and enter a parallel psychic world by utilizing tools and methods unavailable to ordinary people. The transition, Wiccans believe, is achieved via alternative states of consciousness, and the tools to enter these states are familiar. They include fasting, thirst, concentration, hallucinogenics and the infliction of pain. To heighten the psychedelic effect, these are often accompanied by drumbeats, rattles, music, chants and dancing, usually performed in darkness with the added effects of flickering firelight.

These devices are recognizable as ceremonial elements of native cultures throughout the world, which persuades many skeptics that Wicca is nothing more than a WASP-adapted version of rituals performed in old movies of Native American war dances, or racial clichés of lost African native tribes. This ignores the reality that all organized religions, functioning on a supposedly higher intellectual and spiritual plane, have employed their own mystical rituals throughout history. The Catholic Church, for example, "magically" converts wafers to flesh and wine to blood with the assistance of burning incense, stirring music and repeated phrases spoken in unison (and, for hundreds of years, Gregorian chants) to achieve similar objectives. The practice of Communion is an analogy; the objective, however, is similar.

Wiccans no longer use pain as a means of crossing from the physical to the psychic world and most modern practitioners reject the use of hallucinogenics. Yet Wicca remains stigmatized by people who equate its activities with orgiastic rituals, devil-worship, and the use of drugs and narcotics. For this reason many Wiccans, male and female alike, choose to conceal their involvement, fearing ridicule, loss of employment, violence and, among women separated from their partners, the loss of custodial rights to their children. The only defense against this kind of prejudice is secrecy. (With sardonic humor, some Wiccans describe the public admission of their beliefs as "coming out of the broom closet.") As we have seen in other instances, secrecy deepens suspicion, leading to greater motivation for concealment.

Even though Wicca may be considered the most liberal and least regulated of secret societies, an initiation of sorts has evolved over the centuries. The rites are often performed in the presence of a coven although Wiccans may, if they choose, initiate themselves through a process called self-dedication. In the parlance of modern psychology, this becomes a form of "contract with oneself," a ceremony in which the individual considers the path he or she wishes to follow and, once committed to the journey, affirms themselves as a child of the Wicca faith, pledging to abide by the Wicca Rede and to grow spiritually.

Membership in an established Wicca coven may involve a more elaborate ritual and perhaps a waiting period, often "a year and a day," before full membership is granted. Covens may also recognize various levels of status within the group, requiring some evidence of heightened skills or experience, marked by degrees of initiation, before full acceptance is granted. Attaining these degrees could involve sacramental rituals, with specified duties and expectations.

The concept of covens still creates, in the minds of people unfamiliar with and concerned about Wicca, images of black-capped women stirring pots of bubbling brew beneath a full moon, à la Macbeth. Or, in a more contemporary setting, dancing naked in the woods. The Macbeth scene is entirely fictional, but the visions of nudity among modern-day Wicca may well be authentic.

Some members of Wicca prefer to enact their rituals "skyclad," shedding their garments as an expression of pride in the bodies they inherited from their gods. They may practice this alone or in the presence of a coven but, like almost everything else associated with Wicca, the decision is left up to the individual. A number of Wiccans, for example, choose to wear ritual garments, especially for festivals and formal sacraments. And, as we shall see, "skyclad" may owe more to the carnal curiosity of a twentieth-century male than to pagan traditions.

One of the more common group activities among Wiccans involves casting "The Magickal Circle," which is actually conceived as a sphere separating Wiccans from the rest of the world and its negativity, and extending above and below the ground or floor.[11] This presents problems for modern apartment-dwelling Wiccans, since a circle of sufficient diameter could extend into other dwellings directly above and below the Wiccan's residence. As a result, high-rise adherents are advised to cast their circles late at night, when adjacent residents are sleeping and thus unlikely to pass through the "magick space."

A Magickal Circle holds four Watch Towers, one at each quadrant of the compass, and each Watch Tower represents one of the four elements of Wicca: Earth, Air, Fire and Water. North is the location of Earth, and Earth represents the body of Life. As the darkest and heaviest of the four elements, Earth is Mother, the source of our lives, and our final destination. From Earth, Wiccans draw stability, abundance, growth and patience. Air, representing the breath of life and the fresh breezes of change, resides at the eastern point of the Circle, where the sun rises. Air is considered a masculine quality, providing clarity of thought, truth and the conscious expression of the Will.

At the south point of the circle, Fire represents the energy of life, the location of the sun in midsummer. Another masculine quality, Fire provides the Earth Mother with energy, encouraging a bountiful harvest, and provides the Wiccan with courage, conviction and passion. It also threatens anger and hostility if shown inadequate respect.

The womb of Mother Earth is Water, guardian of the western quadrant of the Magickal Circle. This is where the sun sets,

[11] The "magick" spelling in this context was introduced by Aleister Crowley.

A typical Magickal Circle, visualized as a three-dimensional sphere.

and where souls pass into the invisible world. Water also corresponds with the moon, acknowledging the satellite's effect on the tides. It is also an intuitive element, capable of perplexing the logical rationale of Air, and Wiccans look to Water for cleansing, sensitivity, compassion and love.

The technique used to create Magickal Circles suggests a naive Harry Potter–like approach. Everything occurs within the imaginative mind of the Wiccan who, if creating a circle for her individual use, need make it only as large as her own body. The process appears to have as many variations as sources, but among the most common directions are these:

1. The space within which the circle is formed may be a highrise urban apartment or a lush clearing in a forest or jungle. Location is irrelevant.

2. The first step requires cleansing the space, either blessing the area by sweeping the floor or ground, or making a great deal of noise to drive away evil influences (not recommended for apartment dwellers in the dead of night).

3. Solitary Wiccans stand at the circle's center; when three or more are creating the circle they position themselves around its circumference. Relaxing until they feel the energy of the Earth, they turn to face one of the four Watch Towers, gathering its special energy in one hand while pulling energy from the sky with the other hand.

4. Using both hands, they apply the energy to the imaginary spherical shape enclosing them, repeating the process with each of the four Watch Tower locations. Each application builds the sphere's walls, making them thicker and more protective.

5. When the Wiccans sense the invisible sphere is stable, they cease building its walls. The Sphere now may be perceived in various

ways—as a color, a thickening of the air, a wall of electrical power, or simply the source of a low hum.

6. If it is necessary for anyone to leave the circle before the ritual is complete, they must cut a "door" in the "walls" with their hand, holding the fingers straight and describing a rectangular space that they step through, "closing" the door behind them. When returning, they "open" the "door," close it gently, and "smooth" the outline with their hand.

7. Within the Circle, Wiccans may note a marked increase in temperature; opening a "door" creates a rush of cold air, the mark of negativism.

The Circle provides a safe, comforting and effective location for Wiccans to initiate change by focusing their natural powers— change in themselves, in their loved ones and in the world at large. The change, however, must be positive; Wicca prohibits the use of magickal power to harm others.

Derived from the naturalistic roots of Shamanism, Wicca bases much of its beliefs and customs on cycles of life, the moon, and especially the seasons, marking them with eight holiday "sabbats" during the "wheel of the year." Primary sabbats fall on or near traditional equinoxes of the sun; other sabbats occur on "cross-quarter" days, which occur on or near the first day of February, May, August and November. The sabbats include these:

Imbolg (im-molg), also known as Candlemas, celebrated on February 2 to mark the first stirrings of spring and the return of light to the world.

Ostara (oh-star-ah), the day of the vernal equinox March 21 or 22, when light and dark are in perfect balance, with light mastering dark.

Beltane (bell-tane), the first day of May, the Celts' beginning of summer (Beltane is a derivation of the Gaelic "Bel-fire"). On Beltane, fires were lit to commemorate the return of life and fertility, a day adopted by other cultures for similar celebrations. The fertility connection is associated with couples falling in love on this date.

Litha (lee-tha), the summer solstice; it acknowledges the sun's gift of light, warmth and life.

Lammas, or *Lughnasadh* (loon-na-sah), August 1, a prompt for everyone to begin harvesting and make preparations for winter. Lughnasadh is named for the Celtic warrior Lugh, who spared the life of his enemy in return for learning the secrets of agricultural prosperity. This day marks the first of three sabbats dedicated to harvesting.

Mabon (may-ben), the autumnal equinox on September 21 or 22, a joyous day marked again by equal lengths of day and night, with dark now mastering light. This marks the time of the second harvest.

Samhain (sow-in), October 31, a day of much importance because, among other things, it signifies the beginning of the Wiccan year. The word, derived from the Gaelic *samhuinn*, means "summer's end." With the rise of Christianity, Samhain was changed to Hallowmas, or All Saints' Day, to commemorate the souls of the blessed dead canonized that year, and the night before Hallowmas became Halloween, All Hallows Eve, or Hollantide. On Samhain, the major sabbat in Wicca, the veil between the material world and the spiritual world is considered at its thinnest, a time when the spirits of departed loved ones may congregate around Samhain fires to grow warm and express their love for surviving kin.

Yule (yool), the winter solstice, December 21 or 22, marking the longest night of the year and reminding us that the gods must be reborn in order to bring light and warmth back to our earth.

Most benefits of Wicca appear to dwell in the minds of its practitioners, who could rightly claim that this does not invalidate its power. But, as we saw with Rosicrucianism, modern Kabbalah, and the Priory of Sion, the movement's actual history and many of its "ancient" myths are linked to characters of questionable veracity. In this case, at least one of the characters manages to taint the modern Wicca movement with deep skepticism.

Remember the horrific trials of witches during the burning years, especially those conducted at the height of the Inquisition's most appalling activities? The Catholic Church is noted for its methodical recording of events, including Inquisition torture sessions conducted on suspected witches. Detailed accounts of every statement and even every cry of agony were assiduously written and reviewed. In fear and anguish, accused witches would admit or volunteer a host of activities while being tortured. Their confessions frequently included having sexual intercourse with Satan, casting spells upon innocent people, influencing the weather to bring storms and drought upon the land, changing themselves into cats and other animals, and any other iniquity that sprang to the minds of the inquisitors and were demanded of the accused.

Yet nowhere among thousands of accounts do the "witches" identify their Great Goddess or Horned God. No depiction of magic circles exists in any of the transcripts, nor is any information proffered of sabbats and their celebration. Is it possible that, among the thousands of accused witches submitted to questioning under torture, none was either familiar enough with these rituals to describe them, or weak enough to reveal them? Is it likely that no practicing witches were ever submitted to the Inquisition, and thus the torturers had no opportunity to question the only real sources of all the wickedness they were seeking to eradicate?

Or is it plausible that these specific "ancient" rights and tenets are not ancient at all, but modern inventions that sprang from the minds of people who sought glory, wealth and perhaps carnal reward from claiming access to supposedly ancient occult knowledge? If so, at least two individuals, both men of questionable honor, are prime suspects.

One is the familiar Aleister Crowley, who employed the occult as a means of breaking virtually every moral law and precept encountered during his decadent lifetime. Near the end of his life, when he was near-penniless and living in Hastings, Crowley was visited by Gerald Brosseau Gardner. Intrigued by

Gerald Brosseau Gardner. The godfather of modern Wicca or just another dirty old man?

Crowley's claim of access to occult secrets, Gardner was immediately initiated into Crowley's Hermetic Order of the Golden Dawn and the Masonic Ordo Templi Orientis (OTO). As an honored member of these organizations, he met with Crowley several times before Crowley's death in December 1947. Soon after, Gardner declared that he had been appointed Grand Master of the OTO, destined to fill Crowley's position as the unquestioned leader of occult movements through the English-speaking world.

In many ways, Gardner appeared well qualified for the position. Born into an upper-class British family in 1884, he spent much of his youth touring the Mediterranean and Middle East regions, and as a young man lived in Ceylon (now Sri Lanka), Borneo, Singapore and Malaya, acquiring an interest in occult practices encountered along the way. He joined various organizations, including an order of the Rosicrucians, and an English group calling itself The Rite of Egyptian Mysteries.

By the 1930s, Gardner was married and living in England, cultivating an interest in nudism that he nurtured the rest of his life. He also began to write, publishing a couple of so-so novels and, in 1954, *Witchcraft Today*, his *magnum opus* and the first modern book on the subject of Wicca. The book's timing is interesting, coming barely three years after Britain repealed laws banning the practice of witchcraft, and its content is revealing. Building on the writings of Margaret Murray, an earlier occultist whose 1933 book *The God of the Witches* identified witchcraft as a pagan religion predating Christianity, Gardner's book introduced the concept of the Great Goddess and the Horned God. It was also the first book to introduce the term Wicca (spelled by Gardner as "Wica") to describe the movement.

The book proved a great success and elevated Gardner, who cultivated a pseudo-Satanic appearance with pointed goatee and upswept hair, to celebrity status. He followed *The God of Witches* with *The Meaning of Witchcraft* in 1959, and soon began claiming that a "Cone of Power" created by resident witches in Britain had saved the country from a Nazi invasion during World War II. When pressed for details, he was more than vague. "That was done which may not be done except in great emergency," he explained. "Mighty forces were used of which I may not speak. Now, to do this means using one's life-force."

Or perhaps not. Gardner himself noted that "witches are consummate leg-pullers; they are taught it as part of their stock-in-trade." He was either pulling legs or creating a fraud when he claimed to hold a Ph.D. from the University of Singapore, acquiring it in 1934 which, an investigation into his past discovered, was several years prior to the university's existence. His claimed doctorate in literature from the University of Toulouse set heads scratching; no one at Toulouse had any knowledge or record of his attendance.

Other red flags appeared. Along with an interest in the occult, Gardner maintained a similarly powerful interest and pursuit of something his followers excused as "fleshly fulfillment," a means perhaps of attaining spiritual development through physical excesses. One of Gardner's guidelines to female adherents of Wicca included performing rituals sky-clad, especially within his sight and, perhaps, more for his carnal enjoyment than for the witches' spiritual communication. He also advocated The Great Rite, which involved Gardener having sexual intercourse on a metal-clad table with the Great Priestess selected from among female members of the coven. When no volunteers were available, Gardner employed the practical solution of hiring a prostitute to play the role.

Gardner died in 1964. Within a few years his movement, which may have been conceived by its founder more as a libertine sex cult than a means of spiritual fulfillment, arrived in North America, where it rode to great heights on rising tides of psychedelia and hippiedom. Later enthusiasts, in the cooler light of a 1970s dawn, transformed Wicca into a staid neo-

Puritanism, expressing its gentle near-narcissistic character in visions of angelic nymphs dancing in diaphanous gowns beneath the moon and along the shores of star-dappled waters.

Wicca remains a secretive tradition by adherents who fear being ridiculed and ostracized by conformist society, making it impossible to accurately judge the number of followers who create magickal circles and join covens. Their actions may satisfy spiritual longing and bring inner peace to many people unable to tap these resources elsewhere. But their claim that Wicca represents a fount of ancient wisdom and mysteries remains doubtful.

ELEVEN

SKULL & BONES
AMERICA'S SECRET ESTABLISHMENT

MOST SECRET SOCIETIES ARE EITHER FRATERNAL ASSOCIATIONS with convoluted rituals or criminal groups whose activities could be curtailed by willful law enforcement.

One, however, exerts day-to-day influence over the lives of virtually everyone on the planet, and it achieves this end not with a tightly structured organization but via an association of privileged young men attending a prestigious university. Its existence is verifiable, its history is linked to Masonic traditions and Illuminati objectives, its practices remain shadowy, and its activities are replete with suspicious behavior. It is Skull & Bones, a hatchery of American leadership whose members have not only achieved power and prominence on a scale far in excess of their numbers, but retain their close bond throughout their careers, creating at least the semblance of a cabal and perhaps something much more than that.

Officially, Skull & Bones resides in a windowless mausoleum-like building on the campus of Yale University. Known as The Tomb, the brownstone structure was built in 1856 and remains the site of the group's meetings each Thursday and Sunday evening. Only fifteen new members annually are selected from the junior class for membership in Skull & Bones, serving during their senior year. This important distinction means the organization's focus is on its members' future activities in the outside world, not on their temporary campus life. Let everyday fraternities engage in juvenile bouts of binge drinking and pranks; Skull & Bones members fix their attention on bigger things, including the exercise of global influence.

Bonesmen—no longer an accurate term, but one still applied to the group's members—display a veneer of enmity towards the outside world, or at least that part that intrudes on the Yale campus. Nonmembers who enquire about its actions and membership are openly referred to as "outsiders" or "vandals." All Skull & Bones members are required to deny any connection with the organization; if the group's name is mentioned in public, they must leave the room or area with no comment. Nevertheless, enough data regarding its members and procedures have been revealed over the 160-plus years of its existence to substantiate all but the most hysterical speculation about its purpose and influence. Despite its serious mode, the organization employs at least a few aspects, especially of its initiation rites, that fans of the movie *Animal House* may find familiar but perhaps more disturbing.

In 1876, long before Skull & Bones was being viewed with increasing alarm by outsiders, a group of Yale students calling themselves The Order of File and Claw broke into The Tomb and gleefully described its interior. Sounding more like a nineteenth-century boy's club than a gathering place for future world leaders, the most evocative description was of an interior room identified as Parlor 323, where

> on the west wall hung, among other pictures, an old engraving representing an open burial vault, in which, on a stone slab, rest four human skulls, grouped about a fool's-cap and bells, an open book, several mathematical instruments, a beggar's scrip, and a royal crown. On the arched wall above the vault are the explanatory words, in Roman letters, "Wer war der Thor, wer Weiser, wer Bettler oder Kaiser?" And below the vault is engraved...the sentence: "Ob Arm, ob Reich, im Tode gleich." ("Who was the fool, who the wise man, beggar or king? Whether rich or poor, all's the same in death.")

A century later, the girlfriend of a Skull & Bones initiate (who was obviously ill-chosen for membership in a secret society) reported that she had been escorted by him on a tour of The Tomb. Her most vivid memory of its interior was the sight of a wall covered with license plates. Every plate bore the number 322, alluding to the death of the famed Greek orator Demosthenes in 322 BC, the mythical year in which Skull & Bones was supposedly founded. All Skull & Bones members, she was informed, were obligated to "confiscate" any license plate on which the figures 322 appeared, returning them to The Tomb where they were displayed on the wall.

Undergraduates in universities less prestigious than Yale have been committing more serious vandalism than license plate theft over the years, so this may be considered a trivial matter. But it is interesting to speculate on the occasions when an inner-city youth, lacking the privilege of social standing as a result of his circumstances of birth, was brought on similar charges of "confiscation" before a judge or prosecuting attorney who happened to be a Yale graduate and a Skull & Bones member. Was the less privileged perpetrator always forgiven his transgression?

The human skulls are another matter.

Reportedly, each class of Skull & Bones was required to "confiscate" the skull of a famous individual, bringing it to The Tomb as proof of that class's mettle. Many skulls remain on display in The Tomb. "Confiscating" license plates bearing the mystical 322 symbol involves little more than stealth and a screwdriver, but stealing a skull entails nothing less than graverobbing, apparently a long tradition of Skull & Bones members, many of whom seek to take their place in the seats of American power.

Howard Altman, an award-winning U.S. writer and editor, reported that in 1989 a man

The "322" beneath the symbols inspired the "liberation" of automobile license plates.

For over 150 years, strange goings-on have occurred in the depths of The Tomb on the Yale campus.

named Phillip Romero visited him, claiming to be the great-great-grandson of the celebrated Apache warrior and chief Geronimo. According to Romero, his ancestor's bones were among those on display in the Skull & Bones collection. It had been removed from the warrior's grave, Romero charged, in 1918 by Prescott S. Bush, father of the forty-first U.S. president and grandfather of the forty-third.

When Altman explained that he needed verification of the claim before publicizing it, Romero put Altman in contact with a man named Ned Anderson, who resided on an Apache reservation in San Carlos, Arizona. According to Anderson, a few years earlier a public debate between him and another family regarding the relocation of Geronimo's bones from Fort Sill, Oklahoma, to Arizona attracted the attention of a Bonesman who wanted to be identified only as Pat. The bones, Pat declared, had not been in Oklahoma for seventy years, but had been used in rituals conducted by the mysterious Yale society known as Skull & Bones.

The story rang true: Prescott Bush had been stationed at Fort Sill in 1918, when the theft of Geronimo's skull was alleged to have taken place. Adding to the story's veracity is the reported existence of a privately printed document authored by F.O. Matthiessen, a Skull & Bones member, describing the expedition and the recovery of Geronimo's skull from the grave. A sample of the document has been placed in a library at Harvard where, under an agreement between both Skull & Bones and the executors of Matthiessen's estate, it remains unavailable to public view.

Anderson had recruited his senator, John McCain, to pursue the matter in 1986 with George H.W. Bush, who was then

U.S. vice-president. McCain reportedly arranged a meeting between Anderson and a number of Skull & Bones representatives including Jonathon Bush, the vice-president's brother. According to Anderson, the Skull & Bones members presented him with a skull they claimed to be his ancestor's, offering it in exchange for a document preventing him and representatives of Skull & Bones from discussing the incident. Anderson refused, objecting to the gag order and not believing that the skull being offered was actually Geronimo's. Like most states, Connecticut bans ownership of human remains except for specialized legal or professional purposes, a charge that, like "confiscating" license plates, Skull & Bones believes is not applicable to them.

The controversy over Geronimo's skull launched a number of charges regarding the Skull & Bones collection, including one that The Tomb housed the skull of legendary Mexican revolutionary Pancho Villa, and that a child's skull was among those on display. Hard evidence is lacking, not surprisingly considering both the charges and the nature of Skull & Bones. Compared with other activities of the group and its secretive members, however, confiscated license plates and purloined skulls are petty concerns relative to espionage, drug smuggling, war profiteering and interference in the internal affairs of sovereign nations, all involving Bonesmen. On these subjects, proof galore exists.

The origins of Skull & Bones are well documented and not flattering. In 1832 William Huntington Russell, whose family operated a firm called Russell & Company, returned from an extended visit in Germany to begin his senior year at Yale. At the time, Germany was in the grip of Hegelian philosophy, which sprang from the mind of Georg Wilhelm Friedrich Hegel, who died while a professor at the University of Berlin the year before Russell arrived for his visit.

Hegel promoted the concept of Absolute Reason, claiming that the state "has supreme right against the individual, whose supreme duty is to be a member of the state." Building on writings from earlier members of the German idealistic philosophy school, such as Immanuel Kant, Hegel's concepts were enormously influential and served as the theoretical underpinnings of both communism and fascism. Russell returned to Yale overflowing with admiration for Germanic society and Hegelian assumptions. Soon after arriving in New Haven, he partnered with fellow student Alphonso Taft to form "The Order of Scull and Bones," which later became the Order of Skull & Bones.

Something about the atmosphere at Yale during those years encouraged the founding of secret societies among its bright and privileged undergraduates. By the mid-1800s at least seven groups dedicated to surreptitious rituals and identities were flitting around the campus in the dead of night, their members sharing secret signals and names to identify themselves as members of Scroll & Key, Book & Snake, File & Claw, Wolf's Head or some other organization delighting in the exclusivity of its name and rituals. The most exclusive, most secretive and most ritualistic was Skull & Bones.

The original Germanic connection of Skull & Bones has produced speculation about a direct connection between Skull & Bones and the Illuminati. Those who subscribe to this notion point to Illuminati founder Adam Weishaupt's words: "By the simplest means, we shall set all in motion and in flames. The occupations must be so allotted and contrived that we may, in secret, influence all political transactions." Little else connects the two, but the family of founder Russell was involved in activities far more destructive than anything the fabled (and likely fictional) Illuminati had been proven to pursue.

When Russell cofounded Skull & Bones, his family and their company were acquiring massive wealth as a direct result of supplying the Chinese people with opium purchased in India and Turkey. Chinese authorities tried desperately to ban the narcotic, which was draining the country not only of hard currency but of productivity as well. Nothing proved effective; China, in the nineteenth century, was seen by Western countries as a market and a people subject to unfettered exploitation.

The Russell firm became the third largest opium trader in the world, behind Scottish merchants Jardine-Matheson and the British company Dent, and for a time it remained the only opium importer in Canton. The hypocrisy of the British and U.S. governments in this matter remains breathtaking to this day, since both countries had banned the import and use of opium by its own citizens, yet they insisted on the right to ship hundreds of tons of the narcotic into China each year.

Continued efforts by Chinese authorities to ban opium, and resistance to these laws by the importing countries, led to the First Opium War in 1840. The two-year conflict saw China beaten by the technical superiority of the British armed forces. Under the 1842 Treaty of Nanking, Britain humiliated China by negotiating favored rights of opium importation to that country; France and the U.S. added their signatures to the treaty two years later. Russell profited directly from this formalization of opium rights. While the fortunes of Skull & Bones members may have been acquired from myriad sources over its 175-year history, the group's financial roots are deeply embedded within one of the most scandalous and inhuman episodes of mercantile history.

The chief of operations for the Russell company's Canton office was Warren Delano Jr., grandfather of future U.S. president Franklin D. Roosevelt. Delano's position marked the first of a lengthy list of influential families associated with the company and Skull & Bones, which has acted as an incubator for men who sought and seized power out of all proportion to their actual numbers. Skull & Bones founder Russell became a general of the U.S. Army and a state legislator, while his cohort Taft rose through government and ambassadorial ranks to become secretary of war—a post held by many Skull & Bones members—and fathered William Howard Taft, the only man in history to serve as both president and chief justice of the Supreme Court.

The list of Skull & Bones members sounds like a culling of the most prominent males in the U.S. edition of *Who's*

Who: Whitney, Bundy, Harriman, Weyerhaeuser, Pinchot, Rockefeller, Goodyear, Sloane, Stimson, Pillsbury, Kellogg, Vanderbilt, Lovett and, of course, Bush, a list made even more impressive when it is remembered that only fifteen individuals were selected for membership each year.

The selection process for Skull & Bones initiates is suitably dramatic. On a chosen night in April, Skull & Bones seniors arrive outside the rooms of each of the selected juniors, one by one, and pound loudly on the door. When the junior opens the door, a Bonesman slams the candidate on the shoulder and bellows, "Skull and Bones—do you accept?"

If the candidate accepts the invitation, a note wrapped in black ribbon and sealed with black wax is handed over. Inside, along with the Skull & Bones mystical number 322, the message instructs the candidate to appear at The Tomb on initiation night and not to wear any metal.

Through most of its history, the initiation rites for Bonesmen remained among the best-kept secrets of the group, although bit by bit certain activities have come to light. The most enduring ritual, up to recent years at least, obligated the initiate to relate the story of his life in two installments. The first episode, delivered on a Thursday night, covered general aspects of the new member's life, a tale as bland or as entertaining as he chose. The second episode, conducted the following Sunday evening, required him to lie naked in a coffin while recounting details of his sexual history from prep school masturbation to his latest Saturday night conquest, which may have occurred less than twenty-four hours earlier.

With the arrival of coeds on Yale's campus in the late 1960s, the sexual accounts provided substantial titillation for other Bonesmen in attendance, and angry embarrassment for the women whose privacy was invaded in the presence of fourteen male students with greater allegiance to Skull & Bones than to their lovers. One woman confessed an intensely personal experience to her partner, who swore that he would never reveal it to another person. On his return from the Sunday night sex session, she knew instantly by the way he avoided her eyes that he had divulged her darkest secret to his Skull & Bones buddies.

Variations on the ritual seem to have come and gone. During the years between the two world wars, initiates such as future Washington heavyweight W. Averell Harriman and *Time* founder Henry Luce reportedly underwent the sex-tales-in-a-coffin rite of passage. In the late 1930s, when future U.S. Supreme Court Justice Potter Stewart was a Bonesman, seniors dressed in skeleton suits and howled at new candidates, whose initiation into the group required them to wrestle each other naked in a pit of mud.

The reward for Bonesmen may have been worth the humiliation. Acceptance by Skull & Bones reportedly brought with it a $15,000 cash gift to a successful candidate and, upon his marriage, a wedding gift of a good-quality grandfather clock.

Reaction to Skull & Bones from nonmembers on campus was negative from the beginning. The response might by categorized as sour grapes by those overlooked for selection, but the criticism was, and always has been, specific to the enormous power enjoyed by this network of privileged men. In October 1873, a periodical called *The Iconoclast* appeared in New Haven for the first time, with much of its premier edition devoted to disparaging Skull & Bones. Among its points were these:

> We speak through a new publication, because the college press is closed to those who dare to openly mention 'Bones'....
>
> Out of every class Skull and Bones takes its men. They have gone out into the world and have become, in many instances, leaders of society. They have obtained control of Yale. Its business is performed by them. Money paid to the college must pass into their hands, and be subject to their will....
>
> Year by year the deadly evil is growing. The society was never as obnoxious to the college as it is today....Never before has it shown such arrogance and self-fancied superiority. It grasps the College Press and endeavors to rule it all. It does not deign to

show its credentials, but clutches at power with the silence of conscious guilt.

...It is Yale College against Skull and Bones. We ask all men, as a
question of right, which should be allowed to live?

At least part of the answer arrived quickly. *The Iconoclast* was
never heard from again.

Even before the appearance of this article, a pattern of questionable alliances and activities by Skull & Bones members had
been established at Yale. In 1856, three Skull & Bones members
traveled, as Russell had, to the University of Berlin for studies
in philosophy. Upon their return one of the young men, Daniel
Gilman, incorporated Skull & Bones as the Russell Trust
Association, appointing himself as treasurer and the group's
founder, William H. Russell, as president.

The Russell connection has tainted Skull & Bones since its
inception. In some instances, such as the Russell family's
involvement in the Chinese opium trade, the connections are
tenuous; no evidence exists that any Skull & Bones members
outside the Russell family were directly engaged in that activity.
But as time passed the relationship continued, with suspicions
fueled by unusual coincidences and, from time to time, confirmed with hard facts.

Perhaps one of the most startling revelations in recent years
has been an alleged association between the German Nazi party
and Skull & Bones members led by Prescott S. Bush, father and
grandfather of two U.S. presidents.

Prescott Sheldon Bush, Yale '17, was ideal Skull & Bones
material, active in all the right places on campus including the
Glee Club, the cheerleading squad, the University Quartet, the
varsity baseball team and the famous Yale Wiffenpoofs. After
graduation, Bush shrewdly married the daughter of George
Herbert Walker, one of the wealthiest men in the U.S., and one of
the least admired for anything beyond his penchant for squeezing
as much money as possible out of partners and friends. Walker's
earlier career as a heavyweight prizefighter established his person-

ality; according to his contemporaries, Walker's hobbies were golf, hunting, drinking Scotch and beating his sons to a pulp.

Among Walker's business associates was Averell Harriman, a Bonesman from the class of 1913, who founded W. A. Harriman & Co. in 1920, naming Walker president of the firm. Two years later, Harriman traveled to Germany, a country that appears to have held special interest for early Skull & Bones members, and established a branch in Berlin. On the same trip, he established a close acquaintance with August Thyssen, patriarch of the family that dominated Germany's iron and steel industry. In the years between the two world wars, the value of Thyssen's industrial empire was estimated at $100 million, a figure that would be perhaps fifty times higher in today's currency.

August's son Fritz stood to inherit the family wealth. Concerned about the socialist waves that swept his country following Germany's surrender in 1918 and the hyperinflation that followed it, Fritz Thyssen began searching for two saviors: an effective political leader for Germany, and an offshore bank that would serve as an economic anchor in future perilous times. He found them in Adolf Hitler and George Herbert Walker.

Hitler mesmerized Thyssen as, in fact, he mesmerized virtually an entire country desperately in need of strong, decisive leadership. At their first meeting in late 1923, Hitler informed Thyssen that the Nazi Party urgently needed money to grow into a national party, defend itself against attacks from the Communist/Jewish conspiracy, and realize its dream of a fascist state capable of returning the country to its glory. Almost without being asked, Thyssen pulled out his checkbook and handed Hitler 100,000 German marks and a promise to persuade other industrialists to follow his lead. They did, overflowing the Nazi coffers and providing the nascent party with enough funds to survive the aftermath of Hitler's Beer Hall Putsch.

Fritz Thyssen. As part-time banker to the Nazis, he maintained a curious relationship with many Bonesmen.

Meanwhile, Fritz Thyssen's younger brother, who had married a Hungarian aristocrat and acquired the title Baron Thyssen Bornemisza de Kaszon, moved to Rotterdam, where he took over the reins of the Netherlands-based Bank voor Handel en Scheepvaart. In 1924, while Fritz remained in his early rapture over Hitler's charisma and plans, Harriman's bank, with Prescott S. Bush at the helm, joined forces with the Thyssen family's Dutch bank to form Union Banking Corporation (UBC), whose corporate offices were at 39 Broadway in New York City, the same address as Harriman's bank. Through UBC, over $50 million in German bonds were sold to U.S. citizens, financing the rise of Germany's industrial muscle in a close parallel to the growing strength of Hitler and the Nazis.

With this success, Walker provided his son-in-law with a hand up the corporate ladder by naming Bush a vice-president of Harriman & Co. Once settled in the executive suite, Bush added two old friends from Yale to his team, Bonesmen Roland Harriman and Knight Wooley. Bush worked hard, as did everybody under Walker's thumb. He may have worked harder than others, however, because his next career boost involved supervision of a new German steel operation named the Thyssen/Flick United Steel Works, which included the Consolidated Silesian Steel Corporation and the Upper Silesian Coal and Steel Company, both located in Poland.

While Prescott S. Bush was running one of Germany's leading steel producers, Hitler encountered new financial troubles and once again turned to his old friend Fritz Thyssen for money. This time, Thyssen handed over between 250,000 and 800,000 German marks—he claimed the lower figure, others estimated the higher amount—which Hitler used, among other things, to convert a Munich palace into elaborate new headquarters for the Nazi Party.

The Great Depression in the early 1930s sent Germany and the rest of the world on a slide towards disaster. Through a series of political manipulations and the application of brute force, by 1934 Hitler completely controlled Germany, promising to build an intricate system of high-speed highways and launch "a rebirth of the German army." For the latter, he turned to Thyssen's steel mills, whose profits soared in the following years, overflowing into the coffers of the Bank voor Handel en Scheepvaart in Rotterdam and the Union Banking Corporation in New York.

Walker and his son-in-law, through their direction of the Harriman financial organization, seem to have tolerated, if not favored, antidemocratic regimes. In 1927, they were dealing both with Italy's fascist leader Benito Mussolini and Russia's Communist party while Stalin held his country in an iron grip. The bank's Russian connection inspired Lord Bearsted of Britain to recommend that Union Banking cease its dealings with Stalin, prompting Walker to retort: "It seems to me that the suggestion in connection with Lord Bearsted's views that we withdraw from Russia smacks somewhat of the impertinent.... I think we have drawn our line and should hew to it." Business was, after all, business.

Four years later, Harriman and Co. merged with Brown Brothers, a British-American investment firm, creating Brown Brothers Harriman, whose New York office was managed by Prescott S. Bush.

Through the 1930s, Bush's involvement with Nazi Germany's finances expanded beyond Union Banking into shipping via the Hamburg Amerika Line, managed out of Bush's office through a wholly owned firm called the American Ship and Commerce Corporation. In September 1933, Bush helped orchestrate the merger of Hamburg Amerika, or Hapag, with the North German Lloyd Company to create Hapag Lloyd. Meanwhile, another spin-off from the same parent firm was set up to coordinate all trade between the U.S. and Nazi Germany, and Bush arranged refinancing for the German-Atlantic Cable Company, providing the only direct communications linkage between Germany and the U.S. The legal details of this latter arrangement were finalized by a Wall Street lawyer named John

Foster Dulles, who would later become a hard-line secretary of state under President Eisenhower.

Union Banking Corporation grew into the leading financial connection between Nazi Germany and the rest of the world, and by the mid-1930s the relationship was bonded at the highest levels. Consider the identity of its eight members of the board of directors:

E. Roland Harriman
    Skull & Bones, '17   Vice President, W. A. Harriman &
                              Co., New York
H. J. Kouwenhoven   Member of Nazi Party; Managing
                              Partner, Bank voor Handel
                              Scheepvaart N.V. (transfer bank
                              between August Thyssen Bank
                              and UBC)

Knight Wooley
    Skull & Bones, '17   Director, Guaranty Trust, New York
                              (a subsidiary of W. A. Harriman & Co.)
Cornelius Lievense   President, UBC; Director, Holland-
                              American Investment Corp.

Ellery S. James
    Skull & Bones, '17   Partner, Brown
                              Brothers & Co., New York.
Johann Groninger   Member of Nazi Party; Director,
                              Bank voor Handel Scheepvaart N.V.,
                              and Vereinigte Stahlwerke (steel plant
                              owned by Fritz Thyssen)
J. L. Guinter   Director, UBC

Prescott S. Bush
    Skull & Bones, '17   Partner, Brown Brothers Harriman,
                              New York

Of these eight powerful men, six either belonged to Skull & Bones or were members of the German Nazi Party. And although the parent firm of Brown Brothers Harriman employed several Yale graduates in positions of authority and responsibility, only Skull & Bones members sat on the UBC board.

Networking, especially among university alumni, is neither new nor, on its own, worthy of concern. The existence of several members of the same university fraternal organization on the board of a company dealing with an international power of such murderous reputation as the Nazis could be a mere coincidence. Alarmists raise another possibility: the networking was agenda-based, connecting successive generations of very wealthy and highly privileged families whose career-oriented sons belonged to a society pledged to exceptional levels of secrecy and focused on financial and political manipulation on a global scale. This would apply if the organization itself were consciously oriented towards these activities or if its interests reflected the agenda of the families who dominated it, especially in the critical years between 1920 and 1980.

The latter possibility—the idea that an organization could maintain its focus across several generations—raises the specter of a conspiracy among Skull & Bones members to effect its secretive goals. This likelihood is dismissed by skeptics who note that, among the hundreds of surviving Skull & Bones members, many have revealed insights into its operations but none has hinted at such a broadly based conspiracy. Yet, as events such as the collapse of WorldCom, and the exposed relationship between Enron executives and its auditors Arthur Andersen revealed, it takes only a few well-placed individuals to orchestrate an activity that involves an entire organization and benefits a selected few.

Besides, it's not only the administration by Skull & Bones members of UBC and other organizations that's of interest and concern; it's also evidence of sly manipulation of the media and government, such as coverage of the demise of Union Banking, Hitler's Wall Street financier.

The year 2003 saw the publication of *Duty, Honor, Country*, a glowing tribute to Prescott S. Bush by Mickey Herskowitz, a Houston, Texas, sportswriter. Author Herskowitz had produced

previous books on celebrities such as cowboy film star Gene
Autry, TV commentator Howard Cossell and baseball hero
Mickey Mantle, men he admired with a level of adulation
matching his apparent reverence for Prescott Bush.

In glowing prose, *Duty, Honor, Country* traces the career of
this father of one U.S. president and grandfather of a state governor and another president as he blazes the political trail for
his offspring, winning a seat in the U.S. Senate in 1952 and acting as a political confidant for Richard M. Nixon.

Throughout the tale, the book is an uncritical paean to the
Bush family patriarch, one that any Beverly Hills public rela-
tions firm would take pride in producing on behalf of a client.
In one mild effort to present an objective portrait of his subject,
Herskowitz refers to a front-page story that appeared in the
New York *Herald-Tribune* during World War II, revealing close
connections between Union Banking and Nazi Germany.
"Thyssen Has $3,000,000 Cash in New York Vaults," the head-
line announced, followed by the sub-head: "Union Banking
Corporation May Hide Nest Egg for High Nazis He Once
Backed." The article, written by *Herald-Tribune* reporter M. J.
Racusin, provided details of UBC's connection with Thyssen
along with the speculation: "Perhaps it wasn't Herr Thyssen's
money at all, some persons suggest. Maybe he sent it here for
safekeeping for some of the Nazi bigwigs—perhaps for
Goering, for Goebbels, for Himmler, or even Hitler himself."

Whoever had a right to claim the money—no evidence surfaced to suggest that it was anyone but Thyssen—the revelation
was an embarrassment for everyone, especially Prescott Bush
who already had expressed his political ambitions.

According to Herskowitz, UBC president Prescott Bush took
immediate action when the story broke. "[He] acted quickly and
openly on behalf of the firm, served well by a reputation that
had never been compromised. He made available all records
and all documents. Viewed six decades later in the era of serial
corporate scandals and shattered careers, he received what can
be viewed as the ultimate clean bill."

Then the fawning Herskowitz notes:

"Earlier that year [Bush] had accepted the chairmanship of the USO (United Service Organizations). He traveled the country over the next two years raising millions for the National War Fund and...putting himself on the national stage for the first time...[and] boosting the morale of U.S. troops."

The records show that Bush indeed jumped aboard the USO bandwagon in the spring of 1942. Unfortunately, Herskowitz makes a critical error of timing in his subject's favor. The *Herald-Tribune* article, he states, appeared in the summer of 1942, suggesting that Prescott Bush had already assumed an anti-Nazi stance with his participation in the USO several months earlier. How could anyone question the patriotism of a Wall Street financial heavyweight who takes an active role in supporting U.S. troops (the U.S. joined the war effort against Germany in December 1941) well in advance of a revelation that might have put his ethics in doubt?

But the *Herald-Tribune* revelation did *not* appear in the summer of 1942, as Herskowitz stated. It appeared on Thursday, July 31, 1941, a fact that Herskowitz could not have missed, since he quoted directly from the article itself. In that context, Bush made his patriotic move to the USO *after* the appearance of the story connecting him and his bank with a Nazi regime that was well advanced in its murder of millions of innocent civilians and Allied soldiers. No longer an obvious altruistic enlistment, Bush's move now appears more like frantic fence mending, and Herskowitz's story looks like a conscious whitewash.

Bush and his UBC cronies managed to sweep other dusty smudges under the rug wherever possible, as indicated by this innocuous one-line announcement that appeared in the financial pages of the December 16, 1944, issue of the *New York Times*:

The Union Banking Corporation, 39 Broadway, New York, has received authority to change its principal place of business to 120 Broadway.

The announcement conveniently ignored the fact that UBC had been taken over by the U.S. federal government under the Trading with the Enemy Act more than two years earlier, and that 120 Broadway was actually the address of the Office of the Alien Property Custodian. By this time, of course, Prescott Bush and his other Skull & Bones cronies had moved on, parading on behalf of Victory Bonds in their starched shirts and wrapped in Old Glory, ready to assume the next stage in their shining careers which, in Bush's case, included election to the U.S. Senate.

It's this apparent financial/political linkage among Skull & Bones members that alarms many people. With so much smoke swirling among both the organization and the U.S. federal service, they contend, there has to be some fire. Predictably, and most disturbingly, the secret Skull & Bones society has made its biggest impact on that most influential of all government-administered secret societies, the U.S. Central Intelligence Agency.

Consider this partial list of Bonesmen associated with the U.S. intelligence community via the Office of Strategic Services (OSS) and the CIA during their careers:

Hugh Wilson	'09
Robert D. French	'10
Archibald MacLeish	'15
Charles R. Walker	'16
F. Trubee Davison	'18
Amory Howe Bradford	'34
Hugh Cunningham	'34
Richard A. Moore	'36
William P. Bundy	'39
McGeorge Bundy	'40
Reuben Holden	'40
Richard Drain	'43
James Buckley	'44
George H.W. Bush	'48

Sloane Coffin Jr.	'49
V. Van Dine	'49
William Buckley	'50
Dino Pionzio	'50
David Boren	'63

By definition, Bonesmen are bright, ambitious and, based upon their membership in the secret society, eminently qualified to serve in a covert organization like the CIA. On the surface, this makes a good deal of sense. Concerns arise, however, when layers of secrecy concealing many Bonesmen associations and activities are peeled away, revealing suggestions of extracurricular clandestine actions and evidence of remarkable coincidences.

Remember Russell Trust Association, the official corporate name of Skull & Bones? According to records of the state of Connecticut, where the organization was registered, Russell Trust Association no longer exists. But of course it does, since Skull & Bones remains more active and, apparently, more solvent than ever. The parent organization of Skull & Bones is now known as RTA Incorporated, a name it surreptitiously assumed at 10:15 AM, April 14, 1961.

It's an interesting date and time, because less than two hours later the CIA launched its self-financed and self-directed invasion of Cuba, resulting in the disastrous Bay of Pigs debacle. The CIA's mastermind of this folly was Richard Drain, a Bonesman of '43. The White House liaison was McGeorge Bundy, Skull & Bones '40, working closely with his brother William P. Bundy, Skull & Bones '39, at the State Department. Together, these three cooked up one of the great foreign misadventures in U.S. history, boosting Cuba's prestige in the Third World, highlighting Fidel Castro's claims of U.S. imperialism, and leading directly to the Cuban missile crisis, the closest the world has yet come to nuclear war.

The timing of the change in corporate identity and the Bay of Pigs invasion could be dismissed as coincidence, but with the perspective of history and our knowledge of CIA operations over the years, there may be a more practical explanation.

While no one has revealed the source of funding that enabled 1500 Cuban Americans to launch the invasion, suspicion remains that it was the U.S. government, via a CIA operations group. Without a defined conduit, however, a financial linkage cannot be verified. And without an existing Russell Trust Association, any record of a potential involvement of the Skull & Bones parent organization as covert manager of the funds was neatly erased on the morning of the invasion. One fact remains, however: the individual who handled the paperwork on the name changeover and the incorporation of RTA was Howard Weaver, a '45 Bonesman who had conveniently retired from covert work at the CIA less than two years earlier.

Coincidences grow curioser and curioser. George H.W. Bush may or may not have been working on behalf of the CIA in the years between 1958 and 1966, encompassing the timing of Bay of Pigs. His official record identifies him only as chairman of the board and president of Zapata Offshore Oil, a company headquartered in Houston, Texas. Without some experience in espionage, however, Bush's selection as CIA director in 1974 seems strange to say the least, and more than one reliable source has claimed the Zapata company was a cover for CIA operations.

In any case, Zapata happens to be the CIA's code name for the Bay of Pigs invasion and, for an extra measure of conspiracy spice, two of the support vessels for the operation were identified as the *Houston* and the *Barbara*. The latter designation is intriguing because, during his World War II escapades

Three generations of the Bush family—one senator and two presidents—all proudly declared their association with Skull & Bones.

as a pilot, Bush named every aircraft for his wife, the indomitable Barbara Bush.

Another coincidence involves the same former president George H.W. Bush and the assassination of President Kennedy on November 22, 1963. One week after that calamitous event, an official FBI document noted that information on possible Cuban exile involvement in the president's death had been received "orally furnished to Mr. George Bush of the Central Intelligence Agency and Captain William Edwards of the Defense Intelligence Agency on November 23, 1963, by Mr. W.T. Forsyth of this Bureau."

When a reprint of this document appeared in the July 1988 issue of *The Nation*, on the cusp of Bush's run for the U.S. presidency, the CIA quickly issued a statement claiming that "Mr. George Bush" was not really the current candidate for the highest office in the land but a different man with a similar name: George William Bush. This appeared to deflect suspicion about the presidential candidate's hidden career as a spook, but only until George William Bush emerged from obscurity to admit that yes, he had once been employed by the CIA among other government offices, but only as a low-level research and analyst clerk. He also blew the CIA's claim out of the water with an affidavit swearing,

> I have carefully reviewed the FBI memorandum to the Director, Bureau of Intelligence and Research, Department of State dated November 29, 1963 which mentions a Mr. George Bush of the Central Intelligence Agency....I do not recognize the contents of the memorandum as information furnished to me orally or otherwise during the time I was at the CIA. In fact, during my time at the CIA, I did not receive any oral communications from any government agency of any nature whatsoever. I did not receive any information relating to the Kennedy assassination during my time at the CIA from the FBI. Based on the above, it is my conclusion that I am not the Mr. George Bush of the Central Intelligence Agency referred to in the memorandum.

Which leaves the logical conclusion that George H.W. Bush was a CIA operative at a time when he claimed not to be. No surprise there, given the CIA's understandable reluctance to admit anything it doesn't have to. But Bush also had, at the time, an alliance with Cuban exiles who were furious with Kennedy's disassociation with the Bay of Pigs failure, encouraging some observers to make a linkage between Bush and two catastrophic events in U.S. history: the 1961 Bay of Pigs invasion, and the 1963 assassination of John F. Kennedy. The media chose to discount both connections, leading conspiracy buffs into a round of speculation that has endured for years.

From time to time, Skull & Bones lashes out at those who dare probe too deeply into its operations, as it apparently did when Netherlands TV producer Daniel de Wit completed a documentary on the group. De Wit's premise connected Skull & Bones with the CIA in drug-smuggling activities as a means of financing unapproved covert operations, a tactic confirmed during the Iran-Contra hearings of 1988. Before his production could air, de Wit was ordered by the Netherlands government to remove all reference to the CIA and drugs, and soften its criticisms of Skull & Bones. The deletions reduced the program's running time from its original 80 minutes to barely 30 minutes. Completed in 1998, the show was aired once in the U.S. on a Friday at 5 PM when, as de Wit notes, "every possible viewer is in traffic going home." It was never repeated.

In August 2003, de Wit recalled his experience with the CIA and Skull & Bones, noting, "These...institutions and their members show a brute force and an enormous concentrated power that is overwhelming and could make everyone very cynical very easily. That also must be a reason people like to stay away from these realities."

Skull & Bones is no more immune to the passage of time and its changes than anything or anyone else, and whatever influence and impact it had beyond the Yale campus may be waning. The 2004 U.S. presidential election, after all, featured Bonesmen

George W. Bush, '68, against John Kerry. Depending upon your point of view, this proves either that Skull & Bones members dominate the U.S. political arena to an extent no one imagined, or that the vaunted conspiracy did not exist, because why would two conspirators face each other across an ideological divide?

Whatever the answer, the innermost secrets of Skull & Bones have been leaking through the stone walls of The Tomb for several years now, even as the reality of the outside world has been seeping into it. Surely the most important change occurred in 1992 when, after a bitter rear guard battle by old Bonesmen (one, a prestigious Washington-area lawyer, suggested a coed membership "would lead to date-rape"), the organization actually agreed to admit women. By 2000, six of the fifteen Skull & Bones members that year were female.

The changes wrought by the last forty years of social upheaval—Skull & Bones now taps Jews and blacks as potential members, something it avoided during the first 150 years of its existence—make it doubtful that many of the old initiation rites, such as relating one's sexual history while stretched out naked in a coffin, are still practiced. With an estimated $4 million in assets in 2000, however, Skull & Bones could still afford to pay the $15,000 stipend and award a grandfather clock at marriage.

The spectacle of both U.S. presidential candidates being Skull & Bones members may represent the dying echo of the society's excessive influence on the country's political and judicial systems. In a day of hand-held instant messaging, global economics and tech-based fortunes, the networking arrangement that boosted the U.S. privileged class even higher in the pecking order is not nearly as influential or even necessary. The male WASP contingent of American society is no longer as exclusive as a generation ago, and secret societies on campus are considered at best anachronisms, a throwback to days of panty raids and silly rich boys in raccoon coats. Skull & Bones appears to be stumbling towards extinction; in recent years, more Yale juniors have declined the invitation to become a member than have accepted it.

Yet its influence during the past century deserves consideration. Too many of its "best and brightest" were involved in too many economic and foreign policy disasters, from Bay of Pigs through the Kennedy assassination to Vietnam and Iraq, to assess it as an exclusively campus crowd, a bunch of advantaged young men playing silly games in a dark, tomb-like room. There is more to be told. But by whom?

TWELVE

SECRET SOCIETIES IN POPULAR CULTURE
AN ENDLESS FASCINATION

THE MORE CERTAINTY WE HAVE IN OUR LIVES, THE MORE WE are intrigued by mysteries. Their entertainment value is obvious, but we may also need threats to our security in order to fully appreciate it. In the process, we speculate about things we cannot explain, and often become fixed on threats and events well removed from our day-to-day lives. It's more comforting that way, which perhaps explains why the greatest concentration of secret society concerns rests in urban Europe and affluent North America, whose residents have the most to lose materially and spiritually.

For those of us detached from direct association with shadow people, it is the secrecy that is most worrisome, and the potential impact on our lives that is most threatening, an attitude that varies according to proximity. To citizens of Calabria and Sicily, the Mafia is a reality that need not be speculated about, because its presence and influence are evident. Similar attitudes may be found among residents of Hong Kong and Macau, who experience Triad activities first hand, and Japanese businessmen encountering crimes committed by Yakuza. To both groups, the "secret" in secret societies is something of a contradiction when their direct impact is confronted daily.

At the other end of the spectrum, Yak farmers in Mongolia, refugees in Somalia and Inuit on Baffin Island grapple daily with a range of challenges to their survival that middle-class Americans and Europeans cannot grasp. Plotting their very existence occupies too much of their consciousness to speculate about the impact of millennia-old and foreign-based conspiracies, even as entertainment.

To the rest of us, "secret" denotes mystery, and mysteries demand solutions. Where solutions are unavailable, speculation will do. And when speculation is unleashed from reason and motivated by innuendo, we begin to sense that we are surrounded by conspiracies, believing in their existence even when faced with evidence to the contrary.

The more comfortable and predictable our lives become, the more positively we react to the notion of widespread conspiracies because their existence provides a resolution to various unsolved mysteries. Conspiracies supply blame for terrible events that remain beyond our ability to fathom them. No better example exists than the assassination of John F. Kennedy. Those who cannot accept that Lee Harvey Oswald, acting alone, could gun down one of the most admired men of his time look for evidence to support their disbelief. In this incidence there may be much yet to be found, as we saw with the examination of Skull & Bones. On a grander scale, we may ascribe the failure of our economic dreams to an unfathomable and shadowy cartel, the defeat of a favored politician to an international cabal, and unexplained climatic events to supernatural forces controlled by covens.

The growing appeal of secret explanations for catastrophic events has paralleled the impact of contemporary popular culture, with each element feeding the other. Popular novels and movies once dealt with people engaged in direct association with each other; their motivations varied between love and war, often involving both, but they were for the most part open, not shadowy, occurrences. Today's popular culture vehicles find more inspiration not in events we can fathom but in secrets that defy our explanation, held by organizations operating within shadows.

Consider the mystery novel. Most observers trace its origins back to Edgar Allan Poe's 1843 tale *The Gold Bug*. Poe's literary descendant Dashiell Hammett created the prototypical private eye to solve crimes committed by individuals whose closest association with an international conspiracy was usually "The Syndicate," code for the Mafia. Others, such as Arthur Conan Doyle, John Buchan, Sax Rohmer (creator of Fu Manchu) and Sapper (pen name for Herman Cyril McNeile, author of the Bulldog Drummond series), pursued criminals who functioned on a one-to-one scale with their victims while committing robbery, murder and similar unsavory and intriguing activities.

Secret societies rarely appeared in popular literature until relatively recently. Readers of Ayn Rand suggest that her novel *Atlas Shrugged* deals with values associated with the Illuminati, which may explain the basis for the book's popularity. Communists were a familiar target in American novels of the 1950s, but in this case familiarity appears to have bred boredom; communists were an everyday element in news broadcasts, which made them feckless villains in fiction for the most part.

It took Ian Fleming, and progeny such as Robert Ludlum and John Grisham, to address readers' fears of shadowy conspirators exerting widespread power over the lives of ordinary people. A variation on this plot device blasted the Harry Potter series into the records as history's most successful publishing phenomenon in children's books and literature generally. At least three secret societies, such as the Order of the Phoenix, are involved in the Potter plots, each threatening not only the hero and his cohorts but the security of the world itself.

Harry Potter is fun, of course, even when he's scooting over the moors pursued by shadowy villains. This is unusual. In spite of near-farcical aspects of organizations such as the Rosicrucians, likely born of a college-student prank, and the unfortunate death of a Freemason initiate, secret societies are rarely subject to parody in popular culture. On television, Jackie Gleason's early 1950s comedy *The Honeymooners* frequently included the International Order of Friendly Sons of the Raccoons, whose lodge members acted suspiciously like Masons and Shriners, engaging in code words and flapping the tails on their coonskin caps to each other. More recently, and more acerbically, the television series *The Simpsons* has included the Stonecutters in several of its plots. Clearly based on Freemasonry, the Stonecutters meet weekly in a pyramid-shaped building where they honor their Sacred Parchment before drinking heavily and playing Ping-Pong. For proof of their power, the Stonecutters claim to control the British monarchy and prevent the metric system from being used in the USA. It is an accurate, devastating and hilarious parody of the lighter side of secret societies.

In a semi-serious vein, film adaptations of Ian Fleming's James Bond series were among the first to spark Hollywood's interest in international conspiracies, partially because Fleming managed to tap the public's fascination with evil secret societies. Bond's nemesis SPECTRE (Special Executive for Counter-intelligence, Terrorism, Revenge and Extortion) elevated the idea of foreign-accented men with sociopathic qualities and unlimited sources of wealth to an over-the-top level that was consistently entertaining but never within the realm of reality. Similarly, later films based on books by Robert Ludlum, Len Deighton and others usually based their conspiracies and conflicts on clashes between the American CIA, the British MI6 and the Russian KGB, with periodic excursions into the realms of Nazi revivals and the Israeli Mossad.

It took Frances Ford Coppola's *Godfather* trilogy to depict Cosa Nostra with shocking realism, and *Raiders of the Lost Ark*, the first of Steven Spielberg's *Indiana Jones* series, to explore contemporary antics of ancient secret societies with a healthy injection of clichéd Nazi villains.

Perhaps because its current existence is, for the most part, unconfirmable, the Bavarian Illuminati often serves as murky villains in movies and video games. The 2001 film *Lara Croft: Tomb Raider* reversed the traditional order of games spinning off movies when it adapted a best-selling video game into a major film production starring Angelina Jolie and John Voight. The plot, not surprisingly considering its source, suggests a new definition for silliness, pitting Ms. Jolie's character against the

Illuminati's ability to control time as part of that organization's plans for world domination.

Another popular computer game, *Deus Ex*, also features the Illuminati as a secret society controlling the world in company with the Knights Templar. In addition to its political and economic powers, exerted via the World Trade Organization, in *Deus Ex* the Illuminati maintains a hidden store of viruses to be unleashed on groups or entire countries that fail to meet its demands. The Templars are less clearly drawn, representing one of four forces the player may join to achieve the game's objectives. Neither group, as presented here or elsewhere, bears much similarity to the actual namesake organizations.

Through all of these literary, cinematic and computer game productions, readers and viewers found it easy to draw a distinct line between fantasy and reality. Viewers of *The Godfather*, for example, left the movie theater feeling they had acquired an insight into the operations of Cosa Nostra, but few felt any new threat to their lives. Both the film and the book it was based upon ignored the historic heritage behind the organization, choosing to focus on actions of ruthless criminals united by blood and marriage who saw their work as simply a means of doing business. The groups were real, but the threat, while also real, remained distant, and the Mafia's historical roots were never addressed.

Not until Umberto Eco's philosophical satire *Foucault's Pendulum*, in which three Italian editors become caught up in an apparent linkage between historical secret societies extending back to the Crucifixion, did a major novel deal with historical facts. In Eco's rampant and often hilarious tale, organizations such as the Templars, Freemasons, Priory of Sion, Assassins, Rosicrucians, Kabbalah, Druids, Gnostics—the entire pantry of secret societies and their primary characters—pop up both as historical relics and contemporary participants. Part Marx Brothers movie script, part Robert Ludlum thriller and part philosophical treatise, Eco's 1988 narrative satisfied two widely disparate groups: conspiracy buffs who suspect that 8 billion

lives on the planet are controlled by a handful of shadowy plotters, and skeptics who revel in the delight of seeing the
emperor's new wardrobe finally being revealed.

Foucault's Pendulum was clearly inspired by a 1982 book
ostensibly published as non-fiction, but widely assessed as a
work of fantasy loosely based on fact. *The Holy Blood and the Holy
Grail* appeared six years before Eco's opus, and while the latter
was amusing and enlightening to readers who could follow its
meandering plot and respond to its cynical humor, the former
ignited something else among a more gullible public.

The Holy Blood and the Holy Grail was inspired by the experience of a British film producer and former actor named Henry
Soskin, whose previous claim to fame had been performing bit
parts in the 1960s TV series *The Avengers*. Changing his name to
Henry Lincoln, and changing his position from in front of the
camera to behind it, Soskin detected a missing translation of an
encrypted message in an obscure book on Rennes-le-Chateau.
After researching the tale of Father Saunière and his mysterious
wealth, Lincoln produced a documentary film about the supposed
treasure, milking the story of every nuance to heighten the drama.

Some time later, Lincoln encountered a university lecturer
and budding novelist named Richard Leigh, who harbored a
fascination with the Knights Templar. Perhaps the Templars
and the Saunière mystery could be linked together, tracking a
tale extending from Christ's crucifixion down to contemporary
times. Leigh recruited a former photo-journalist named
Michael Baigent, and together this triumvirate invested four
years researching, speculating, postulating and finally writing a
book that spun 100,000 words of conjecture into a theory connecting virtually every secret society extant, in reality or fantasy,
over two thousand years. At the core of the tale were three
unproved (and unconfirmable) assertions:

1. Christ did not die on the cross; an impostor took his place, per-
    mitting Christ to escape across the Mediterranean to the south of
    France.

2. Christ was not single and celibate; he married Mary Magdalene and fathered at least one child, who accompanied the parents on the journey.

3. The descendants of Christ's children have been active in determining the fate of the world for twenty centuries.

As the premise for a historical novel, this is splendid stuff. In the hands of authors as divergent in their periods and styles as Thomas B. Costain or Don de Lillo, it could have been a respectable flight of fancy and an entertaining, even informative, peek at some of history's most interesting events.

The authors and their publisher did not see it this way. They believed that the impact of a non-fictional hypothesis had a better opportunity of generating interest and sales than a historical novel, and they were proven correct when *The Holy Blood and the Holy Grail* appeared on the best-seller list almost from the day of its publication in 1982. It also managed to inspire the only book that has seriously challenged the Harry Potter series for sales volume in recent years: Dan Brown's *The Da Vinci Code*. Until that point, Brown had hardly distinguished himself as a writer destined for greatness. His previous work, *Angels and Demons*, blended the Illuminati and Syrian Ismailis in a laughingly awkward manner, and included the author's erroneous assumption that Muslims in Syria, Iraq, Iran and India all speak and write the same language.

Holy Blood and *Da Vinci* are as closely linked as any literary parent and progeny can be, even to the extent of each mirroring the other: *Holy Blood* is imaginative fiction posing as reality, and *Da Vinci* is pseudo-reality posing as fiction.

Despite his assertions that many of the organizations, characters and events in his book are real, Brown can neatly sidestep criticisms about his novel by pointing at the "fiction" designation. The trio of authors who concocted *Holy Blood* have no such defense except their protests of unfair attacks by skeptical critics, delivered with great passion and conviction in later editions of their book. But complaints of unfair criticism cannot overcome weaknesses that fail to suspend disbelief among perceptive readers.

Throughout their tale, the authors frequently pose the query, "What if?" What if the power of the Templars rose to the same extent as a prominent individual who happened to be their contemporary? Does that point to a relationship? Perhaps, but it hardly proves it. Once their "what if?" premise is established, it is treated from that point forward like a proven assertion on which an entire network of suppositions can be strung. The result is a spider web that supports its builder, but is quickly swept away in the first fresh breeze.

Most serious works of non-fiction base their premise on accessible facts, established by a credible source identified to the reader. The *Holy Blood* authors take a startling new stance. History can only be seriously interpreted, they claim, when the researcher seeks conclusions from among apparently unrelated events, even when the events are, at best, apocryphal. In effect, they are suggesting that documented facts are no more important—and perhaps less so—than colorful myths. If this is truly the case, an enormous volume of new information awaits discovery by imaginative historians who link, for example, the early-1944 consolidation of Nazi power in Europe with that winter's unprecedented levels of snowfall in North America.

The analogy of a spider's web may favor the strength of the web over the ability of *Holy Blood* to sustain close examination, because the authors themselves ask the reader to forgive their frequent sleight of hand. Consider these exit doors for truth, appearing on consecutive pages of the 1996 paperback edition:

> This, of course, was only a speculative hypothesis, with no documentary confirmation. (p. 115)

> The possibility cannot be proved, but neither can it be dismissed out of hand. (p. 116)

On the basis of these connections, we have formulated a tentative hypothesis. (p. 117)

Repeatedly, Lincoln *et al.* seize on colorful speculation that advances their theories while discarding any hard evidence that discredits them. They also proffer, as corroboration for their argument, material that is not only suspect in veracity but often confirmable as fraudulent. Much of their case rests on *Les dossiers secrets de Henri Lobineau*, supposedly containing detailed lineages tracing the Merovingian dynasty from the fifth-century Frankish leader Meroveus through the mysterious Giselle de Razes to the ninth-century Sigisbert VI. These had already been declared a forgery by the man acknowledged as their creator, the prankster and dipsomaniac Philippe de Chérisy, when he filed court documents suing Pierre Plantard to recover payment for producing the fraudulent documents. Plantard, who declared himself a direct descendant of Dagobert and Giselle, and director of the Priory of Sion, never disputed de Chérisy's claim, although he later concocted the story that de Chérisy had merely copied originals in Plantard's possession. Nowhere in *Holy Blood* is de Chérisy's lawsuit against Plantard mentioned, nor anything about de Chérisy's questionable background.

Noel Corbu, who invented much of the fable as a means of building traffic to his hotel and restaurant, is mentioned in *Holy Blood* only as the purchaser of Villa Bethania, a man left frustrated by the death of Marie Denarnaud before she could relate details of her past. Nothing more is said of him or of the tale played to guests at Corbu's restaurant while they dined. Both facts, of course, would trip up the entire thesis presented by the authors, who prefer that nothing obstruct their claim to solving perhaps the greatest mystery of all time.

Holy Blood challenges its readers to prove the existence of a negative reality by asking them to show that a hypothesized event did *not* occur. Proof that something does not exist may work in mathematics, where negatives can be theorized and assessed, but not in history. To demonstrate the vacuity of *Holy*

Blood's premise, imagine a non-fiction work on the existence of Santa Claus, based upon evidence that no one has yet proven he does *not* exist.

This could all be a matter of literary bashing, suitable for bookish nabobs to lob back and forth in *The New York Review of Books* and *The Times Literary Review*, producing little more than bruised egos and fits of jealousy among authors and editors ("Why didn't *I* get the idea for that book!!??"). If this were the sole by-product, none of us would or should give it a thought. There may be more to the picture, however.

While it may be entertaining to trace the tracks of stampeding minds among historical clues, stitching dozens of links together to create an apparent chain of proof, the practice creates risks from certain unstable members of society. The more outrageous of this group reside on the far fringes of the left and right wings of political thought, who are quick to identify every problem in life, on either a personal or global scale, as rooted in a secret cabal of power brokers. On the surface, this should be of little consequence. Paranoia is not new nor, when spread among groups with nothing better to do with their spare time, is it necessarily cause for concern. Unfortunately, the basis for much of this paranoia is often racial, and that's where the game grows serious.

If *Holy Blood* can lend credence to such easily proven frauds as Priory of Sion, it can also convince those who are open to such persuasion that aberrations like *The Protocols of the Elders of Zion* are rooted in reality.

The *Protocols* are mentioned in *Holy Blood* in an unfortunately typical manner. First, the authors disown its veracity ("Experts today concur—and rightly so, we concluded—that the *Protocols*, at least in their present form, are a vicious and insidious forgery."). Later, after agreeing with respectable sources that the *Protocols* are a forgery, they claim this discredited tome is "of paramount importance to the Prieuré de Sion."

How and why are they important? No details are given. Almost 230 pages later, the *Protocols* are mentioned again, but only briefly and for the last time, when a reference to them is used to support the authors' claim that a new king will carry "the holy seed of David." If the *Protocols* are "a vicious and insidious forgery," why rely upon the document for anything at all? The authors are performing a dance here, waltzing around a scurrilous text while remaining close enough to use it for support when it serves their purposes.

Nothing established about the *Protocols* suggest they are anything more than a fable presented as fact to achieve questionable, often nefarious, goals. Here, in brief, is their history:

In 1868 a German novelist named Hermann Goedsche, using the English pen name Sir John Retcliffe, published a novel titled *Biarritz.* The plot centered on a Jewish cabal intent on taking over the world. Goedsche appears to have been inspired by the French writer Maurice Joly, whose *Dialogues in Hell Between Machiavelli and Montesquieu* spun a tale based on opposition to Napoleon III. Goedsche, a notorious anti-Semite, lifted Joly's plot device, introducing Jews to the story line as the villains.

All of this might have slipped out of sight beneath the waves like similar bad writing except for the precarious position of Russian czar Nicholas II near the end of the nineteenth century. In a move designed to strengthen his hand among the Russian people and weaken his political opponents, the czar demanded a device that would expose his enemies as allies in a conspiracy involving world domination. From our perspective today, the "world domination" motive sounds like a Hollywood scriptwriter's pitch for yet another James Bond movie, but in the heady paranoia of Russia in 1895, it carried enough whiffs of validity to convince some of the people some of the time.

With the czar's directive, the Russian Okhrana secret police force plundered various sources for inspiration. They found it in Goedsche's novel, and in 1897 published as fact the section dealing with the Jewish plot. Eight years later, the Protocols were translated into English and widely circulated as minutes recorded during the First Zionist Congress held in Basel,

Switzerland, in 1897 presided over by "the Father of Modern Zionism," Theodor Herzl.

The *Protocols*, intended to be read like an instruction manual for running the world, are either chilling or absurd, depending on your gullibility and appreciation for black humor. Assisting in the ambitious project of global domination, the documents declare, are the Freemasons, whose agenda is being manipulated by the Elders, and the Bavarian Illuminati, who are either dupes or willing participants.

Practical lessons in the Protocols vary between chilling generalizations and outright farce. Protocol No. 1, for example, lectures, "Therefore, in governing the world the best results are obtained by violence and intimidation, and not by academic discussions," while Protocol No. 23 proposes that the general public should be made unhappy, and thus subdued, by passing laws prohibiting drunkenness.

Many of the most troubling Protocols were adopted by right-wing politicians of their day as a means of motivating their most ardent supporters. By selecting the elements that best served their needs and loading them on the always-rolling anti-Semitic bandwagon, everyone including Adolf Hitler claimed the *Protocols* were authentic.

They became a treasure-trove of rationales for racists. "We shall destroy among the masses the importance of the family and its educational value," Protocol No. 10 declared. Protocol No. 12 promised, "We shall saddle and bridle [the press] with a tight curb....Not a single announcement will reach the public without our control." To tighten the thumbscrews a little more, Protocol No. 14 proclaimed, "It will be undesirable for us that there should exist any other religion than ours....We must therefore sweep away all other forms of belief."

In the economic and political chaos that fol-

Theodor Herzl, "the Father of Modern Zionism," is assumed in some quarters to be the creator of *The Protocols of the Elders of Zion*.

lowed World War I and the Russian revolution, it took only the briefest of references to the *Protocols* for much of American and European popular culture to seize on them as proof of a secret conspiracy. Among the advocates was automotive magnate Henry Ford, who launched the Dearborn *Independent* newspaper in 1920 partially as a means of disseminating the *Protocols*, along with periodic attacks on Communists. For a time, Ford clung stubbornly to his opinion that the *Protocols* were indicative of a Jewish conspiracy for world domination. In an interview appearing in the February 17, 1921, issue of the New York *World*, Ford said: "The only statement I care to make about the *Protocols* is that they fit in with what is going on. They are sixteen years old [*sic*], and they have fitted the world situation up to this time. They fit it now." Meanwhile, Hitler was quoting the *Protocols* in *Mein Kampf*, and selections from the book were being read in the Romanian parliament as a rationale for expelling Jews from that country.

Little by little, thanks to serious investigation conducted by skeptical journalists, the truth of the *Protocols'* origins became known. Among the first to expose their fraudulent basis was a London *Times* reporter named Philip Graves, who traced their genesis back to Joly and Goedsche. Slowly, the weight of proof rose to such a mass that even crusty Henry Ford admitted he had been mistaken. In 1927, in a public retraction, he apologized for his support of the *Protocols* hoax, blaming his assistants for duping him.

The perception persists, however. *Holy Blood's* weak denunciation of the *Protocols* before employing them later as support for its premise adds to the suspicion, among those who grasp at any available straw, that such wild speculation bears heeding.

Among the political and industry leaders who promoted the truth of the *Protocols* was Henry Ford.

Hitler quoted from the Protocols in *Mein Kampf.*

By inserting the *Protocols* into their opus, the authors of *Holy Blood* create the mirroring effect mentioned earlier. In their case, a work of reputed non-fiction treats a fictional event as though it contained vestiges of reality. In his book *The Da Vinci Code*, author Dan Brown uses a work of fiction to deride a real organization, Opus Dei, as though it were a threat to humanity as genuine and treacherous as the fictional *Protocols.*

Brown's reckless use of facts to add verisimilitude to his work of fiction has been criticized in great detail by numerous critics elsewhere; in this context, only the author's skewed depiction of Opus Dei will be dealt with.

Opus Dei is the de facto villain in Brown's tale, so dedicated to protecting the secret of Christ's supposed bloodline that it employs hired assassins, at least one of whom is a decidedly sadistic character. This may be suitable for James Bond stories and the fictional SPECTRE, or Len Deighton tales involving familiar evils of Nazism, but ascribing such illusory qualities to an existing organization in support of a fantastic premise strikes many people, Catholics and non-Catholics alike, as outrageous.

The Roman Catholic Church is as appropriate a target for criticism as any, and considering many of its less admirable activities over the past millennium, more suitable than most. But the family-oriented agenda of Opus Dei, as much as liberal Catholics may disagree with its conservative bent, is portrayed in an especially bizarre manner by Brown. Key to the author's plot involving a sadomasochistic albino monk is the premise that Opus Dei operates as a monastic order. This is a fabrication and a complete reversal of the organization's actual premise: monks seek holiness by withdrawing from society; Opus Dei chooses to function in the midst of secular society.

Other aspects of Brown's tale can be considered nothing less than character assassination. These include references to Opus Dei recruits being drugged into silence, the use of a barbed *cil-ice* belt as a masochistic tool, and the suggestion that Opus Dei "bailed out" the Vatican when its bank encountered financial difficulties, purchasing special favors from the papal office in the process. In a manic effort to denigrate the organization, Brown even got the entrances to the Opus Dei Manhattan headquarters wrong. Men and women may enter any door to the building they choose, but since the headquarters includes separate residences for celibate men and women, occupants of each section enter through one door or another to reach their own quarters more directly. Brown stretches this to claim that all men must enter through the main door on Lexington Avenue, and all women must enter through a side door. Not only is this gender restriction false, it is backwards regarding the residents: women enter their residence area off Lexington; the entrance for male residents is via the adjoining street.

Apologists for Brown and his publisher note that *Da Vinci* is, after all, a work of fiction and carries the familiar disclaimer opposite the dedication page ("All of the characters and events in this book are fictitious, and any resemblance to actual persons, living or dead, is purely coincidental."). Turn that page, however, and you encounter Brown's claim that the Priory of Sion "is a real organization," that Opus Dei has been alleged to conduct "brain-washing, coercion and a dangerous practice known as 'corporal mortification,'" and that "all descriptions of artwork, architecture, documents, and secret rituals in this novel are accurate." All three claims are made without any hint of irony.

How seriously should we take these and other discrepancies in the book? After all, it *is* merely a novel, and not a very serious one at that. Authors must be permitted the luxury of freedom when giving their imagination rein to create tales whose primary goal is entertainment, whether their basis is a cheap detective novel or a tome worthy of Dickens or

Hemingway. This premise will not be challenged in this book or, it is hoped, elsewhere.

Imagination is one thing; unfairly and inaccurately maligning an existing organization or individuals for the purpose of adding realism is another matter. It is no exaggeration to compare the initial and extended impact of *The Protocols of the Elders of Zion* with *Da Vinci*, and their first appearance in a work of fiction; while the Catholic Church is not nearly as vulnerable to the kinds of abuse the *Protocols* created for Jews, the principle remains unchanged.

For hundreds of years Masons, Rosicrucians, Druids, Gnostics, Wiccans and others whose practices were benign, if out of the mainstream, suffered attacks from people who see a conspiracy behind every innocent symbol and plots behind every unforeseen event. In many cases, these fringe elements influenced the main fabric of society with unfortunate results. For almost a century now, the hysterical and anti-Semitic scribblings of Nesta H. Webster have been accepted as factual by otherwise astute readers of her book *Secret Societies & Subversive Movements*.

Webster's work, turgid almost without exception, has nevertheless remained in print for almost eighty years. Impressively comprehensive (her references to often obscure sources are exceptional in their scholarly approach), it represents an ideal example of a blend of good academic research leading to a shaky premise and motivated by deeply rooted racism. From her viewpoint immediately following World War I, Webster identified the major threats to world peace as Grand Orient Freemasonry, Theosophism, Pan-Germanism, International Finance and World Jewry.

As a superpatriotic Briton, her concerns about German nationalism were not quite as prescient as they appear; the entire British Empire remained furious at the inhuman Huns while Webster was writing her book in the early 1920s. Her political stance was extreme right wing, her hatred of any socialist goals was almost palpable, her anti-Semitic stance was

Secret societies investigator Nesta H. Webster has been praised despite her overt racism.

unwavering, and her blinkers were large and narrowly set—she made no mention, for example, of Marx, Lenin or any reference to Communism at all, and she continued to insist that the French Revolution was conducted according to an agenda of various secret societies. Interestingly, the American Revolution received as much attention from her as Communism did.

Webster had a right to express her views, and readers should continue to maintain the freedom to absorb them. The same freedom, it can be argued, should be provided Hitler's *Mein Kampf* and Mao's Little Red Book.

These freedoms must bring with them an appreciation of the risk that social organizations, and individuals within them, may be targeted in a manner that defies their ability to prove their innocence, a principle of freedom of the press that we neglect at our peril.

On the reverse side of this coin is the risk that truly menacing organizations could be underestimated and disregarded if grouped among the darlings of the fringe-dwellers. Like wolves concealing themselves among the sheep, at least a handful of secret societies may represent a genuine source of concern easily grouped in the minds of the public as either benign or misunderstood.

It is easy to dismiss these organizations in this manner. It may also be dangerous.

THIRTEEN
CRITICS, ALARMISTS AND CONSPIRACY THEORISTS
WHEN DOES PARANOIA MAKE SENSE?

WITH THE EXCEPTION OF EXTREME FUNDAMENTALIST RELI-
gious sects, most people assume a laissez-faire attitude towards
neighbors and co-workers who profess a belief in fairies, UFOS,
personal angels or similar entities. As long as the acceptance or
skepticism has no impact on our lives, we feel free to harbor our
own convictions and tolerate those of others.

Should our response to a neighbor's belief in secret societies
be different? Since most organizations qualifying as secret societies—with the exception of Cosa Nostra, Triads and
Yakuza—are for the most part benign fraternal groups, how
seriously should we take claims that they are manipulating our
lives without either our knowledge or our approval? And how
far should we go in investigating the agenda of these groups?

The latter question is a practical one, with practical
limitations.

Anyone with an Internet connection and a search engine can
summon up dozens of societies whose stated beliefs and agenda
range from promoting alchemy (Central Ohio Temple of
Hermetic Science) and "Benevolent Satanism" (United Luciferan
Church of France) to conducting telepathic relations with Mars
(Aetherius Society). Many such organizations are, in reality, variations on long-established societies such as Masons and Gnostics,
or alternative religions pursuing a belief in karma and reincarnation. Their activities, no matter how much or how little we
subscribe to their tenets, should remain entirely their concern.

From time to time, however, the curtain is drawn back to
reveal disturbing, often tragic, activities stemming from a

clandestine group. Among these was the Order of the Solar Temple. Its impact may have been minimal and limited, but the lesson of its birth and demise is important if only because it determines the transition point between a cult and a secret society. Solar Temple began as the former, and almost morphed into the latter.

Solar Temple consisted of several dozen trusting members and their children under the command of two charismatic leaders: Joseph Di Mambro, a French citizen born in Zaire, who became something of an expert in audio-video effects; and Luc Jouret, a Belgian physician who reportedly drew strength to conduct the group's ceremonies from having sex with one of the female members of the congregation. The Order of the Solar Temple was founded by Jouret and Di Mambro in 1984; its formal name, revealed only to the highest qualified members, was International Chivalric Organization of the Solar Tradition. Di Mambro had abandoned his trade as a jeweler after becoming a member of AMORC, the dominant Rosicrucian group. He left AMORC under circumstances involving a charge of swindling, and in 1970 moved to a region of France near the Swiss border where he posed for several years as a psychologist.

In 1978, Di Mambro met Luc Jouret, and together they joined the Renewed Order of the Temple, dedicated to Templar and Rosicrucian themes. Jouret became the Grand Master, but within a year he was forced out for, rumor has it, misappropriation of the order's funds. Di Mambro and many other followers left with him, and the ragtag group eventually formed the Order of the Solar Temple with Jouret filling the post of Grand Master.

Originally a licensed physician, Jouret proved to be a charismatic leader who attracted a number of recruits to the organization during a lecture tour of Switzerland, France, and Quebec, Canada. As

The Order of the Solar Temple, founded by Luc Jouret, might have achieved secret society status.

the organization grew, Jouret and Di Mambro established three levels of membership. The entry level, Amanta, was for new initiates attracted by Jouret's lectures and seminars. The next level, Archedia Clubs, was reserved for members who wished to further explore the ideas and teachings of the order. The most highly qualified members were added to the International Chivalric Organization of the Solar Tradition.

Jouret continued on the lecture circuit, promoting himself as "Luc Jouret, Physician, Revealing Secrets of Love and Biology." The sessions segued from "love and biology" to a hectoring message of spirituality and apocalypse, with Jouret warning of volcano eruptions, vanishing forests and other environmental disasters. Only a small core of people physically and intellectually strong enough would survive the catastrophe, Jouret cautioned his audiences. The Solar Tradition was seeking those who qualified, preparing them to inherit the earth when all others were gone.

In his lectures, Jouret claimed he had been a Knight Templar in a previous life, and asserted he would lead the most loyal of his followers to a planet orbiting Sirius. He also claimed to be a third reincarnation of Jesus Christ and that his daughter had been immaculately conceived. Over time, he and Di Mambro crystallized the Solar Temple's philosophy into a blend of neo-Templarism, New Age philosophy, Christianity and survivalist paranoia. Life was an illusion, members were taught. "Liberation is not where human beings think it is," Jouret warned. "Death can represent an essential stage of life." The end was nigh, the world would end by fire, and only the most trusted members of the Solar Temple would escape the flames. Meanwhile, Jouret pledged to lead the group towards a number of vaunted objectives reminiscent of Templar goals, including the following:

1. Re-establishing the correct notions of authority and power in the world.
2. Affirming the primacy of the spiritual over the temporal.
3. Giving back to man the conscience of his dignity.

4. Helping humanity through its transition.
5. Participating in the Assumption of the Earth in its three frame-
    works: body, soul, and spirit.
6. Contributing to the union of the Churches and working towards
    the meeting of Christianity and Islam.

Each ceremony began with a confession of sins. Instead of
the privacy accorded to this process in Roman Catholicism, this
confession was conducted as guided group meditation, the
effect enhanced by luminous particles that appeared to materi-
alize from the participants' bodies courtesy of video tricks
performed by Di Mambro.

Things grew more bizarre. Before conducting ceremonies,
Jouret sought a female member to provide the strength he
needed to deliver his lectures by having sex with him. During
many of his ceremonies, spiritual beings seemed to appear at
Jouret's command, thanks not to Jouret's spiritual powers but to
expensive electronic projection devices operated by Di
Mambro. While Di Mambro's primary duties occurred back-
stage, he also was fond of engaging in sexual liaisons with
female members of the order, presumably to give him strength
to operate the projector.

Membership grew to about 500 in the early 1990s, which is
when trouble arrived. Jouret had advised members to stockpile
weapons in preparation for the end of the world, which led to
Jouret being charged with illegal gun possession in Canada.
Shortly after a member of the order named Tony Dutoit publicly
spoke out against the Solar Temple he, his wife Nicky and their
child were murdered in their home in Morin Heights, Quebec,
killed with shocking savagery—Dutoit suffered more than fifty
stab wounds, his wife was stabbed four times in the throat and
eight times in the back and once in each breast, and their infant
child had been stabbed six times before his body was wrapped in
a black plastic bag suspended from a wooden stake. An investigation discovered that Dutoit had told other members that the
apparition illusions used in the order's ceremonies were a sham.

The order began to crumble, with Jouret and Di Mambro subjected to humiliation by defecting members. It was too much for their egos to accept. On the night of October 4, 1994, residents of Chiery, Switzerland, reported fires raging in the area of the Solar Temple quarters. The remains of fifty-three members, including Jouret and Di Mambro, were found the next morning in the building's ruins. Autopsy reports showed that two victims died of suffocation and twenty-one had been administered sleeping pills before being shot in the head. Others were found with plastic bags over their heads, and many showed signs of struggle, indicating that the deaths were not part of a mass suicide pact.

A year later, the charred bodies of another sixteen members, arranged in a star pattern with their feet towards the source of the fire, were found in a burned-out chalet in the Swiss Alps. The dead included both the wife and son of Jean Vuarnet, who had made a fortune in ski wear and sunglasses. All the victims had been shot, stabbed, suffocated or poisoned. Two years later, a final five lives were taken in St. Casimir, Quebec, in the burned home of Didier Queze, a member of the order. Four bodies in an upstairs bedroom had been arranged in the shape of a cross; the fifth, Didier's mother, was on a sofa in the living room with a bag over her head.

A total of seventy-four members died at the hands of this neo-Templar order. Charges of murder were brought against a Solar Temple member and former symphony conductor named Michel Tabachnik, but he was found not guilty and released. No one was ever convicted, nor were the weapons used to murder the victims located.

Enough was revealed about the order, however, to generate wild speculation based on minimal facts. Stories began circulating among newsletters and Internet sites that Solar Temple financing had been achieved by running weapons between Europe and South America, leading to claims of a "military-occult complex," all to achieve goals of "the fascist-Masonic lodge." Unless, of course, the reader subscribed instead to allegations that Radio Canada reporters discovered the organization actually earned its money by laundering hundreds of millions of dollars through the infamous Bank of Credit & Commerce International (BCCI). Closed in 1991, BCCI indulged in fraudulent record-keeping, rogue trading, flouting of bank ownership regulations and money laundering within a structure so complex that a complete picture of its activities is still not available. (For the record, no legitimate news source, including Radio Canada, has ever published stories about either activity by the Solar Temple beyond identifying them as "rumors.")

Di Mambro and Jouret were disturbed and dangerous men cut from the same warped fabric as was James Jones, who led hundreds to their deaths in the 1978 Jonestown massacre in Guyana, and David Koresh, whose Branch Davidians died in a fiery standoff with the FBI in 1993.

What are we to make of leaders who hold life-and-death control over their adherents, and what happens if these leaders choose to exert their powers on a global stage? The line between cult and secret society grows blurry and indistinct when the organization grows in scope and power.

Any search for serious threats from secret societies on a wider range could begin, perhaps, with a snatch of dialogue from a 1948 Hollywood western movie entitled *Ft. Apache* between Owen Thursday, a newly arrived Lieutenant Colonel played by Henry Fonda, and the crusty captain of Fort Apache played, of course, by John Wayne.

> *Lt. Col. Thursday:* I suggest the Apache have deteriorated, judging by a few of the specimens I have seen on the way out here.
> *Captain Yorke:* If you saw them, sir, they weren't Apaches.

Like the Apaches referred to by Wayne's character, any clandestine group posing a threat to broad sectors of the public will seek to either conceal or camouflage its true motives. Thus, the most dangerous organizations are either unknown or have achieved success at the practice of "hiding in plain sight." On that basis, "recognizable secret societies" is both an oxymoron and a clue that the danger they represent, if any, is minimal.

Assessing the risk that each known group represents could begin by categorizing them according to four classifications:

1. fictional or historical societies that may be operating in a clandestine manner,
2. organizations whose stated premise is demonstrably benign or non-threatening,
3. groups whose conspiratorial relationship has yet to be revealed, and
4. government departments exerting power beyond their formal mandate.

FICTIONAL AND HISTORICAL GROUPS. Of this grouping, the Bavarian Illuminati draws the most persistent attention from conspiracy advocates, as it has for 200 years. Its founder Adam Weishaupt, an ex-Jesuit who nevertheless is labeled a Jew by some members of the right-wing conspiracy crowd, managed to attract a few prominent individuals to his society before it collapsed, first from suppression by the Bavarian government and later by Weishaupt's own rejection of his philosophy.

Coincidental with the expansion of the Illuminati came the radical upheavals of the French Revolution, an event so apocalyptic in nature that many conservative observers insist on viewing it as the product of a vast conspiracy. They refuse to accept that common French citizens, outraged at the antics of the ruling class for so many years, could succeed without the aid of powerful assistance from various clandestine organizations. Surely the overthrow of the French throne, they argue, could never

Critics of the Illuminati acknowledge that Adam Weishaupt founded the movement, but few know he repudiated it.

spring from the minds and intentions of a mass of near-illiterates, echoing skeptics who reject the notion that William Shakespeare could be so erudite and prolific. The revolutionists, they propose, must have been manipulated by a secret society, and the Number One culprit is the Illuminati.

Established as a secret group concealed beneath the skirts of the Masons, and with the success of the French Revolution as assumed proof of its power, the Illuminati became a fixation among conspiracy theorists. No group was more industrious in promoting this idea, nor as classic in its use of the paranoia that secret societies can generate, than the John Birch Society, founded in 1958. Birchers joined the blatantly anti-Semitic Nesta H. Webster in the contention that the Illuminati had masterminded the French Revolution for its own ends. Interestingly, both ignored the fact that the French monarchy was reinstated after the fall of Napoleon in 1815.

Birch Society founder Robert Welch went on to assert that the Illuminati's agenda had been hijacked in the early 1800s by the Rothschild banking family as a means of controlling U.S. foreign policy. The family's banking success and closed structure provided all the raw material Welch needed. Established in the late eighteenth century by Mayer Rothschild, the financial house owed its success to Rothschild's tactic of installing each of his five sons in various centers across Europe, including Frankfurt, Vienna, London, Naples and Paris. He set up marriages for his sons to various closely related family members, keeping the bank's operations entirely within the family and operating it in a closed, clandestine manner. This latter aspect enabled the company to maintain total discretion about the size of its wealth as well as its multiple business connections and achievements, providing a fertile ground for people like Welch. Meanwhile, the family shield, a clenched fist gripping five arrows, suggested a belligerent attitude not normally associated with bankers.

Robert Welch lectured John Birch Society members to achieve their goals by operating as a secret society.

The Rothschild connection, according to Welch and others, also explained how an organization as large and powerful as the Illuminati managed to escape detection for 200 years. Obviously, the wealth of the Rothschilds had been employed, but the group's association with Masonry was at the heart of the cover-up, Welch declared. Various other commentators, from the inexorable Nesta H. Webster to Jacob Katz, author of *Jews and Freemasonry in Europe*, argued that the Illuminati had assumed control of German Freemasonry and relocated its headquarters to Frankfurt. There, it recruited a number of prominent Jewish leaders and financiers, including Rabbi Zvi Hirsch and Rothschild chief clerk Sigismund Geisenheimer, creating, as one observer described it, "a secret society within a secret society." Welch put all the weight of his once influential power behind this idea, generating sufficient momentum to keep the speculation rolling fifty years later.

The importance we should place on the idea that a society managed to obscure proof of its existence over two centuries while manipulating global economics, politics and armed conflicts is minimal. How, for example, could the Illuminati maintain total secrecy among its members when various elements of the Mafia have divulged that organization's deepest secrets, defying in some cases even blood bonds? Have the lips of Illuminati supporters really been hermetically sealed for over 200 years?

Convinced that the U.S. was threatened by the Illuminati, whose goals of world domination included betraying U.S. sovereignty to the United Nations and running the world via a global socialist government, Welch began urging his followers in 1960 to support a "Get Us Out of the UN!" campaign. They should, Welch advised, create influential cells of opposition and covert action by "joining your local PTA at the beginning of the school year, get your conservative friends to do likewise, and go to work to take it over." Perhaps only Welch failed to recognize that he was proposing the creation of a new secret society, masquerading as a public service organization to aid the education of children but actually dedicated to effecting its own international agenda.

Nothing exists to prove that the Illuminati did not die with its founder, who regretted and rejected the principles originally proposed by him. Until trustworthy evidence to the contrary appears, the Illuminati remains alive only in the fertile imaginations of computer game creators and their players, and in the minds of anyone who still believes wisdom may be found among the detritus of Robert Welch's cold war meanderings.

BENIGN OR NON-THREATENING ORGANIZATIONS. Employing a "hide in plain sight" strategy, these may openly declare their membership, announce their intentions, and declare that they function on behalf of the greater good. They may also avoid the trappings associated with "traditional" secret societies, including initiation rites, mystical ceremonies and vows of silence.

With so much latitude, every group from the Salvation Army to a neighborhood investment club could qualify as a dangerous secret society in the minds of the incessantly paranoid, but one organization in recent years has led all the rest as a candidate for evil intentions: The Bilderberg Group.

Bilderberg is often associated with the Trilateral Commission, founded in 1973 to promote closer cooperation between Europe, Japan and North America; and the Council on Foreign Relations, a think tank dedicated to increasing America's understanding of the world. These associations leave the group open to accusations that it is actively involved in various schemes to exert global control of financial, military and diplomatic activities. Those concerned about Bilderberg's objectives note that it is not merely a question of how this control is applied; it's also a question of by *whom*. Heads of state in democratic monarchies such as Britain, Sweden, the Netherlands and others are prevented from playing an active role in the political process, they claim, but Bilderberg provides precisely this arena, subverting the will of democratic nations and recalling hints of the Divine Right of Kings.

Decisions made during Bilderberg conferences supposedly include the selection and approval of candidates to run for top political office in all of the world's great democracies; without Bilderberg approval, the argument contends, presidential candidates in the U.S. and potential prime ministerial leaders in Britain, Australia, Canada and other parliamentary countries cannot achieve power.

Other condemnations include wide-ranging but nonspecific claims that Bilderberg members pull the world's strings either in concert with each other or in conjunction with the Illuminati, Masons and the rest of the usual suspects. On a bizarre note, the group has been accused of eliminating warfare as a means of controlling and directing nationalistic goals and ideas among European nations, as though substituting warfare with diplomacy were a dangerous activity.

Curiously for a society with such alleged power and influence, its members and the locations of its gatherings, where upcoming agendas regarding world domination are submitted and approved, are proclaimed in advance.

The Bilderberg Group owes its existence and notoriety to the skill, connections and vision of one man who, almost fifty years after his death, is still referred to as *l'éminence grise*. Joseph H. Retinger, raised by Jesuits, possessed enormous political instincts, incisive intelligence and much charm, all of which enabled him to influence the bureaucracy of the Catholic Church to the point where he became the key linkage between the pope and the father-general of the Jesuit Order. At Retinger's funeral in 1960, one of the eulogizers recalled: "I remember Retinger in the United States picking up the telephone and immediately making an appointment with the President, and in Europe he had complete entrée in every political circle as a kind of right acquired through [the] trust, devotion and loyalty he inspired."

Retinger's original goals in life attest to a socially conscious system of values. He spent some time in Mexico as a youth, supporting efforts to launch an effective trade union movement

Joseph H. Retinger (*right*): The pope and the U.S. president always took his calls.

there during the 1920s, and convincing the Mexican government to nationalize U.S.-controlled oil interests. If the scant biographical information available on Retinger is true, he was the stuff of legends. During World War II, he acted as a political aide to Polish general Sikorski, and in 1943, at age fifty-eight, he parachuted into Nazi-occupied territory near Warsaw to direct sabotage missions.

Retinger's interests and achievements encompassed the revival of devastated postwar Europe, and in 1949 he was instrumental in launching the Council of Europe, headquartered in Strasbourg. As a member of the council's executive committee, Retinger began fulfilling his dream of avoiding conflicts similar to the world wars that engulfed Europe in 1914–1918 and 1939–1945 by creating a European economic, political and military union. One way to achieve this was via international organizations whose long-term commitment to progress would neutralize the short-term ideological conflicts that continually erupted between governments. The benefits, to anyone with the slightest understanding of the morass that sucked nations into World War I, would prove inestimable. A neutral multinational group expressing the will of powerful interests within a multitude of countries could defuse the kinds of outbursts, strung in a chain of explosive treaties and obligations, that detonated war in 1914.

Having secured left-wing support from his work in Europe, and employing right-wing connections resulting from his Vatican ties, Retinger was the best man to serve as a catalyst for such an organization. He proved it in May 1954 when he persuaded Prince Bernhard of the Netherlands to host a secret conference for representatives of NATO countries. The prince, a major investor in Royal Dutch Petroleum, now Shell Oil, chose the Bilderberg Hotel in Oosterbeek, Holland, as the site. Attendees at the first conference included U.S. general Walter Bedell Smith, director of the CIA, and representatives of the Rockefeller family, who controlled Standard Oil, Shell's largest competitor.

The group has met almost annually over the fifty-plus years since, their meetings sending conspiracy buffs into a frenzy of speculation with Chicken Little concerns about the sky, and virtually everything else, falling to the ground. Powerful men (and increasingly numbers of women) meeting in luxurious surroundings while engaged in private discussions inspire dark speculation.

American critics on the right suspect that Bilderberg attendees are plotting a world government to override hard-earned rights and freedoms. Should the Bilderbergers have their way, they argue, the U.S. would be burdened with a national healthcare system and disarmed by draconian gun laws. Meanwhile, the left wing sees Bilderberg representatives manipulating currencies, negotiating resource rights and eviscerating trade unions as a means of tightening their grip on global economics. A few broad-minded (or perhaps merely confused) Web sites support both interpretations of the group's motives.

On a more realistic basis, serious criticism of the Bilderberg Group tends to address four specific concerns:

They are a supragovernmental organization. All nongovernmental organizations representing international interests deserve monitoring. Other groups in this category might range from OPEC to university research scientists delving into munitions development and genetic manipulation. A dash of practicality and trust is surely prescribed, however. Given the disdain by democratic governments to recognize long-term global concerns and deal with them in an appropriately expeditious manner, is it surprising that a group such as the Bilderbergers would gather to discuss priorities and exert influence in implementing them?

They manipulate currencies and set global monetary rates.
Currency manipulation and its impact on markets and individuals may indeed be a legitimate concern. But is it
reasonable to expect that discussions on this matter would
involve presidents and prime ministers agreeing to any plan
that would negatively affect their constituents and thus
damage their prospects for re-election? It is more logical—
and potentially dangerous to the public—for central banks
and others to carry out this manipulation in private than in
a session whose location, timing and participants are widely
known. Conspiracy buffs counter this notion by suggesting
that the election prospects of democratic leaders are tightly
controlled by Bilderbergers, eliminating any serious objection the leaders may have to decisions made at the
conferences. Perhaps, but a large segment of the world population familiar with machinations conducted during the
U.S. presidential elections of 2000 and 2004 are convinced
that, if election manipulation exists, its perpetrators likely
reside closer to home than among Bilderbergers.

*They select political figures to become future rulers and tar-
get current rulers to be removed from power.* A few dozen men
and women gathering to name and approve the next president of the United States, the next prime minister of Great
Britain, and the next sheikh of Qatar is indeed a chilling
prospect. If that's the case, however, the rejected leaders
tend to accept their fate with remarkable grace and silence.
The Bilderberg gathering that took place in Stresa, Italy,
from June 3 to 6, 2004, reportedly included U.S. president
George W. Bush, British prime minister Tony Blair and—
surprise, surprise—U.S. vice-presidential candidate John
Edwards who, along with running mate John Kerry, lost the
U.S. election to Bush five months later. Was the decision
awarding Bush his re-election actually made on a June day
in Italy? Did Edwards meekly accept the ruling, perhaps
with the promise of being elevated to U.S. presidential status in 2008? Was Steven Spielberg directing?

They decide which countries will wage war on others. The extended period of peace enjoyed by Europe since 1945 is unprecedented given the potential for conflict over those sixty-plus years, and much of the harmony can be directly ascribed to Retinger's vision. Conspiracy advocates may argue that the Bilderberg Group controls the peace as well as the war, but most conflicts since the group's inception have involved nations and communities beyond the group's membership, including Vietnam, Iran, Iraq, the former Yugoslavia and other jurisdictions. This does not eliminate the Bilderbergers' thumbs from these particular pies, but...

Some criticisms remain valid, however, and the roots of most can be laid at the feet of Bilderberg participants. Bilderberg founder Prince Bernhard himself identified the source of these concerns when he said, "It is difficult to re-educate people who have been brought up on nationalism to the idea of relinquishing part of their sovereignty to a supranational body."

This attitude, coupled with the scope of the discussions conducted at Bilderberg sessions and the influence of its participants, fosters concern among normally unruffled folk. The Bilderberg Group's agenda, according to available evidence, appears to focus more on the propagation of its own power and the enrichment of its members than on concerns about global health, energy supply, environmental crises and widespread hunger.

Supporters of the Bilderberg Group will argue that free-ranging discussions between people of widely disparate views must be held in confidence to encourage openness and honesty. They also point out that all political and business decisions, made in both corporate board rooms and political cabinet rooms, are subject to various levels of secrecy. True enough. It is the international aspect of Bilderberg that disturbs most people. The crux of concern over Bilderberg is this: We like to think that, as members of a pseudo-democratic society, we exert at least periodic control over events within our own state, provincial and national borders, and we are reluctant to relinquish that control to foreigners.

GROUPS WITHOUT APPARENT CONSPIRATORIAL ACTIVITIES. The members of Skull & Bones have no influence on matters beyond the campus of Yale while they remain students there. But what of the relationship among members after they enter the business and political world?

The concept of networking has existed since humans first organized themselves into tribes. It would be fruitless to monitor and attempt to control activities between fraternity brothers, sorority sisters, lodges, service clubs, Scout troops and similar associations. What happens, however, when members of these organizations operate in collusion, extending the secrecy vows that appeared innocent within a campus environment onto the world stage?

Consider a group of bright, privileged men actively seeking high positions of power in order to pursue goals that reflect the values of the closed society to which they once swore eternal allegiance. Then recall the activities of the Bundy brothers, the lineage of the Bush family, and the questionable antics of the Russell Trust and Union Banking Corporation, among various Skull & Bones escapades.

It is highly unlikely that middle-aged Skull & Bones members still lie naked in coffins while reciting their sexual exploits to each other (especially now that it is a coed organization), or that they exchange some secret ritual upon meeting without grinning in embarrassment. The idea, however, that men of this high caliber, ambition and focus could easily discard their association when planning international financial and political strategies in concert with each other is equally difficult to accept.

OFFICIAL GOVERNMENTAL ASSOCIATIONS EXERTING POWER BEYOND THEIR MANDATE. If covert decisions are made that adversely affect democratic societies, the source may prove to be not secret organizations with centuries-old traditions but powerful interests functioning within government apparatus, their actions concealed beneath the impenetrable cloak of national security.

While it may be true that these organizations do not follow practices associated with secret societies, such as elaborate initiation ceremonies, in a world where computer recognition of palm prints and iris patterns instantly identifies a friend or foe, who really needs code words and gestures to confirm identities?

The idea that an acknowledged federal government organization such as the U.S. National Security Council (NSC) is subject to assessment in the same context as the Assassins and Cosa Nostra may be offensive to some, and if this were the only point of comparison the criticism would be justified. But on a broader scale, evidence exists that secret decisions made by this organization have greater negative impact than any confirmable act committed by Masons, Templars, Rosicrucians, Kabbalah, the Illuminati and other favorite targets of conspiracy buffs.

The NSC has been described as "the ultimate Washington insider's club, a who's who of those with the power to shape history." Created by President Harry Truman in 1947 as a means of keeping himself informed of international events, the NSC grants membership to a select group of people whose careers have intertwined throughout years of involvement in matters of defense policy, intelligence gathering and diplomatic relations.

Dominating the NSC from the first day of his entry into the group during the Nixon administration is Henry Kissinger, a man who has never been elected to public office yet whose forty-odd years of activity in clandestine international affairs qualifies him as the most influential figure of our time.

Unlike other U.S. federal organizations, the NSC functions according to an open-ended mandate, its vague purpose supposedly limited to helping the president decide and coordinate military and foreign policy. This intentional haziness permits personalities such as Kissinger and his various sycophants to exert a disturbing level of control over U.S. affairs which, by definition, involve international activities.

The pinnacle of Kissinger's power in this regard occurred in the latter days of Richard Nixon's presidency. Crippled by revelations of Watergate and tumbling towards his inevitable doom, Nixon abdicated management of the NSC. Into the vacuum stepped Kissinger, seizing the group's direction and, immediately prior to Nixon's resignation, placing U.S. armed forces on a high DEFCON (DEFense CONdition) alert status, an act that constitutionally belongs exclusively to the president.

This might be considered an aberration, a rare response to an unprecedented situation, but two factors are worthy of concern here. One is Kissinger's widely acknowledged role in illegal international activities including the bombing of Cambodia and the overthrow of Salvador Allende, the democratically elected president of Chile. Both are disturbing examples of the power granted to members of the NSC, who lack both the official authority and direct accounting under the country's constitution.

The other is the matter of openness and transparency. Supporters of the NSC and Kissinger will argue, with great conviction, that the pursuit of national security demands certain decisions be conducted in secrecy without prior consultation or later confirmation that the decisions were made at all. The same assertion may be submitted by corporate chiefs justifying board room secrecy from shareholders. NSC decisions, however, are often global in impact and influence, well beyond the scope of the largest corporations. Clearly, it would be a more effective application of energies if rabid concerns about supposed power exercised by groups such as Templars, Masons, Illuminati, Priory of Sion and others were applied instead to existing and acknowledged organizations, including the NSC, whose power and potential for abuse are both evident and extensive.

The world wobbles. Its lack of perfect balance should alert us to the realization that nothing is as stable and predictable as our senses tell us and our preferences desire. Orbital aberrations and tidal forces occur beyond not only our ability to alter them, but also our means to sense them. We acknowledge their existence and the dangers they represent when catastrophe strikes in the form of an oncoming ice age or a cataclysmic earthquake. Otherwise, we treat such possibilities the same way we treat our own mortality: as a rumor that can only be confirmed when fulfilled.

Rather than deal with cosmic risks, many of us prefer to worry about other dangers, including the threat posed by shadowy groups whose existence may be limited to the speculations and imaginations of overly imaginative authors and Web site owners. We can never, it seems, have too many secret societies on which to project our fears, whether justified or not. Nor, it appears, are we prepared to retire shadowy groups whose last acknowledged act occurred hundreds of years ago.

New secret organizations germinate each year. Most wither under the glare of study and scorn, but others manage to blossom and survive long enough for ancestors a century or two in the future to name them as sources of evils we cannot imagine today. One near-contemporary example illustrates the origins of secret societies, the events that fertilize their growth, and the individuals who cultivate their ground.

The discovery of wreckage on an open ranch near Roswell, New Mexico, in 1947 proved to be a seminal incident among those suspicious of government conspiracies and the secret societies that foster them. More than half a century after the event, millions of American citizens still believe the detritus was the remains of either a spaceship from another planet or a top-secret military aircraft capable of exceptional flight performance. Both theories, their adherents propose, explain their government's steadfast refusal to reveal details. The actual truth, as available evidence and logic contend, is that a military weather balloon, designed to sample temperature, wind force and other meteorological factors, descended to the ground, as all such equipment will. The military's haste in recovering the material and equipment before a curious heifer stomped it into

July 4, 1947: flying saucers are spotted and new conspiracies are born.

the soil, or a ranch hand gathered it to display his treasure back in the bunkhouse, is understandable. Military minds are superb at constructing cover fiction in the name of security but this tale had the ring of truth for most people.

But not everyone. Legends have been constructed around this otherwise mundane event, and outlandish tales suggest how and why nothing more of substance has been revealed. This has led to the supposition that a secret organization monitors the public's curiosity, maintains necessary secrecy, protects evidence, and deflects any public investigation that comes too close to "the truth." In this case, the clandestine group is known as the JASON Society, supposedly established to conceal evidence of alien entry into the U.S., including the "flying saucer" crash at Roswell.

Created by President Eisenhower, the fable goes, JASON consists of thirty-two prominent men, many with CIA connections, responsible for keeping U.S. citizens and the world at large from discovering the true facts about Roswell, including the "fact" that the bodies of two alien creatures were found among the wreckage. Twelve members of JASON, identified by the code MJ-12, direct the group's income, which is earned by running most of the world's illegal drug traffic; in this manner, JASON is concealed from members of Congress who might be alerted to its existence through budget appropriations. As a by-product of generating its funds through narcotics, the organization is able to identify and eliminate, if necessary, weak elements of U.S. society.

The rest of the alleged actions and attributes of JASON provide a clinic in tying together elements of multiple conspiracy theories to create a conclusion that is not only larger than the sum of its parts, but distinctly different.

President John Kennedy's discovery of JASON, its believers claim, prompted his assassination by MJ-12 members within the CIA. These CIA operatives disagreed with his plans to reveal the presence of aliens, along with samples of their weapons and materials, to the American public, a move that would cut off the group's funding. JASON determined that the president of the United States must be killed, and hidden in the JASON vaults is a film showing the driver of Kennedy's limousine turning in his seat with a pistol in his hand to deliver the coup de grace while guiding the limo through Dallas streets. Bizarre? Of course. But how much more weird than the idea of descendants of Jesus Christ manipulating world events for 2000 years while managing to conceal their existence? Weirdness is relative, after all.

Secret societies prosper when their believers can coalesce around some individual whose unique powers of perception serve as a beacon to his followers. When that leader becomes a martyr, whose violent death serves as proof that he possessed information that cost him his life, so much the better. In the case of JASON, this role was played with great effect by Milton William Cooper, who alleged that he owned an immense trove of government secrets regarding the events at Roswell and other actions, including John F. Kennedy being shot by his own chauffeur. Cooper had examined evidence of these events while serving as a U.S. navy intelligence officer with access to top secret files.

Believers on the far right fringe of U.S. society, especially those who tuned to Cooper's daily radio show or plodded

Milton William Cooper claimed flying saucers exist, aliens had landed, and he would be killed by the government. Only the last has proved true.

through his 1991 book *Behold a Pale Horse* (Light Technology Publications, 1991), called him "America's greatest patriot," an accolade awarded even after he claimed *The Protocols of the Elders of Zion* were authentic (although he suggested to his listeners that they replace "Jews" with "Illuminati"). Cooper supported many of his claims by saying he had once been a member of the Order of de Molay, providing him with insight into the secret powers of Freemasonry.

Cooper constantly railed against a litany of secret societies, always boasting that he possessed hard evidence of their existence and evil influence. Too bad he didn't possess a world atlas. In attacking the Bilderberg Group, he claimed their headquarters was located in "The Hague, in Switzerland" and pointed out that Switzerland was the only European country that avoided invasion and bombing during World War II, attributing this fact (which is not entirely true) to the influence of Bilderberg participants. Perhaps he should have acquired a calendar as well, since the Bilderberg Group was not formed until nearly ten years after World War II ended.

Whatever his Masonic credentials, Cooper was no naval intelligence expert. According to official U.S. military records, he rose no higher than a second-class petty officer in the navy before being discharged in 1975. Twenty-five years later, living as a recluse in a remote corner of Arizona, Cooper was killed during a shoot-out with several sheriff's deputies attempting to serve him with a warrant for, among other charges, tax evasion and aggravated assault with a deadly weapon.

Since that day in November 2000, legends have crystalized around Cooper and his revelations. He was killed, the stories say, because he knew too many government secrets. His military records, his followers contend, had been altered to remove any evidence of his intelligence work. The truth about Roswell, the Kennedy assassination, the 9/11 attacks, the JASON Group, Richard Nixon's real reasons for resigning, and other events manipulated by secret societies were buried with him, they insist.

It is not difficult to imagine Cooper's "martyred" death and his claimed knowledge of dark secrets and dangerous conspiracies evolving over several generations into a foundation promulgating the existence of clandestine plans and treacherous activities, all based on "unassailable facts." The legend will undoubtedly attract individuals who choose to believe that the failings of this world in general, and their fortunes in particular, are the result not of flaws in our economic system or their own lack of initiative, but the realized goals of covens and committees employing secret oaths and rituals. They will rely upon unproven activities of secret societies that they wish, or even need, to believe in. And they will take comfort in a certainty that exists purely, exclusively, in their own imaginations.

AFTERWORD
OF DEMONS AND BALONEY

I SET OUT TO WRITE THIS BOOK WITH THE HOPE, IF NOT THE expectation, of discovering centuries-old conspiracies among the world's power elite. I hoped to meet shadowy men in subterranean caverns manipulating the world's currencies, concealing proof of extraterrestrial visitors, or confirming the location of Christ's bones. I sought evidence of brilliant minds dealing with eternal questions of the cosmos, or engaged in accumulating wealth and power over a grand scale of time and geography. For the most part, all I encountered was ill-defined paranoia expressed in juvenile babble, supported by sporadic tales in the mainstream media, stories designed to titillate readers and build circulation rather than deliver real news or knowledge.

Evil and invisible powers lie at the heart of every conspiracy theory, the tales too often delivered with half truths, outright fiction, and an absurd blend of historical and imaginary events. These wild assertions carry weight because, especially in advanced and industrialized cultures, they tap widespread anxiety over our potential loss of control and identity as individuals. They address the fears many of us harbor, and accounts of their existence, no matter how outlandish, are comforting to some degree.

I concluded that buying into these theories without exercising logic and reasoning is dangerous, because it diverts attention from concrete risks. Too many of us spend too much time wrestling with imaginative secret society–based explanations and not enough time probing the validity of false presumptions leading to catastrophic events...or have we forgotten those weapons of mass destruction? Instead of making gullible readers aware of actual risks and providing a means of dealing with them, as conspiracy authors claim to do, their tales aggravate a sense of helplessness while diminishing the ability to deal with serious social and political situations.

Amid the myths, a few glimmers of reality appear from time to time. The linear connection between the Assassins and Al Qaeda, for example, is obvious, although whether an understanding of the Assassins' methods and structure will assist in the battle against extremist Muslim terrorism remains to be seen. The influence of the NSC extends well past the borders of the U.S., and their inclination to act unilaterally in the pursuit of U.S. interests remains a reason for monitoring their power. Beyond these exceptions, our fascination with secret societies appears rooted more in the entertainment value they afford than in the global menace they suggest.

It took the esteemed scientist Carl Sagan, in his book *The Demon-Haunted World: Science as a Candle in the Dark* (New York: Ballantine Books, 1997), to point his finger at the core of the secret society phenomenon. Sagan's primary topic was the enduring fascination with flying saucers in his country and the extraterrestrial demons piloting them, prompting him to note that 95 percent of Americans are scientifically illiterate and seek bizarre explanations for natural events. Instead of parsing superstition-based tales of alchemists and occult masters behind many ancient societies, Sagan suggests, we should pay attention to things even more awe-inspiring and comprehensive that lie all around us waiting to be explored, deciphered and appreciated. "We want so much to be roused from our humdrum lives," Sagan writes, "to rekindle that sense of wonder we remember from childhood." Secret societies provide a link with that phase of childhood wonder, but while immersing ourselves in their allure we risk accepting legends of their existence as true and avoid the application of logic and reason. Too often, we settle for superstition instead of scientific analysis.

Sagan especially decries a "celebration of ignorance" among those who favor rigid dogma over reasonable deduction. "Sooner or later," he warns, "this combustible mixture of ignorance and power is going to blow up in our faces. When governments and societies lose the capacity for critical thinking, the results can be catastrophic, however sympathetic we may be to those who bought the baloney."

It seemed to me, as I reviewed and assessed all the sources, viewpoints, evidence and opinions regarding secret societies, that it has been a seller's market in the baloney business for some time now.

December 15, 2005

NOTES

Introduction—Fools, Fears and Fanatics, p. 11

An infant covered with their meal, p. 11: Minicus Felix, *Octavius of Minucius Felix*, Chapter 9. Felix was a Christian, and the quoted passage was from an imagined dialogue between a pagan and a Christian, with the former simply repeating the tales of Christian activities exchanged among the Romans.

An Instrument of Torture as Symbol and Identity, p. 14: Christians also used a fish as a symbol, a less threatening depiction of their identity. The fish, however, had long been used by cultures in China, India, Egypt and Greece to designate fertility (again with strong sexual implications). Its use by Christians has never been as pervasive or as unifying as the cross. Have you ever seen a Christian making the sign of a fish?

Kabbalah, p. 16: A multitude of spelling variations exists, including *Qabbala, Cabala, Cabalah, Cabbala, Cabbalah, Kabala, Kabalah, Kabbala, Qabala* and *Qabalah*. "Kabbalah" appears to have won election, but only with a plurality.

1. Assassins—Nothing Is True, Everything Is Permitted, p. 19

He renamed the fortress Alamut, p. 32: It has also variously been identified as *Eagle's Guidance* and *Vulture's Nest*.

"caused to be made a vast garden in which he had water conducted", p 33: This description is retold by Thomas Keightley in his 1837 work, *Secret Societies of the Middle Ages—The Assassins, the Templars & The Secret Tribunals of Westphalia* (Boston: Weiser Books, 2005), p. 74. Keightley's research was impeccable and his conclusions were drawn long before the topic was subject to the sensationalist theories of Hollywood and fact-based fiction writers.

And they were the first to be known as the *hashshashin* or assassins, p. 36: An alternative explanation to the name claims that *assasseen* in Arabic translates to *Guardians of the Secrets*. The hashish connection is more widely accepted, however. In fact, this may be a situation of reverse definition, with *assasseen* derived from the assassins and not the other way around. In any case, *assassins* was almost exclusively a European term for the group; to Muslims they reportedly were known as *Nizaris*.

Thought Reform and the Psychology of Totalism, p. 38: Robert Jay Lifton (Chapel Hill: University of North Carolina Press, 1989).

...also called Aladdin (Height of the Faith), p. 41: This is not the Aladdin of the fabled lamp.

...where they became known as the *Khojas*, p. 41: The Khojas are not to be confused with the Thugees, a Hindu tribe of strangler bandits who terrorized parts of India before being hunted down and hanged by British colonial administrators in 1861.

2. Templars, Freemasons and Illuminati—The Secret Seat of Power, p. 43

...including many signers of the U.S. Declaration of Independence, p. 43: The number of Masons who signed the Declaration of Independence varies with the teller. Some sources claim that most were Masons. Historian Jasper Ridley, who had unfettered access to Masonic archives, could confirm only nine of the fifty-six signers as members.

...the result not of chivalrous intent or even a dedication to the Christian faith, but of feudalist obligation, p. 45: Much of the information on the Templars was obtained from Keightley's *Secret Societies of the Middle Ages*.

..."sweet-tempered, totally dedicated, and ruthless on behalf of the faith...", p. 50: Robert Payne, *The Dream of the Tomb: A History of the Crusade* (New York: Stein & Day, 1984), p. 64.

"But both names suit them, for theirs is the mildness of the monk and the valor of the knight", p. 52: Keightley, p. 193.

...offering to convert to Christianity if the Templars would forego the tribute, p. 54: F. W. Bussell, *Religious Thought and Heresy in the Middle Ages* (London: R. Scott, 1918), p. 796.

...he faced death by protracted torture., p. 54: Keightley, p. 206.

...the Germanic language acquired a new description for a house of ill-fame, p. 55: *Tempelhaus:* The description of the Templars' extracurricular activities comes from G. Mollat, *Les papes d'Avignon* (Paris: Unknown bindery, 1912), p. 233.

...they engaged in a battle launched by the Templars reportedly in pursuit of their rival's treasure, p. 56: Keightley, p. 219.

"unspeakable apostasy against God, detestable idolatry, execrable vice, and many heresies", p. 56: Nesta H. Webster, *Secret Societies & Subversive Movements* (London: Boswell Print & Co, 1924; reissued by A&B Publishers Group, 1998), p. 51. Webster's work is sound in a scholarly manner but her racist views, especially her anti-Semitism, color many of her conclusions.

"...should be so forgetful of their salvation as to do these things, we are unwilling to give ear to this kind of insinuation", p. 56: As quoted by Webster from Michelet, *Proces des Temploiers* (1841). Some historians claim the Templars left their riches with the French king, but this contradicts the king's later actions against them.

"The flames were first applied to their feet", p. 58: Keightley, p. 326.

No fewer than sixteen U.S. presidents have proudly declared their Masonic status, p. 61: But not necessarily concentrated power. In this category, Skull & Bones may well dominate.

"Although our thoughts, words and actions may be hidden from the eyes of man...", p. 62: Thomas Smith Webb, *The Freemasons Monitor or Illustrations of Masonry* (Salem, Mass.: Cushing & Appleton, 1821), p. 66.

"In the bosom of the deepest darkness...", p. 67: Marquis de Luchet, *Eassai sur la secte des illuminees* (Paris, 1789).

In spite of Washington's objections..., p. 69: Various attributions, including Albert Pike, *Morals and Dogma: Of the Ancient and Accepted Scottish Rite of Freemasonry* (New York: Nuvision Publications, 2004). This is from TOTSE.com.

Among the symbols impressed on Washington's street layout..., p. 69: Various graphic interpretations of Freemason and satanic symbols on the street grid of Washington DC exist.

....the initiate experiences the point of a compass being pressed against his chest..., p. 71: There seems to be some confusion about this ritual. Apparently some Mason chapters continue to follow it while others have discarded the practice.

Recently, their image has been tarnished by revelations suggesting that barely 25 percent of their $8-billion charity endowment is spent on actual charitable activities, p. 72: *TORO* magazine, "Black Shadow" (Summer 2005), pp. 41–45.

"'Frater' meaning male brothers....", p. 73: *Ibid.*, p. 45.

The shots were to be fired by 77-year-old Albert Eid, p. 75: *Newsweek* (March 11, 2004). Eid pleaded guilty to criminally negligent homicide and was sentenced to five years' probation.

3. Priory of Sion—Keepers of the Holy Grail, p. 77

A Priory is defined as an offshoot of an abbey, whose superior officer is a *prior*. Sion is the Latin term for Mount Zion, the hill on which David founded Jerusalem.

Despite certainty among Christians, Mary Magdalene was no Jerusalem strumpet, p. 78: As noted, multiple variations exist of the tale of Mary Magdalene giving birth in France. The basis for this version came from several sources, most notably Jim Marrs, *Rule By Secrecy* (New York: HarperCollins, 2000).

Thanks to several geographic advantages, Rhaede boasted a population at the time of more than 30,000 inhabitants, p. 80: Details of Renne-le-Chateau's past were obtained from the town's official Web site, www.renneslechateau.com.

Plantard sometimes assumed the clichéd manner and appearance of French underworld characters, p. 89: Details on Plantard's life were obtained from *GNOSIS* magazine, "The Priory of Sion Hoax" (Spring 1999), and from the Rennes *Observer,* "The Templars of the Apocalypse," by Jean-Luc Chaumeil, (June 15, 1997) pp. 19–20.

The latter is easily confirmed via French police archives, p. 90: This information was provided in response to an inquiry concerning a two-page letter dated 8 June 1956 from the Mayor of Annemasse to the Sub-Prefect of St. Julien-en-Genevois, held in the File containing the original 1956 Statutes of the Priory of Sion [File Number KM 94550]: "...in our archives we have a note from the I.N.S.S.E dated 15 December 1954 advising us that Monsieur Pierre Plantard was sentenced on 17 December 1953 by the court in St. Julien-en-Genevois to six months imprisonment for a 'breach of trust' under articles 406 and 408 of the Penal Code." Articles 406 and 408 of the old-style Penal Code correspond to Articles 314–1, 314–2 and 314–3 of the present Penal Code. These articles are classified in Book III of the Code, "Crimes and offences against property"—theft, extortion, blackmail, fraud, and embezzlement.

Evola supported a philosophy similar to the Divine Right of Kings, p. 97: Evola's teachings continue to fascinate fringe groups, including substantial numbers of skinheads and young people caught up in the "Goth" culture. For details on his life and teachings, read Nicholas Goodrick-Clark's *Black Sun: Aryan Cults, Esoteric Nazism and the Politics of Identity* (New York: New York University Press, 2001).

Correspondence seized from Saunière's church, p. 99: Details of Saunière's mail-order business in masses were provided by Jean-Jacques Bedu in *Autopsie d'un myth*, published in 1990.

The myth lives on, p. 100: A final note to the Priory fable: Two of the most exhaustively researched books on this general topic–Keightley's *Secret Societies of the Middle Ages* (1837) and Webster's *Secret Societies & Subversive Movements* (1924)—fail to make any mention of the Merovingian bloodline or the Priory of Sion. Both were published long before Plantard's claim of their existence and their influence on world events. Books published on this topic since 1970, claiming various degrees of authenticity, are legion, of course.

4. Druids and Gnostics—Knowledge and the Eternal Soul, p. 101

Those seeking to become Druids at the height of the movement's influence, p. 104: The source for this account is Manly P. Hall, *The Secret Teachings of All Ages—Readers Edition* (New York: Jeremy P. Tarcher/Penguin, 2003).

Caesar, as talented at observing and recording social structures as he was at commanding armies, p. 106: Julius Caesar, *The Gallic Wars*, Book 6, paragraph 13.

Followers of the Gnostic sect led by Carpocrates, p. 113: Epiphanius (*ca.* 310–403 AD), Bishop of Constantia in Cyprus, provided this commentary. His zeal for the monastic life, ecclesiastical learning and orthodoxy gave him extraordinary authority and may also have encouraged him to exaggerate some of the more licentious activities of the Gnostics whom he undoubtedly disliked.

A follower of John the Baptist, Simon gathered his own disciples around him and was viewed, not surprisingly, as a potential competitor to early Christian leaders, p. 114: Simon has his defenders, who note that, as a Samaritan, he was viewed with distaste and suspicion by Jews, and that his words and intentions may have been distorted. The legacy, nevertheless, lives on in English dictionaries.

As Christianity grew in strength it became less tolerant of Gnosticism, p. 117: Webster, *Secret Societies & Subversive Movements*, p. 32.

Whether or not Gnostics suffered abuse at the hands of Christians, p. 117: *Ibid*, p. 32.

"In the ancient world," Jung wrote, p. 118: Dr. Carl Jung, *Aion*, *Collected Works*, Vol. 9, 2 (Princeton: Princeton University Press, 1959), p. 10.

5. Kabbalah—Origins of the Apocalypse, p. 119

In addition to these biblical writings, three other books dominate ancient Kabbalah philosophy, p. 123: Eliphas Levi, *The Mysteries of the Qabalah: Or Occult Agreement of the Two Testaments* (New York: Samuel Weiser Inc., 1974; reissued Weiser Books, 2000) p. 123.

...the "pagans" may well have been Jews seeking to satirize Christianity for their own amusement and ends, p. 123: Hall hints at this theory in *The Secret Teachings of All Ages*, and then discounts it. Others are not so sure.

The base of the Sephiroth (Malkut) represents the world, with all of its flaws and perfections. The pinnacle (Keter) represents God, or the Supreme Crown, p. 124: Spellings and interpretation of the Sephirots vary according to sources.

Three triangles are formed by the nine sephirots and connecting pathways above the Malkut. These symbolize the human body; the topmost represents the head, the middle represents the trunk and arms, and the bottom represents legs and the reproductive organs, p. 125: Other methods of interpreting the Sephiroth are promoted by various factions of Kabbalah. One, for example, teaches that the centers are arranged in three columns. The left column is called the Pillar of Severity and represents the female side. The right column is called the Pillar of Mercy and represents the male side. The middle pillar is called the Pillar of Equilibrium and represents the balance between the male and female pillars.

According to Webster, the Zohar's original wise counsel has been "mingled by the Rabbis with barbaric superstitions, p. 128: *Secret Societies & Subversive Movements*, p. 11.

"His chamber is lighted up by a silver candlestick on the wall", p. 129: *The Jewish Encyclopedia*.

From there it was a small step to associate this with the Holy Grail, supposedly possessed by Templars and later Masons, inspiring fresh connections to new galaxies of secret conspiracies, p. 130: The linkage between Kabbalah and the Holy Grail is presented with some detail and a straight face in *The Holy Blood and the Holy Grail*.

Crowley died penniless in 1947, p. 132: Crowley's fame did not entirely disappear, in pop culture at least. His face appears amid the crowd on the album cover of the Beatles' *Sergeant Pepper's Lonely Hearts Club Band*, and Jimmy Page, lead guitarist with Led Zeppelin, lives in Crowley's mansion in Scotland, surrounded by various Crowley memorabilia. Most surprising of all perhaps were the results of a poll conducted by the BBC in 2002 to name *The 100 Greatest Britons*: Crowley was rated 73, ahead of Lloyd George, Chaucer, Field Marshall Montgomery and Sir Walter Raleigh.

His name was Feivel Gruberger, p. 132: Details of Feivel Gruberger/Philip Berg and the origins of Kabbalah Center are drawn from several sources, including a lengthy account in the *Daily Mail (UK)*, (May 22, 2004).

6. Rosicrucians—The Pursuit of Esoteric Wisdom, p. 139

None of these discussions took place during the remarkably long life Rosenkreuz led, p. 140: The actual publication date of the *Fama* remains controversial. Most sources say 1614, a few suggest 1610, and *The Catholic Encyclopedia* is adamant that it was published in 1604. This latter date is curious, since it is precisely 120 years after the death of Rosenkreuz, a period of time that bears some significance—it is the number of years that the founder requested secrecy following his death and, as readers of works such as Umberto Eco's novel *Foucault's Pendulum* will recognize, it represents cycles of secrecy demanded by Templars.

…the man was "unfamiliar with the use of a pen, and it is obvious either that he copied the signature or that his hand was guided while he wrote.", p. 142: As quoted by Manly P. Hall in *The Secret Teachings of All Ages*. First published in 1928 (and reissued in 2003 by Penguin), Hall's book is considered a classic of its genre. It includes an extensive discussion of the role of Bacon as the true author of Shakespeare's works and serves as a prime source of the discussion of Bacon as a Rosicrucian.

Is it possible that the greatest single fount of English literature is merely a series of envelopes containing clandestine messages in murky codes?, p. 143: The source of these claims (other sources and other claims are legion) is Hall's *The Secret Teachings of All Ages*, pp. 543–51.

In Henry IV, Part One, the word "Francis" appears 33 times on one page, p. 143: The multiple mentions of Francis occur early in act 4, scene 1.

"Bacon is not to be regarded solely as a man but rather as the focal point, p. 144: Hall, pp. 548–49.

A contemporary of Lippard, Paschal Beverly Randolph, was also acquainted with Lincoln, p. 150: Details of Randolph's life are found in his work *After Death, or Disembodied Man* (Boston: Rockwell & Rollins, 1868).

AMORC takes great pains to identify itself not as a religious order but as "a non-profit educational charitable organization", p. 153: As reported on the Rosicrucian Order Web site www.rosicrucian.org.

"We do not propose a belief system, nor a dogmatic decree", p. 153: AMORC Web site.

"A true Rose Cross does not indulge in secret hand signs or shakes, celebrations, vain displays of wealth", p. 154: R. S. Clymer, *The Rose Cross Order* (Quakertown: The Philosophical Publishing Co., 1916).

"Unlike Masons, Rosicrucians have no special rings", p. 154: R. S. Clymer, *The Fraternitatis Rosae Crucis* (Quakertown: The Philosophical Publishing Co., 1929).

Johansson's lengthy and meandering article, readers are informed, was drawn "from discourses presented by the Grand Masters and the Imperator at the World Peace Conference", p. 155: Data from the Johansson article is from *Rosicrucian Digest* (No. 1, 2005) p. 10.

7. Triads—Cultural Criminals, p. 157

For much of the information on triads and tongs, I am deeply indebted to author and criminal investigator James Dubro, who summed up much of the history of these groups in his excellent book *Dragons of Crime: Inside the Asian Underworld* (Toronto: Octopus Publishing Group, 1992).

Resident Chinese usually refer to the organizations as *hei she hui*, literally translated as "black (or secret, sinister or wicked) society", p. 162: South China *Morning Post*, Macau Edition (December 12, 1999).

Royal Canadian Mounted Police investigators claim 14K and other triads maintain a presence in every Chinese community of substance across North America", p. 165: RCMP Triad files: ecdp0062.doc.

"I was not required to pay any percentage of profits to the 14K leadership", p. 168: Discussion Paper by the Australian Parliamentary Joint Committee on the National Crime Authority (February 1995).

One Hong Kong businessman who chose to defy triad threats was sent the severed head of a dog, p. 169: Jan Morris, *Hong Kong* (New York: Random House, 1988), p. 44.

In Britain, the National Criminal Intelligence Service conducted a study of triad activities, p. 170: ERRI: *Evaluation of Chinese Triads in Great Britain*— EmergencyNet NEWS Service (July 21, 1996).

In 1988, an Australian government study estimated that 85 to 95 percent of all heroin entering that country was controlled by Chinese triads: *Asian Organised Crime In Australia—A Discussion Paper by the Parliamentary Joint Committee on the National Crime Authority* (February 1995).

...a U.S. investigation indicated that triad dominance had been reduced by competition from South east Asian countries: Statement of Steven W. Casteel, Assistant Administrator for Intelligence, before the U.S. Senate Committee on the Judiciary (May 20, 2003).

"The leaders of the early gangs came out of the aftermath of the Vietnam war", p. 171: Interview with the author (August 6, 2005).

8. The Mafia and Cosa Nostra—Wise Guys and Businessmen, p. 173

In AD 1000, a wave of invasions brought Normans, p. 174: Much of the information in this section was derived from Gaia Servadio's excellent *Mafioso: A History of the Mafia from Its Origins to the Present Day* (New York: Stein & Day Publishers, 1976).

The code of *omerta* decreed that any man who appealed for law enforcers to right a wrong was either a fool or a coward, p. 179: Rick Porello, *The Rise and Fall of the Cleveland Mafia* (Ft. Lee, NJ: Barricade Books, 1995).

A high-ranking Italian government official recently described 'Ndrangheta, p. 180: Italian government news release, Ministry of the Interior (September 22, 2004).

"Only blood does not betray": S. Accardo, as quoted by M. La Sorte, see *ff.*

...in 2004 the Italian government suggested the 'Ndrangheta consisted of 155 family clans and a total membership of over 6000, p. 182: M. La Sorte, *The Calabrian 'Ndrangheta* (SUNY: *The 'Ndrangheta Looms Large*, December 2004).

Promoting the region as a holiday destination, the Calabrian tourism office admits "you will find no Florences or Venices in Calabria", p. 182: *Ibid.*

...you may also enter a Calabrian village and encounter a sight similar to that witnessed by the citizens of Taurianova, p. 182–183: *Ibid.* from P. Lunde, *Organized Crime* (New York: DK Publishing, 2004).

FBI lurkers heard Deluca instructed to repeat an oath spoken by the boss, p. 192: "FBI tapes offer a rare inside look at Mafia induction," the Boston *Globe* (March 27, 1990).

D'Amato was head of the DeCavalcante family, the largest in New Jersey and reputed to be the basis of the popular *Sopranos* television series, p. 193: "Mafia Head Killed for Being Gay, Mobster Testifies," *National Post* (May 2, 2003).

This was a matter of personal pride that the prospect of having 5000 volts of electricity blasting through his body within a few hours could not divert, p. 196: Interestingly, Buchalter was Jewish, not Italian. It is a tribute of sorts to the power of the Mafia's code that he chose to make his statement and be assessed as a man of honor to the end.

9. Yakuza—Traditions and Amputation, p. 199

"The nobles, courtiers and even the ladies in waiting of the women's quarters were slashed to death", p. 202: J. N. Leonard, *Early Japan* (New York: Time-Life Books, 1968), p. 58.

In addition to incomplete pinkies, Yakuza members may be identified by their extensive tattoos, p. 204: Davis E. Kaplan and Alex Dubro: *Yakuza— The Explosive Account of Japan's Criminal Underworld* (Reading, Mass.: Addison-Wesley, 1986).

The *sokaiya* are chosen for their vehement style, capable of shouting down anyone who tries to silence them, p. 207: Christopher Seymour, *Yakuza Diary—Doing Time in the Japanese Underworld* (New York: Atlantic Monthly Press, 1996).

10. Wicca—The Great Goddess and the Horned God, p. 209

"Without witches, some late medieval theologians were left facing their questions as to why bad things happen", p. 213: Walter Stephens, *Demon Lovers: Witchcraft, Sex and the Crisis of Belief* (Chicago: University of Chicago, 2002), p. 100.

...celebrated on February 2 to mark the first stirrings of spring and the return of light to the world, p. 223: On this basis, the sabbats do not apply to countries south of the equator.

"That was done which may not be done except in great emergency", p. 227: Philip Heselton, *Gerald Gardner and the Cauldron of Inspiration—an Investigation into the Sources of Gardnerian Witchcraft* (Milverton: Capall Bann Publishing, 2003).

NOTES 309

"witches are consummate leg-pullers; they are taught it as part of their stock-in-trade", p. 227: G. B. Gardner, *Witchcraft Today* (San Francisco: Citadel Press, 1954/2000), p. 27.

11. Skull & Bones—America's Secret Establishment, p. 229

"On the west wall hung, among other pictures", p. 230: *Fleshing Out Skull & Bones* (Walterville, OR: TrineDay Press, 2003), p. 473.

Howard Altman, an award-winning U.S. writer and editor, reported that in 1989 a man named Phillip Romero visited him, p. 231–232: *Ibid.*, pp. 33–36.

Adding to the story's veracity is the reported existence of a privately printed document, p. 232: Rob Rosenbaum, "More Scary Skull and Bones Tales," the New York *Observer* (2002).

The reward for Bonesmen may have been worth the humiliation, p. 237: Ron Rosenbaum, "The Last Secrets of Skull and Bones," *Esquire* magazine (September 1977), p. 89.

"We speak through a new publication, because the college press is closed to those who dare to openly mention 'Bones'", p. 237: *Fleshing Out Skull & Bones*, pp. 3–4.

Prescott Sheldon Bush, Yale '17, was ideal Skull & Bones material, p. 238: *Ibid.*, p. 40.

Hitler mesmerized Thyssen as, in fact, he mesmerized virtually an entire country desperately in need of strong, decisive leadership, p. 239: Thyssen described this transaction, along with his motivations, in his tell-all book *I Paid Hitler* (New York: Farrar & Rinehart, 1941).

For the latter, he turned to Thyssen's steel mills, whose profits soared in the following years, overflowing into the coffers of the Bank voor Handel en Scheepvart in Rotterdam and the Union Banking Corporation in New York, p. 241: A postwar investigation of the Thyssen family's role in arming Nazi Germany estimated that the family's interests had provided the following proportion of Germany's national output in 1938:

50.8 percent of pig iron
41.4 percent of standard plate steel
36.0 percent of heavy plate steel
38.5 percent of galvanized sheet steel
45.5 percent of steel pipe
22.1 percent of wire

35.0 percent of explosives
Source: *Elimination of German Resources for War*, U.S. Congress report, Sub-Committee on Military Affairs (July 2, 1945), p. 507.

The bank's Russian connection inspired Lord Bearsted of Britain to recommend that Union Banking cease its dealings with Stalin, p. 241: W. Averell Harriman papers, Library of Congress (September 12, 1927).

Consider the identity of its eight members of the board of directors, p. 242: *Fleshing Out Skull & Bones*, p. 205 and p. 249.

The year 2003 saw the publication of a *Duty, Honor, Country*, a glowing tribute to Prescott Bush, p. 243: Quotations from *Duty, Honor, Country— The Life and Legacy of Prescott Bush* (Nashville: Rutledge Hill Press, 2003), p. 72.

Consider this partial list of Bonesmen associated with the U.S. intelligence community, p. 246: *Fleshing Out Skull & Bones*, p. 9 .

The individual who handled the paperwork on the name changeover and the incorporation of RTA was Howard Weaver, p. 248: Ron Rosenbaum, *The Secret Parts of Fortune: Three Decades of Intense Investigations and Edgy Enthusiasms* (New York: HarperPerennial, 2000), pp. 155–67.

Coincidences grow curiouser and curiouser, p. 248: Joseph McBride, "George Bush, CIA Operative," *The Nation* (July 16, 1988).

Zapata happens to be the CIA's code name for the Bay of Pigs invasion, p. 248: Michael R. Beschloss, *The Crisis Years: Kennedy and Khrushchev, 1960–63* (New York: Edward Burlingame Books, 1991), p. 89.

Another coincidence involves the same former president George H.W. Bush and the assassination of President Kennedy, p. 249: The complete document, as provided by Joseph McBride, *op. cit.*, reads:

Date: November 29, 1963 To: Director, Bureau of Intelligence and Research, Department of State

From: John Edgar Hoover, Director Subject: assassination OF PRESIDENT JOHN F. KENNEDY NOVEMBER 22, 1963

Our Miami, Florida, Office on November 23, 1963 advised that the Office of Coordinator of Cuban Affairs in Miami advised that the Department of State feels some misguided anti-Castro group might capitalize on the present situation and undertake an unauthorized raid against Cuba, believing that the assassination of President John F. Kennedy might herald a change in US policy, which is not true.

Our sources and informants familiar with Cuban matters in the Miami area advise that the general feeling in the anti-Castro Cuban community is one of stunned disbelief and, even among those who did not entirely agree with the President's policy concerning Cuba, the feeling is that the President's death represents a great loss not only to the US but to all Latin America. These sources know of no plans for unauthorized action against Cuba.

An informant who has furnished reliable information in the past and who is close to a small pro-Castro group in Miami has advised that those individuals are afraid that the assassination of the President may result in strong repressive measures being taken against them and, although pro-Castro in their feelings, regret the assassination.

The substance of the foregoing information was orally furnished to Mr. George Bush of the Central Intelligence Agency and Captain William Edwards of the Defense Intelligence Agency on November 23, 1963, by Mr. W.T. Forsyth of this Bureau.

"I have carefully reviewed the FBI memorandum to the Director, Bureau of Intelligence and Research, Department of State dated November 29, 1963", p. 249: United States District Court for the District of Columbia, Civil Action 88-2600 GHR, Archives and Research Center *v.* Central Intelligence Agency, Affidavit of George William Bush (September 21, 1988).

In August 2003, de Wit recalled his experience with the CIA and Skull & Bones, p. 250: *Fleshing Out Skull & Bones*, p. 212 .

With an estimated $4 million in assets in 2000, p. 251: Yale University archives, *Light & Truth's Guide to Society Life at Yale*. Interestingly, the competitive secret society Scroll & Key has substantially higher assets of $6 million.

12. Secret Societies in Popular Culture—An Endless Fascination, p. 253

"Experts today concur—and rightly so, we concluded—that the *Protocols*, at least in their present form, are a vicious and insidious forgery", p. 262: Baigent *et al.*, *The Holy Blood and the Holy Grail* (London: Arrow Books, 1996), pp. 198–203. All references are from this edition.

The *Protocals*, intended to be read like an instruction manual for running the world, are either chilling or absard, depending on your gullibility and appreciation for black humor, p. 264: Several sources for the *Protocols* exist. These herein have been selected from Jim Marrs, *Rule By Secrecy* (New York: HarperCollins, 2000), pp. 145–53. The author is a secret societies alarmist, but his work on this topic at least is accurate in its selection of the *Protocols* contents.

The Roman Catholic Church is as appropriate a target for criticism as any, p. 266: For the record, I have no Roman Catholic affiliation—in fact, I have no religious affiliation.

13. Critics, Alarmists and Conspiracy Theorists—When Does Paranoia Make Sense?, p. 271

The Rothschild connection, according to Welch and others, p. 279: Sources for this section include *Jews and Freemasonry in Europe* (Boston: Harvard Press, 1970) and William T. Still, *New World Order: The Ancient Plan of Secret Societies* (Lafayette, LA: Huntington House Publishers, 1990), pp. 104–41.

At Retinger's funeral in 1960, one of the eulogizers recalled, p. 281: The speaker was Sir Edward Beddington-Behrens, President, Central and Eastern European Commission, European Movement. The quote is available at dozens of Web sites purporting to deliver the "true" story behind the Bilderberg Group, although most misspell his name.

The NSC has been described as "the ultimate Washington insider's club", p. 287: Dan Dunsky, "*Two Degrees of Domination,*" Toronto *Globe & Mail* (June 25, 2005) p. D3.

The pinnacle of Kissinger's power in this regard occurred in the latter days of Richard Nixon's presidency, p. 288: A detailed and disturbing examination of the NSC and the risk it poses is available in David J. Rothkopf's excellent *Running the World: The Inside Story of the National Security Council and the Architects of American Power* (New York: PublicAffairs Books, 2005).

Afterword—Of Demons and Baloney, p. 295

"We want so much to be roused from our humdrum lives", p. 296: *The Demon-Haunted World: Science as a Candle in the Dark*, p. 123.

"Sooner or later," he warns, "this combustible mixture of ignorance and power is going to blow up in our faces", p. 297: *Ibid.*, p. 209.

PICTURE CREDITS

ACKNOWLEDGMENTS

THE INSPIRATION FOR THIS BOOK ORIGINATED WITH ANNA Porter and the clarity of her publishing vision. Anna marked the route, set the tracks and built up steam in the engine, and left the actual journey to me; I thank her for this opportunity and others.

Helping to shape the project was Clare McKeon. Her warmth and editorial skills at trimming the flab and extending the ideas, where each was appropriate, were exemplary and always appreciated.

Many sources were tapped for much of the content and, given the nature of the tale and certain aspects of their occupations, their identity cannot be revealed. Each knows of my appreciation, and I trust all are satisfied with my use of the data they so kindly provided.

Finally, every honest author (especially males, curiously enough) is compelled to admit that his work could never have traveled from inspiration to completion without the assistance and encouragement of two people: his agent and his spouse. Once again, my heartfelt thanks and affection to Hilary MacMahon and to Judy.

INDEX